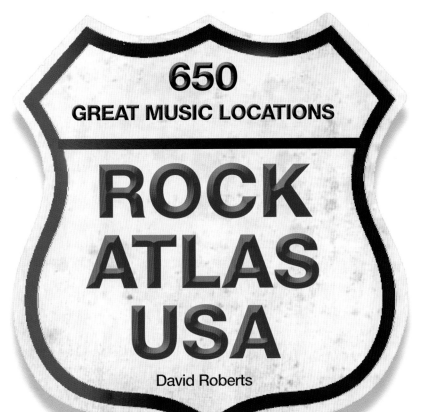

650
GREAT MUSIC LOCATIONS

ROCK ATLAS USA

David Roberts

RED PLANET

Rock Atlas USA

First Published November 2013
Reprinted May 2017

For more information visit: www.redplanetzone.com
Front cover photo of Crosby, Stills & Nash by Henry Diltz

Rock Atlas is a trade mark of Red Planet Publishing Ltd

650
GREAT MUSIC LOCATIONS

ROCK
ATLAS
USA

David Roberts

Alabama · Alaska · Arizona · Arkansas · California · Colorado · Connecticut · Delaware · Florida · Georgia · Hawaii · Idaho · Illinois · Indiana · Iowa · Kansas · Kentucky · Louisiana · Maine · Maryland · Massachusetts · Michigan · Minnesota · Mississippi · Missouri · Montana · Nebraska · Nevada · New Hampshire · New Jersey · New Mexico · New York · North Carolina · North Dakota · Ohio · Oklahoma · Oregon · Pennsylvania · Rhode Island · South Carolina · South Dakota · Tennessee · Texas · Utah · Vermont · Virginia · Washington · West Virginia · Wisconsin · Wyoming

Introduction
Welcome to Rock Atlas USA

Popular music is well served by books about the people and the songs that make it such an emotionally engaging art form; less so when it comes to the amazing places associated with it. So here's a guidebook with a side order of stories about America's great rock music locations. It's called Rock Atlas but the word "Rock" is a catch-all for any genre that combines with it. So, country, folk, blues, soul, and even jazz, all get included. Therefore, fans searching for the likes of Dolly

Parton's statue, Woody Guthrie's home, or the B.B. King Museum shouldn't be disappointed.

Every one of the special places has been lovingly written and researched by me, but mostly from a great distance. You may think a British born and based author might not be the best qualified person to write and research a guidebook to US music locations. I certainly haven't visited all of the 650+ places listed in Rock Atlas USA, but then I didn't get round all

the great places in the UK and Ireland edition either when compiling that edition of the book. But, to paraphrase: 'remoteness makes the heart grow fonder.' Mere mention of the words "Asbury Park," "CBGB," "Sun Studios," "Paisley Park," "Galveston," "Hitsville U.S.A.," and "Woodstock" is enough to set my pulses racing.

Remember, us Brits really do love American popular music history with a studious passion. Just as The Beatles, The Rolling

Like thousands of Eagles fans before him, Rock Atlas author David Roberts arrives at the spot where he can honestly say that he's "standin' on the corner in Winslow Arizona..."

Stones, and Led Zeppelin sucked in the amazing sounds invented by Chuck Berry, Buddy Holly, and Muddy Waters, I, in my own small way, have drawn on my obsession for unique American locations such as Laurel Canyon, Muscle Shoals, and Greenwich Village and hopefully come up with an objective and useful guide to the places that musically tug so strongly on our emotions.

I've always remembered Eric Burdon's take on the whole love affair with evocative American music locations. Thinking back to his childhood in Newcastle-upon-Tyne in the industrial North East of England, The Animals vocalist perfectly summed up the British excitement at the music coming out of America before the Second World War when he explained his own teenage infatuation:

❛The River Tyne in my mind became the Mississippi and I was convinced I was already in New Orleans before I left my home town. I knew all of the names of all the top players and hero-worshipped them. I had visions of New Orleans all the time ❜

Eric Burdon

Hopefully, Rock Atlas will enable you (just as Eric Burdon once did) to turn a vision into reality by visiting some of the hundreds of entries included in the pages that follow. My personal favorites are the exact place where fans can get themselves photographed in rock music's most iconic settings. It might be the spot where a much-loved album cover was created, outside

Rock Atlas USA
Acknowledgments

As I haven't personally visited all the locations listed in Rock Atlas USA, I needed some help. And what great help I received. So, here is where I must thank all the generous music fans, local newspapers, photographers, and everyone else across America who shared my enthusiasm for the project. Turning my words and pictures into the beautiful book you are now reading were publisher and long-suffering designer Mark Neeter, proof-reader Matthew White, and my chief supporters, fellow enthusiast and friend Martin Downham, and my wife Janet Roberts.

Big thanks also go to Melinda Abrazado, Wendy and Craig Anderson, Mary Elizabeth Beary, John Berger, Tony Bradshaw, J.C. Brown, Lisa Burks (www.gravehunting.com), Justin Carrasquillo, Chris Chaber, Ron Clamp, Scott Clark, Larry Crane, Andy Davis, Ren Davis Travel Guides, Henry Diltz, Hope Edwards, Bob Egan (www.popspotsnyc.com), John Einarson, Rick Elmore, Katherine England, Todd Fife, Patricia Florio, Fox, Don Fritz, Don Furu, Erick Godin, Alex Hallmark, Andrew Hearn (www.theelvismag.com), Ralph Helmick, Kevin Herridge, Michael Hibblen, Chris Hillman, Jennifer Huber (SoloTravelGirl.com), Jamie Hull, Alison Jordan, Ernie King, Lance and Donna Jost, Peter Lewry, Tom Likes, Gil Markle, Bob Mataranglo-Murals, Keith Miles, Stephen Mitchell, Lars Movin, Ryan Ozawa, Kyle Pelton, John Porcellino, John Powers, Ron Pownall, Lee Pullen, Tim Rice, Paul Ridenour, Jason Robinson, Bob Santelli, Robert Scanlon, Ted Schaar, Ed Scott, Clete Shields, Leni Sinclair, Roderick Smith, Charles Snapp, Lauren Snelgrove, Brian Southall, Erik Thrane, Wayne Toth, Anne Vinci, Mick Wallingford, Gary Wayne, Timothy Webb, Harry Weber, Ken Weiss, Ed Wheaton, Raven Woods, Jennifer Yang and Stephen Zorochin.

The following books were invaluable sources of reference: Billboard Top Pop Singles and Billboard Top 40 Albums (ed. Joel Whitburn), Rock Chronicles (ed. David Roberts), Follow Me to Tennessee by Andrew Hearn and Andrew Snelgrove, Hotel California by Barney Hoskyns, Shout! The True Story of The Beatles by Philip Norman, Canyon of Dreams: The Magic and the Music of Laurel Canyon by Harvey Kubernik and Scott Calamar, The Sociology of Rock by Simon Frith, Detroit Rocks! A Pictorial History of Motor City Rock & Roll 1965-1975 by Gary Grimshaw and Leni Sinclair, Guinness Rockopedia (ed. David Roberts), The Rolling Stone Illustrated History of Rock & Roll, The Guinness Encyclopedia of Popular Music (ed. Colin Larkin), Q Encyclopedia of Rock Stars by Dafydd Rees and Luke Crampton, 1001 Albums You Must Hear Before You Die (ed. Robert Dimery), and Under the Covers (DVD) by Henry Diltz and Gary Burden

a vitally important venue or recording studio, or even beside a plaque, statue, or memorial to one of America's great musicians. Aside from the locations where music sprang from, Rock Atlas USA includes the places that have sprung up to celebrate the music: museums, record stores, and festivals.

Sadly, not all of the important buildings included in Rock Atlas are still standing and your imagination sometimes needs to work overtime to seek out what remains of a demolished treasure now little more than a parking lot. But, writing this book gave me hope that towns and cities across America see the cultural (and financial) value in waymarking and protecting the amazing musical heritage on their doorstep. And, if you are visiting any of the vast majority of the Rock Atlas locations which are still standing, please remember that some of the places included are people's homes and businesses. Please respect the current owners and occupants' privacy.

Finally, Rock Atlas USA is a selection rather than a complete, definitive guide to America's music locations. It's my ambition to make future editions even more comprehensive, so let me have your favorite places and stories and we will add them to the mix for Rock Atlas USA 2.

David Roberts, Wivenhoe, UK

Contact me regarding anything to do with Rock Atlas: poppublishing@gmail.com Visit the Rock Atlas web pages at www.rockatlas.com and our Facebook page at www.facebook.com/rockatlas

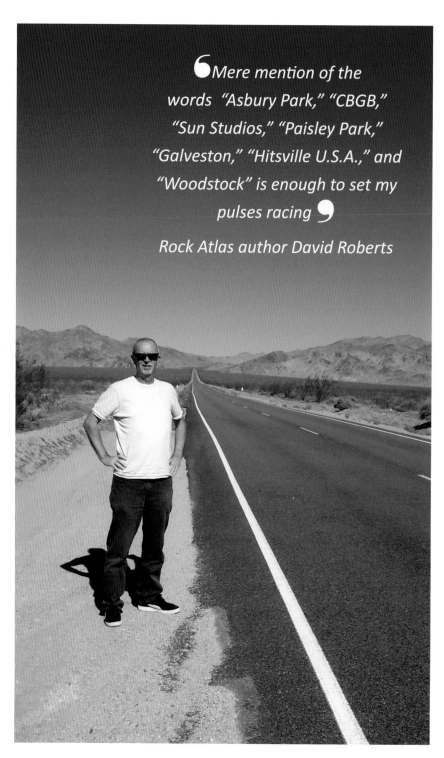

'Mere mention of the words "Asbury Park," "CBGB," "Sun Studios," "Paisley Park," "Galveston," "Hitsville U.S.A.," and "Woodstock" is enough to set my pulses racing '

Rock Atlas author David Roberts

Rock Atlas USA

Contents

RockAtlasUSA

Contents

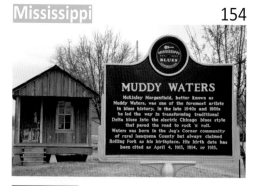

Contents

RockAtlasUSA

Contents

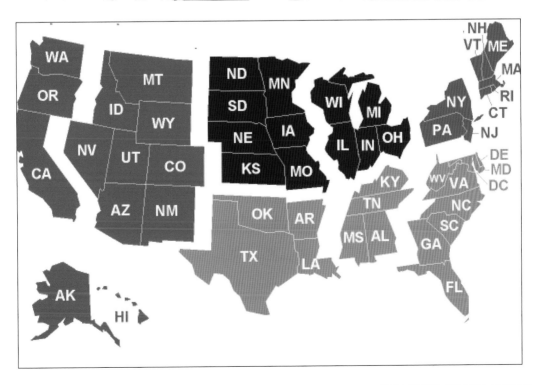

RockAtlasUSA

Alabama

Gulf Shores
Hangout Music Festival

Could a festival be any closer to the ocean? The annual Hangout Music Festival at Gulf Shores takes place directly on the beach. There's rock by day and night and yoga in the morning. Recent years' headliners have included Foo Fighters, Paul Simon, Red Hot Chili Peppers, and Jack White.

Location 001: around 50 minutes west of Pensacola, one hour south of Mobile, and 2.5 hours east of New Orleans, the exact location is 101 East Beach Boulevard, Gulf Shores, AL 36542

On the beach: The Flaming Lips prepare to launch their inflatable shark at Hangout

Dave Vann

Montgomery
Hank Williams' statue, museum, and gravesite

Although born in nearby Mount Olive, Butler County, Hank Williams began and ended his career here in Montgomery. The state's capital promotes the legacy and influence left by the legendary country singer, who died aged just 29 in West Virginia, with a museum and statue. His short career took off following a winning performance at a talent show at the local Empire Theater in 1937 and his final public appearance came at Montgomery Street's Elite Café

for a musician's union meeting, a few days before his death on January 1st 1953. Find out why so many of today's legendary music makers revere the man by visiting The Hank Williams Museum's large collection of memorabilia, featuring his old 1952 Cadillac in which he made his final journey.

Locations 002, 003, and 004: open seven days a week, the museum is in downtown Montgomery at 118 Commerce Street, AL 36104. The gravesite

where his remains are interred is marked by a large memorial stone at the Oakwood Annex Cemetery, 1305 Upper Wetumpka Road, Montgomery, AL 36107, which is a couple of miles north of the museum. Hank's imposing statue stands facing Montgomery's City Hall, where his funeral attracted thousands of fans. The exact spot is on the east side of North Perry Street (Lister Hill Plaza) between the junctions with Monroe Street and Madison Avenue, AL 36104

Tens of thousands attended Hank Williams' funeral inside and outside the building where his statue now looks on

James D. Pellowski, Milwaukee, Wisconsin

Sheffield
Muscle Shoals Sound Studio

This world famous facility has two locations. The original Muscle Shoals Sound Studio first opened for business in April 1969 when a bunch of musicians, who became The Muscle Shoals Rhythm Section (nicknamed "The Swampers"), created their own recording studio in the small city in the northeast corner of the state of Alabama. This former tobacco warehouse has gained the status of a listed building on the National Register of Historic Places. Classic albums recorded here include Traffic's The Low Spark of High Heeled Boys, Sticky Fingers by The Rolling Stones, Rod Stewart's Atlantic Crossings, and several by The Staple Singers and

Bob Seger. Appropriately, Lynyrd Skynyrd's signature tune 'Sweet Home Alabama' was recorded here with a lyrical name check for the place and its owners "The Swampers". In 1978 the studio moved across the city to a state-of-the-art dual studio set-up featuring 24-track recording equipment. However, the original building was the recording base for The Black Keys for what turned out to be a Grammy-winning album, Brothers, in 2009.

Locations 006, and 007: still open for business as a studio, the

The address of the Muscle Shoals Sound Studio is the title and the image on the cover of Cher's sixth studio album, made in Sheffield in 1969

original Muscle Shoals Sound Studio can be booked in advance for both recording and tours at 3614 North Jackson Highway, Sheffield, AB 35660. The second studio is situated two miles west of the original on the riverfront at 1000 Alabama Avenue, Sheffield, AB 35660

Muscle Shoals
Fame Recording Studios

The Muscle Shoals Sound Studio is strictly speaking not in the city of Muscle Shoals at all, although another world famous recording facility is. The Florence Alabama Music Enterprises Recording Studios (FAME Recording Studios for short) have specialized in recording top soul and R&B artists including Aretha Franklin, Wilson Pickett, Otis Redding, Etta James, and Tom Jones. The FAME location has changed three times since those beginnings in 1959. The first premises were above the City Drug Store in nearby Florence across the Tennessee River, then an old tobacco warehouse on Wilson Dam Road, Muscle Shoals, before settling at its current address in a purpose built building in Muscle Shoals.

Location 005: at 603 East Avalon Avenue, Muscle Shoals, AL 35661

Tuscumbia
Alabama Music Hall of Fame

Just inside the lobby of this interactive museum the visitor is introduced to Alabama's legendary music makers by a series of bronze stars which make up the Hall of Fame's Walk of Fame. The variety of Alabama's music output is conveyed through a giant jukebox, 16-foot guitar entrance to the country music area, an actual tour bus belonging to the band Alabama, jazz club, nightclub, exhibits and a working recording studio where visitors can cut their own tracks.

Location 008: the museum in Tuscumbia is in the northwest corner of Alabama, about three miles southwest of downtown Muscle Shoals. Head for 617 Highway 72 West, AL 35674

Alaska

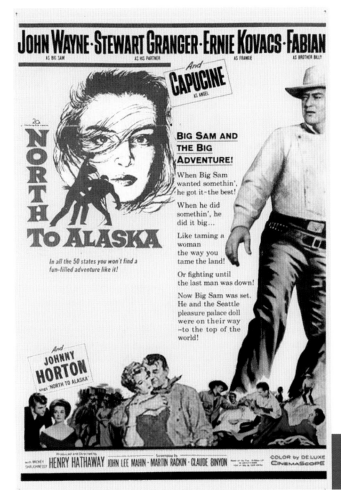

Nome
Johnny Horton's Alaska

The story of two cowboys who headed north in 1892 in search of gold, Johnny Horton's song, 'North to Alaska,' describes a successful conclusion when they find "big nuggets" a little southeast of the small city of Nome. The 1960 Billboard No.4 hit featured in the movie of the same name starring John Wayne and the song started a craze for saga songs. A year earlier Horton's 'When it's Springtime in Alaska' was the first of his three country No.1 records. His Alaska songs were written from experience: the California-born singer-songwriter had headed 'North to Alaska' himself in his twenties in search of gold.

Location 010: at the heart of the century-old gold rush, Nome is on the Seward Peninsula in western Alaska, AK 99762

Johnny Horton's hit song accompanied the movie of the same name

❝One of the great pop songs about that chilly state was 'North to Alaska' by Johnny Horton. And it's a fact that the film [North to Alaska] cost almost as much to make as the state cost to buy from Russia in 1867. Then you have Michelle Shocked with a song called 'Anchorage'; a young singer named Jewel who was very successful in the late nineties and grew up in Alaska; and even I have written a song about Alaska [with Francis Lai]. It was imaginatively called 'Alaska'❞

Tim Rice extols the virtues of America's largest state

Anchorage
Michelle Shocked: 'Anchored Down in Anchorage'

The hit single 'Anchorage' is the best known song by Texan singer-songwriter Michelle Shocked. Recorded for her 1988 album Short Sharp Shocked, the track tells the story of a fractured relationship with a friend who has moved from Dallas, Texas, writing a reply letter from Anchorage.

Location 009: southern Alaska, AK 99501

RockAtlasUSA
Arizona

Courtesy of MIM

Courtesy of MIM

Phoenix
The Musical Instrument Museum

Exhibiting musical instruments from more than 200 countries from around the world, the Musical Instrument Museum has a collection of 15,000 items housed in a striking building designed by award-winning architect Rich Varda. Aside from the comprehensiveness of the exhibits, the MIM displays iconic instruments that once belonged to Carlos Santana, Taylor Swift, John Lennon, and Elvis Presley.

Location 013: about 20 miles north of downtown Phoenix at 4725 East Mayo Boulevard, Phoenix, AZ 85050

Guitar heaven (top) at the sleekly designed Musical Instrument Museum, which is open seven days a week

Monument Valley
The Byrds' cover cheat

The curving staircase on which The Byrds perch on the cover of their 1970 Untitled album appears to be on a building somewhere in Monument Valley. But the Arizona landscape favored by Wild West movie makers which provides the covers' backdrop isn't what it seems to be. Turn to the Los Angeles, California pages of Rock Atlas USA for the real location of the stunning structure.

Location 011: Monument Valley, AZ 84536

Phoenix
Jimmy Webb's sad song begins here

'By the Time I Get to Phoenix' doesn't quite begin here. Songwriter Jimmy Webb's sad song story, made massive by Glen Campbell, must have started someplace else as the subject of the song is only "rising" by the time the narrator gets to Arizona's capital city, then "working" by the time he gets to Albuquerque, and "sleeping" when he makes Oklahoma. When writing the song, Webb was hugely influenced by the domestic story-telling he discovered in Lennon & McCartney's mid-sixties lyrics.

Location 012: a bedroom someplace west of Phoenix, AZ 85006

Tempe
U2 begin and end their Joshua Tree Tour

Tempe saw the first and last concerts of the nine-month-long Joshua Tree Tour that U2 undertook in 1987. Staged in three legs, the tour, which was filmed for their movie Rattle and Hum, began at the Arizona State University Activity Center (now the Wells Fargo Arena) on April 2nd and climaxed with their final gig at the seven-times-larger-capacity Sun Devil Stadium on December 20th. The Sun Devil Stadium had earlier rock pedigree, hosting a 1981 Rolling Stones concert filmed for their Let's Spend The Night Together movie. Tempe was also popular with The Jimi Hendrix Experience, who took a mini vacation break from touring here in February 1968. The trio were in town to play the Sun Devil gym at the University on the 5th of the month, supported by Soft Machine. In 2010, Hendrix was inducted into the Fender Hall of Fame at the city's Tempe Center for the Arts.

Locations 014, 015, 016 and 017: east of downtown Phoenix, the Wells Fargo Arena is at 600 East Veterans Way and the Sun Devil Stadium is a short walk away at 500 East Veterans Way, Tempe, AZ 85281. The smaller arena where Jimi Hendrix played – the University's Sun Devil gym – is now named Physical Education West, still at 451 Orange Street, AZ 85281, and the Tempe Center for the Arts is at 700 West Rio Salado Parkway, AZ 85281

Jimi Hendrix takes time out to make home movies in and around Tempe in 1968

Roger Mayer

Winslow
The Eagles' Standin' on the Corner Park

David Roberts

Winslow is a tourist trap for all Eagles fans. Graphically immortalized in the lyrics of the band's first big hit, 'Take it Easy,' the small city has created an extraordinarily popular homage to the song, released in 1972. Standin' on the Corner Park, an echo of the song's "Well, I'm standing on a corner in Winslow, Arizona" lyric line, features a statue of the guy in the song doing just that. Behind him is a wall mural which illustrates the girl "in a flat-bed Ford" - another line from the track featured on the Eagles' eponymous debut album. The park's paved area is made up of a series of ▶

❝Covering the corner used to be a drug store before the hippie statue was put up. Men like my husband did once used to stand on that corner back in the fifties – but they were railroad men and cowboys❞

Winslow resident Pat Hanno, whose late husband is remembered on one of the park's paving stones

Arizona

Winslow
The Eagles' Standin' on the Corner Park

▶ engraved, sponsored paving bricks where fans of both Winslow and the Eagles have left messages. There's a festival every late September celebrating Winslow's music connection and the town has Eagle Glenn Frey to thank in particular for putting Winslow on the tourist map. The song had been written by friend of the band Jackson Browne, who was never quite satisfied with it. He donated it to the Eagles but it was Frey who reportedly added the all-important verse about Winslow, Arizona.

Location 018: Winslow is on Interstate 40 between Flagstaff and the New Mexico border. The park is situated on the corner (naturally) of old Route 66 at East 2nd Street and North Kinsley Avenue, AZ 86047

The corner, the "flat-bed Ford" from the song (right), and statue on the old Route 66, in Winslow

David Roberts

Arkansas

Black Oak
The town that gave us Black Oak Arkansas

The wild and woolly rock band Black Oak Arkansas took their name from the town where they were formed. The place has a population of less than 300 but became famous worldwide for lending its name to the band fronted by the long blonde-haired showman Jim "Dandy" Mangrum. These bad boys – once busted for grand larceny with an eight-year suspended jail sentence in the early days – would rehearse in a cotton gin bean elevator outside the town before going on to make their fortune as one of the seventies' most colorful rock bands.

Location 019: not to be confused with two other small towns named Black Oak in Arkansas, this one is in Craighead County, AR 72414

Mountain Home
The Black Oak Arkansas Commune

Around 150 miles northwest of the band's hometown at Black Oak lies the tiny town of Mountain Home. Here's where Black Oak Arkansas set up their own idea of heaven. The band's commune in the Ozark Mountain foothills was an oak-fenced stockade where they brewed their own moonshine and barbequed the local fauna most nights. In true rock star fashion, their swimming pool displayed a tiled mosaic of the band's cartoon style lightning bolt, fist, and acorn logo on the bottom. For further relaxation, the Black Oak Arkansas community would head through the trees to the nearby Bull Shoals Lake to access their own privately moored powerboats. The place is now a public resort.

Location 021: the Black Oak Resort is at 8543 Oakland Road, Oakland, AR 72661

Dyess
Johnny Cash's childhood home

Although Johnny Cash's birthplace was Kingsland, Arkansas, his childhood home in Dyess, more than 200 miles northeast, is the location most connected to the Man in Blacks formative years. The town where he grew up from the age of three and worked picking cotton two years later was a location for the filming of the multi-award-winning 2005 Johnny Cash bio-pic, Walk the Line. The Cash family home was on an agricultural resettlement community, part of the "New Deal" government economic program that provided relief to poor families during the depression. The family were one of 500 who received a new colony house, 20 to 40 acres of land, a mule, and seed for farming when they had the good fortune to move to Dyess in 1935. The property, complete with smokehouse, chicken house, and barn in J.R.'s day (as he was called back then), is now owned and cared for by the Arkansas State University and has a historical marker out front. Authentic restoration of the farmhouse was due to be completed in 2013. There are ambitious future plans for a museum to mark the Cash family connections to Dyess, to cater for the growing number of Cash fans visiting the town.

Location 020: a mile west of the town center at 4791 West County Road 924, Dyess, AR 72330

Johnny Cash's childhood home: beautifully restored to its original brand new state as it was when the Cash family moved to Dyess in 1935

Michael Hibblen

Arkansas

Newport
The Highway 67 Museum

The Arkansas Rock 'n' Roll Highway 67 Museum is dedicated to the 1950s venues on the route between Pocahontas and Newport traveled by the likes of Elvis Presley, Johnny Cash, Carl Perkins, Jerry Lee Lewis, Conway Twitty, and Roy Orbison. The museum exhibits artifacts and memorabilia relating to the artists who played joints such as the Silver Moon, Porky's Roof Top, and Bob King's (which is still standing in Swifton) up and down this famous road.

Location 022: a short distance west of Highway 67 at 201 Hazel Street, Newport, AR 72112

Ozark
The Wakarusa Music Festival

The Wakarusa Music Festival is an annual shindig that takes place on Mulberry Mountain in late spring. Here you can catch some great music while watching the spectacular sunsets behind the Ozark Mountains. Acts of the caliber of Wilco, The Black Keys, The Black Crowes, and Mumford & Sons have all performed in recent years since the festival, named after the River Wakarusa, switched location from Lawrence, Kansas. The gathering isn't huge and if you've never been to a music festival, this would be a good place to start.

Location 023: 20 miles east of Highway 540 between Fayetteville (to the north) and Fort Smith (to the south) at Mulberry Mountain Loop, near Ozark, AR 72949

Walnut Ridge
A flying Beatles visit

The 'Fab Four's only visit to Arkansas was in Walnut Ridge. The little place may only have a population of 4,925 but it certainly knows how to celebrate its rock and roll claim to fame in a big way. The town is now an unlikely tourist stop-over because The Beatles did exactly that on the weekend of September 19th and 20th 1964. John, Paul, George, and Ringo were on their way to a dude ranch vacation when they flew in and out of the only convenient airport at Walnut Ridge. Finishing a concert at the Dallas Memorial Auditorium in Texas on Friday September 18th The Beatles flew to Walnut Ridge Airport before heading off to relax at airline operator Reed Pigman Sr.'s Pigman Ranch, 75 miles north at Alton, Missouri. The secret plan to squeeze in a mini vacation between Dallas and New York City concerts, giving the group a break from fever-pitch Beatlemania, worked up to a point. That point came when the group returned to Walnut Ridge to fly onto New York City on Sunday. Several hundred fans and curious Walnut Ridge residents somehow got to hear of The Beatles' imminent arrival and assembled to catch a glimpse of the world famous foursome. During the 15 minutes it took to arrive and depart, the group had time for only a few handshakes and autographs as they made the short walk through the crowd from automobile and plane to the jet booked to fly them onto their tour's conclusion at the Paramount Theater, New York City, later that same day. Proud to be the only Arkansas place The Beatles ever visited, Walnut Ridge still ▶

Above: Ringo Starr and John Lennon snapped during their one very short visit to Arkansas. The Walnut Ridge airport photo is used courtesy of Shelby Wayland and Stacy Rice, daughter and granddaughter of the photographer that day, Newell Mock

Below: George Harrison arrives in Walnut Ridge. This rare photograph is used by kind permission of Carrie Mae Snapp, whose father's box Brownie snapped the moment. Carrie Mae now owns a shop in Walnut Ridge called, appropriately enough, 'Imagine'

The informative Guitar Walk pays tribute to the musicians who established the Rock 'n' Roll Highway 67 which runs through Walnut Ridge

Arkansas

▶ celebrates the fact to this day. A festival, "Beatles at the Ridge," is promoted as "Where Abbey Road meets the Rock 'n' Roll Highway" and the organizers aren't faking. There really is an Abbey Road in Walnut Ridge and a tribute sculpture depicting the famous album cover and a performance area can be found on what was formerly Southwest Second Street. The town's music heritage isn't confined to The Beatles. If you're thinking of completing your own flying visit, don't miss the massive 115-foot Guitar Walk (modeled on the hollow-bodied electric Epiphone Casino) which stretches out across Cavanaugh Park. Here you'll find a series of plaques equipped with audio buttons that both inform and play tracks by the artists that helped establish the local Highway 67 as the Rock 'n' Roll Highway 67 it is today.

Locations 024, 025, and 026:
Walnut Ridge is on a road now designated as Rock 'n' Roll Highway 67 due to the likes of Elvis Presley, Carl Perkins and Johnny Cash using the route to travel to concert bookings in the 1950s and 60s. The Beatles Park tribute site is at 110 Abbey Road, just half a block away from Main Street, at 110 Abbey Road, AR 72476 – formerly Southwest Second Street until the city officially changed the street name in 2011. Main Street is part of Rock 'n' Roll Highway 67, making Walnut Ridge the spot "Where Abbey Road meets the Rock 'n' Roll Highway" as the locals like to say. The Cavanaugh Park Guitar Walk is a couple of blocks walk away at 109 Southwest Front Street. The airport – the only spot The Beatles actually set foot on – is at 11 Airport Access Road, about three miles north of downtown Walnut Ridge.

❛When The Beatles stepped out of the Red GMC Suburban and the small plane, to board the larger plane, the crowd went wild. I could even see an unseen level of excitement in my parents' eyes. The crowd was composed of people I knew. Parents of kids and the kids we ran around with, yet it appeared everyone had been overtaken by some form of magic ❜

Eyewitness Charles Snapp

London's Abbey Road comes to Abbey Road, Walnut Ridge. These Beatles are the creation of local sculptor Danny West and are made from heavy carbon steel plate, with the backdrop ground from thick aircraft aluminum plates

California

Henry Diltz

Agoura Hills
Eagles play cowboys

Where the first Eagles album cover had them playing a sons-of-the-desert vibe for the photoshoot, with the band high on peyote in the high desert, the follow-up Desperado shoot involved a bank raid. Glenn Frey, Don Henley, Bernie Leadon, and Randy Meisner, augmented by friends Jackson Browne and J.D. Souther, played Wild West outlaws while management and roadies acted out the roles of a posse at the Paramount movie

Ranch back lot in Agoura Hills. The 1973 concept album, with its plaintive title track 'Desperado,' pictures the band armed to the teeth and ready for action on the front cover, then shot dead with the victorious posse standing over them on the back. Cover art director Gary Burden summed up the concept perfectly when he drew the parallel between the gunslingers in the 1870s and the guitar players of the 1970s. The photoshoot wasn't that much of a

stretch for the Eagles: most West Coast rock stars dressed pretty much like cowboys anyway. The old Paramount Movie Ranch, where many classic westerns were filmed, is now a Wild West tourist attraction and the admission is free.

Location 027: Agoura Hills is about 40 miles west of L.A. The Wild West town at the old Paramount Ranch is at 2903 Cornell Road, Agoura Hills, CA, 91301

Funded by Asylum Records boss David Geffen, the photoshoot on December 18th 1972 provided the perfect centerfold shot when the Eagles staged the bank raid and photographer Henry Diltz snapped away. Sadly, Geffen changed his mind and nixed the centerfold, although the spectacular gunfight did make it to onto the album's billboard advertisements in the run-up to the LP's release in 1973

California

Altamont
The notorious Altamont Free Festival

On December 6th 1969, just four months after love and peace overflowed from the Woodstock festival, Altamont saw all that positivity come crashing down at the free festival staged at Altamont Speedway track. The symbolism of the tragic ending of the sixties on such a bum note was not lost on the media, who dubbed the event as the end of the hippie dream. The violent atmosphere created by Hells Angels, hired as security to 'police' the event, reached a sickening climax when an-18-year-old gun-toting fan was stabbed to death in front of the stage. As headliners The Rolling Stones began their seventh number, 'Under My Thumb,' Meredith Hunter, who was high on drugs, was murdered by Hells Angel Alan Passaro. His was not the only life lost that day: one fan

was drowned and two were killed when vehicles drove over them in their sleeping bags. Weirdly, Altamont only happened in the first place due to the conscience of The Rolling Stones. Troubled by a bad press over what some had argued were inflated ticket prices on their earlier 1969 tour dates, the Stones agreed to play a free festival accompanied by a supporting cast of the hottest bands of the year. Crosby, Stills, Nash & Young, Jefferson Airplane, Santana, and The Flying Burrito Brothers had all played before sundown heralded the delayed appearance of the Stones due to the late arrival of their bass player Bill Wyman, who had missed the helicopter ride into the site. Even before the Stones took to the stage in front of 300,000 fans, the violence had been simmering.

❛It was also the first time 'Brown Sugar' was played in front of a live audience – a baptism from hell, in a confused rumble in the Californian night.❜

Keith Richards remembers Altamont in his biography Life (2010)

Airplane vocalist Marty Balin received a punch from a Hells Angel, rendering him unconscious during his band's performance, and as a result the next act due to appear, Grateful Dead, pulled out at that moment and refused to take the stage. It seems astonishing today that this infamous festival was only switched to the Altamont Speedway two days earlier, when organizers in open spaces in nearby San Jose, San Francisco's Golden Gate Park, and Sears Point Raceway all declined to host the event. They left Altamont to sully its name as perhaps the location of rock music's darkest hour.

Location 028: now called Altamont Raceway Park, the site of the 1969 festival is 40 miles northeast of San Jose between Livermore and Tracy at 17001 Midway Road, CA 95377

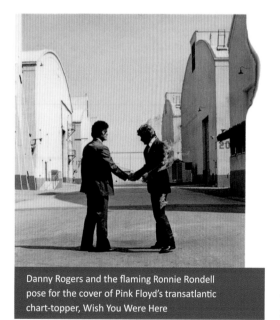

Danny Rogers and the flaming Ronnie Rondell pose for the cover of Pink Floyd's transatlantic chart-topper, Wish You Were Here

Burbank
The burning man Pink Floyd photoshoot

Pink Floyd's striking album cover for Wish You Were Here was photographed at the Burbank movie studios lot. Storm Thorgerson's photoshoot required two men to shake hands – one of whom was on fire. As the cover was created before the common use of computerized imagery, stuntman Ronnie Rondell was kitted out with fire-resistant underclothes beneath a business suit and a wig. Once set alight the precautions worked but the plan hadn't taken account of

the direction of the wind, which blew toward Rondell, burning his mustache before he and fellow stuntman Danny Rogers changed positions.

Location 030: the city of Burbank is north of Los Angeles. The tour guide at Warner Bros. Studios pinpoints the Wish You Were Here photoshoot as taking place at the intersection of the Mill Building and Stage 16 at Warner Bros. Studios, 4000 Warner Boulevard, Burbank, CA 91522

20. **CELEBRATION AT BIG SUR** Color by DE LUXE®

71/144

Big Sur
A hippie celebration on the California cliffs

Founded in 1962 as an alternative educational sanctuary devoted to "the exploration of what Aldous Huxley called the "human potential," the Esalen Institute played host to an extraordinary West Coast festival one month after Woodstock. With little or no security and performers mingling freely with 5,000 fans massed around the estate's swimming pool, the Woodstock vibe carried over into the weekend of September

13th and 14th 1969, on the Pacific coast at Big Sur. The newly crowned kings and queen of the hippie movement, Crosby, Stills, Nash & Young and Joni Mitchell, were the star performers. Some $10,000 richer from their Woodstock appearance, CSN&Y played Big Sur for free. The Celebration wasn't the first time the Esalen Institute had been used as a music venue – concerts were held in the grounds from 1964 to 1971 – but

the 1969 Big Sur folk festival was certainly the most memorable due in no small part to the movie made that weekend. Celebration at Big Sur (now on DVD) featured music and relaxation with David Crosby enjoying emersion in the hot spring baths, a facility offered by Esalen today where, as in 1969, "swimsuits are optional, and nudity common."

Location 029: Esalen estate, 55000 Highway 1, Big Sur, CA 93920

John Sebastian, Stephen Stills, Graham Nash, Joni Mitchell, and David Crosby grooving poolside: a still from the 20th Century Fox movie Celebration at Big Sur

California

Corona, Fullerton, and Santa Ana
The Leo Fender story

The Fender factory in Corona is the place to head for to uncover the history behind the work of famous electric guitar builder Leo Fender. Born in nearby Fullerton in 1909, he helped revolutionize 1950s rock and roll music with the manufacture of a series of new and exciting solid-bodied electric guitars. There's a Fender Visitor Center and Museum which will guide you to other points of interest including the newly recognized landmark building where Fender worked in the

1940s (now an aerospace parts manufacturer) called Fender's Radio Service and Jimmi's Nascar Bar & Grill – formerly the factory where the very first Fender Stratocasters were made. Leo Fender died in 1991 and is buried (with a small illustrated plaque to mark the spot) at the Fairhaven Memorial Park in Santa Ana.

Locations 031, 032, 033 and 034: The Fender Visitor Center is off Railroad Street at 301 Cessna Circle, Corona, CA 92880. Four

miles south of the Visitor Center is a mosaic which marks the spot of the former Fender's Radio Service building at 107 South Harbor Boulevard, Corona, 92882. Jimmi's Nascar Bar & Grill is at the corner of South Raymond Avenue and Valencia Drive, Fullerton, CA 92831, in the city where Leo Fender was born. Eleven miles south of Fullerton's former Fender factory is the Fairhaven Memorial Park where Fender was buried, at 1702 East Fairhaven Avenue, Santa Ana, CA 92705

Left: 'Stratocaster Orange Coast,' a mosaic wall mural by artist Katherine England (pictured) decorates the back wall of the former Fender Radio Service building in Corona

Right: Fender's widow, Phyllis Fender, helps artist Katherine England open the Stratocaster mural

Cotati
Prairie Sun Studios and 'The Waits Room'

Former touring musician Mark "Mooka" Rennick started a residential recording facility when he teamed up with land owner Clifton Buck-Kauffman. Prairie Sun Recording Studios, which started life in 1978, were relocated to the latter's 12-acre chicken farm in 1981. Since then a steady stream of rock's biggest

names have visited Cotati to work and relax in this rustic location north of San Francisco. Tom Waits recorded his 1992 Grammy-winning album Bone Machine mostly in an old storage room here when he couldn't find the right atmosphere in the studios. The room, off Studio C, is now affectionately known

as The Waits Room. Waits has returned on many occasions to the storage room, notably during the recording of another Grammy winner, Mule Variations (1999).

Location 036: Cotati is north of San Francisco. The studios are just west of Highway 101 at 1039 Madrone Avenue, CA 94931

❛I found a great room to work in. It's just a cement floor and a hot water heater. Okay, we'll do it here. It's got some good echo ❜

Tom Waits records a Grammy winner in the old hatchery

Costa Mesa
The Newport Pop Festival

The Orange County Fairgrounds was the setting for the ground-breaking Newport Pop Festival held here in August 1968. Named after the beach and boulevard address of the fairgrounds, the event became the first pop concert to attract a paid attendance of 100,000. The popularity of the event took organizers by surprise. The original location inside the fairgrounds was scrapped, and in just three days fencing, sanitation, and a stage moved out into the fairground parking lots to accommodate the growing number of ticket holders. Although amateurishly organized and with an inadequate sound system, the sun shone and the festival did make a profit. Country Joe & The Fish, Grateful Dead, Canned Heat, Eric Burdon & The Animals, and Alice Cooper were on the bill and a hippie vibe prevailed with helicopters dropping flowers on the crowds. The event's high spirits climaxed on the Sunday when David Crosby of The Byrds instigated a pie fight with Jefferson Airplane which led to a stage invasion as the stockpile of meat and pastry flew back and forth. Was the festival a success? In the eyes of the fans and performers: probably. However, Costa Mesa Mayor Alvin Pinkley was moved to announce: "To say that we would not like it back here would be the understatement of the year." He got his wish, and in 1969 it moved 70 miles north to Northridge.

Location 035: the Orange County Fairgrounds are 37 miles south of L.A. at Newport Boulevard and Fair Drive, Costa Mesa, CA 92626

Daly City
A Who substitute at Cow Palace

Unsurprisingly, with a name like Cow Palace, the indoor arena's very first show back in 1941 was the Western Classic Holstein Show. Aside from rodeo, circus, ice shows, and sports events, its greatest music claim to fame came when it was chosen as the first venue on The Beatles' first tour of North America in 1964. Famously, when The Who opened their Quadrophenia tour at Cow Palace on November 20th 1973 Keith Moon passed out on two occasions during the gig. Fueled by a cocktail of pills and booze the drummer left Pete Townshend, Roger Daltrey, and John Entwistle no option but to continue without drums until Townshend hit on the idea of an appeal to the audience for help. Nineteen-year-old rock fan and drummer Scot Halpin, who had arrived 13 hours early to secure a good spot in a front row seat, was in just the right position to get up on stage and

CAN ANYBODY OUT THERE PLAY DRUMS? THE WHO

Roger Daltrey, John Entwistle, Pete Townsend and hero Scot Halpin end a memorable gig at Cow Palace

made a confident substitute. He and the rest of the band received a thunderous standing ovation at the end of the night. Townshend's appeal even spawned the title of a Who at Cow Palace bootleg album released later called Can Anybody Out There Play Drums?

Location 038: Immediately south of San Francisco, Cow Palace is at 2600 Geneva Avenue, Daly City, CA 94014

Cypress
Eddie Cochran's gravestone

Killed in an auto accident in England when returning to Heathrow Airport at the end of a UK tour in 1960, rock and roll star Eddie Cochran was a guitar hero to many aspiring musicians who grew up in the British Beat boom during the early 1960s. Cochran is buried here at the Forest Lawn Memorial Park alongside his girlfriend Sharon Sheeley, who survived the auto accident but died in 2002. When asked where he was from, Cochran, who was born in Minnesota, would reply "Oklahoma." This is where his parents moved in the late 1940s, before the family moved back to Minnesota and then California.

Location 037: south of L.A., Forest Lawn Memorial Park is at 4471 Lincoln Avenue, Cypress, CA 90630

EDWARD R. COCHRAN 1938 1960

Born in Minnesota, died in England, buried in California

California

Death Valley
U2's Joshua Tree cover

When U2 completed work on their fifth studio album in 1987 it was pretty clear it was going to be big from the outset. Having already photographed the band and directed their video for 'Pride (In The Name of Love),' Anton Corbijn was hired to find suitable locations and travel with the band to find the perfect spot for the album's cover shoot. Once on the road to find the perfect desert landscape, Corbijn described the striking Joshua trees they would see and the band were so enthralled with the tree's image and Old Testament religious significance they immediately named the new album after one. The solitary Joshua tree pictured on the back cover artwork with the band standing in the desert in the freezing cold was shot in Death Valley. That solitary tree

died and keeled over long ago, but enthusiastic fans of the band had already marked its position and next to the remains of the tree now lies a metal plaque bearing the inscription "Have you found what you're looking for" – a play on words from the album's second track 'I Still Haven't Found What I'm Looking For'. Also, right next to the dry, old remains of the tree is a large cylindrical receptacle for fans to post messages called the U2ube. Hundreds have made the pilgrimage but few want to share the secret of the exact location. The discovery of the spot seems to be a badge of honor among fans, partly to protect the shrine from any removal or disapproval from authorities who look after the area. The album's front cover shot, sans Joshua tree, is easier to

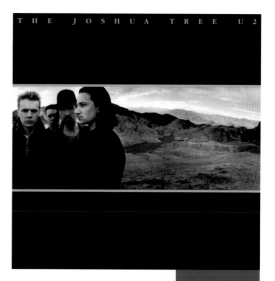

pinpoint. Head for Zabriskie Point, where the iconic black and white photograph was taken.

Locations 039 and 040: the Mojave Desert (back cover) and Zabriskie Point (front cover), Death Valley

Anton Corbijn's front cover photo was taken at Zabriskie Point

Richard and Karen Drive past their family home on Newville Avenue

Downey
The Carpenters family home

The home where the Carpenter family lived from 1963 was immortalized on the cover of Karen and Richard's 1973 album Now & Then. The Carpenters' brother and sister duo are pictured on the cover

driving past the family home in Richard's Ferrari. When Richard sold his parents' home in 1997, subsequent purchasers were still inundated with fans calling at the property.

Location 041: the city of Downey is in southeast Los Angeles County. The former Carpenter home (threatened with demolition) is at 9828 Newville Avenue, Downey, CA 90240

El Cerrito
John and Tom Fogerty's childhood home

El Cerrito is the place where four schoolmates formed a band that later became Creedence Clearwater Revival. Most definitely not 'Born on the Bayou,' as the CCR song goes, two of the band members were brothers Tom and John Fogerty. Their childhood home is on Ramona Avenue, where Tom had an upstairs bedroom and younger brother John slept in the basement. A series of 28 special pavement stones that highlight the cultural history of El Cerrito includes one which acknowledges the local music scene and the contribution Creedence Clearwater Revival have made in putting this small town on the map.

Locations 043 and 044: El Cerrito is just north of Berkeley in northern California. The street paving stone is on San Pablo Avenue and the Fogerty brothers' childhood home is at 226 Ramona Avenue, El Cerrito, CA, 94530

Encino
The Jacksons' family home

When the Jackson offspring had made a significant amount of money from hit records in the 60s as The Jackson 5, manager and father Joe Jackson moved the family from Indiana to a mansion in Encino. The mock Tudor house and grounds, which boasted its own zoo, became the home hub of activity for the constantly touring and recording Jacksons. Michael Jackson lived here until he departed for Neverland in 1988.

Location 045: about 20 miles west of central LA, the house is at 4641 Hayvenhurst Avenue, Encino, CA 91436

El Cerrito
The Metallica house

Sandwiched between Wildcat Canyon and San Francisco Bay on Carlson Boulevard stands a pretty little detached house where Metallica turned their thrash metal experiments into a million-dollar business. Rented by the band's sound engineer Mark Whitaker, the house, more specifically the garage underneath it, was where the band partied, wrote, and rehearsed two albums, Ride the Lightning (1983) and Master of Puppets (1986), that would establish both enduring critical acclaim and commercial success. Originally based in L.A., the band only decided to move to El Cerrito when enthusiastically trying to enlist the services of ace bass player Cliff Burton. Metallica headed north to the Bay Area as Burton's one condition for agreeing to join was that they all moved to him rather than him move south to Los Angeles. His contribution both geographically and musically to the band was key, but in September 1986, with Master of Puppets already a worldwide hit, Burton was killed when the Metallica tour bus overturned in Scandinavia.

Location 042: El Cerrito is 15 miles northeast of San Francisco. The Metallica house is at 3140 Carlson Boulevard, El Cerrito, CA 94530

Fairfax
The Moby Grape album cover

Moby Grape's debut album cover was photographed by Jim Marshall outside former antiques emporium, Junktiques, in Fairfax. The 1967 cover shoot found the band's singer, songwriter, and drummer Don Stevenson in a bad mood. As Moby Grape and Marshall trekked around Fairfax searching for an ideal photo opportunity, Stevenson made sure he flipped his middle finger in all the shots Marshall snapped. Earliest copies of the album carried the photo of Stevenson giving his obscene gesture before Columbia Records had it photographically removed on later printings.

Location 046: sadly, the antique store building appears to be long gone at 341 Bolinas Road, Fairfax (15 miles north of the Golden Gate Bridge), CA 94930

Don Stevenson (with washboard) flips the finger that Columbia later 'removed.' The record company also later substituted the red flag and replaced it with the Stars and Stripes

California

Glendale
Michael Jackson's tomb

Although Michael Jackson's last resting place is hidden from public view, the 'King of Pop''s fans still visit in large numbers to pay their respects, particularly on anniversaries of his birthday and his death in 2009. The Forest Lawn Memorial Park is a maximum security, privately owned cemetery which the Jackson family chose to protect Michael from overzealous fans and press intrusion. The remains of the shy superstar are entombed in the Great Mausoleum's Holly Terrace. It's fitting that a large stained glass window in the Mausoleum depicts a version of Leonardo da Vinci's 'The Last Supper': the painting had been a favorite of Michael's, a copy of which he'd had hung at his Neverland home.

Location 049: Glendale is a short distance north of L.A. The Forest Lawn Memorial Park is at 1712 South Glendale Avenue, Glendale, CA 91205. There is no public access to the tomb.

Glacier Point
David Lee Roth's Skyscraper cover shoot

The cover of David Lee Roth's 1988 Skyscraper album pictures the man himself hanging from the rock face of Yosemite National Park's Glacier Point. The camera doesn't lie. It really is him suspended bravely by one 12-inch-long climbing peg wedged into the rock. The photoshoot was more like an expedition. A lot of walking past Half Dome and Nevada Falls – Lee Roth rejected the offer of a horse to start the journey – and one overnight camp was involved before the crew and Lee Roth found the perfect spot to shoot the cover. Was this rock star at all worried? "Visibly shaking" and "Scared shitless!" according to the climbing expert hired for the trip.

No stunt double: Galen Rowell's shot of David Lee Roth at the top of Glacier Point in 1987

Location 048: assuming no one is attempting to reenact Lee Roth's pose, all you need to know is Glacier Point, Yosemite National Park, 250 miles east of San Francisco, CA 95389

Folsom
Johnny Cash's 'Folsom Prison Blues'

Johnny Cash's musical association with Folsom State Prison would never have begun had he not sat down with fellow US Air Force staff to watch a movie called Inside the Walls of Folsom Prison in 1952. The movie inspired him to write a song about the place that would later provide a turning point in his music career. When Cash first performed a prison concert in 1957 at Huntsville State Prison, Texas, he was responding to inmates who, identifying themselves with his 1955 Sun Records single 'Folsom Prison Blues,' had written requesting a prison appearance. He actually got to play Folsom Prison in 1966 and returned two years later to make a live album that would boost a career that had been recently blighted by drug addiction. The album, Johnny Cash at Folsom Prison, was recorded during two shows in front of enthusiastic inmates on January 13th 1968. Although Columbia Records had agreed to Cash's unusual venue for a live album they invested little time and money promoting it. The record turned out to be an unexpected and enduring hit with added critical acclaim that saw Johnny Cash's career begin to scale new levels. (See also the entry for San Quentin.)

Location 047: Folsom State Prison is 20 miles northeast of Sacramento, at 300 Prison Road, Folsom, CA 95671

❝The concert was down on a makeshift stage and we were recording up in the cafeteria. There were guards walking around up on the balcony with those dark glasses on, so you couldn't see anything, and the guns were loaded. It was a maximum security prison❞

Producer Bob Johnston

Johnny Cash arrives outside Folsom Prison for the recording of the live album that would prove to be the most significant record release of his career

California

Hawthorne
The Beach Boys monument

Although the childhood home of Beach Boys Brian, Carl, and Dennis Wilson was demolished in the 1980s, the exact spot where the house once stood on 119th Street, Hawthorne, is commemorated by a monument to the group. The structure consists of a 3D stone relief reproduction of The Beach Boys image on their 1963 Surfer Girl album cover. As the bronze plaque below the stone image says, "It was here in the home of parents Murry and Audree that Brian, Dennis, and Carl Wilson grew to manhood and developed their musical skills, during Labor Day weekend 1961. They, cousin Mike Love, and a friend Al Jardine, gathered here to record a tape of their breakthrough song 'Surfin'. This marked the birth of the rock group known worldwide as The Beach Boys, and the beginning of an historic musical legacy. The music of The Beach Boys broadcast to the world an image of California as a place of sun, surf, and romance." More than 800 fans plus Beach Boys Brian Wilson and Al Jardine attended the unveiling of the monument in 2005. Aside from Mike Love, all the Wilson brothers and Jardine attended Hawthorne High School, a short distance from the Fosters Freeze hamburger stand said to be the favorite hangout and Beach Boys inspiration for their 1964 hit 'Fun, Fun, Fun.'

Locations 050, 051, and 052:
Hawthorne is in the South Bay area of Los Angeles County. The Wilson family home Beach Boys monument is next to Highway 105 at 3701 West

Monument photo © Gary Wayne of Seeing Stars

Above: California Registered Historical Landmark No. 1041: The Beach Boys

Left: the album cover image that inspired the Hawthorne monument

119th Street, Hawthorne, CA 90250. Fosters Freeze is at 11969 South Hawthorne Boulevard, Hawthorne, 90250, and Hawthorne High School is at 4859 El Segundo Boulevard, Hawthorne, 90250

Indio
The Coachella Festival

This is one of the hottest festivals: literally so due to its California desert setting, where daytime temperatures frequently rise well above 100 degrees. The whole thing started in 1993 when Pearl Jam played on the lawns of the Empire Polo Club in Indio. The concert would seem to have been a success attracting 25,000 fans and paving the way for another music event featuring Beck and Morrissey in 1999 before today's annual Coachella Festival began in 2001. The festival made the news worldwide in 2012 when, during Dr. Dre and Snoop Dogg's set, deceased superstar rapper Tupac Shakur joined the duo on stage courtesy of an astonishing projection technique likened to a hologram. The festival has specialized in attracting some of the biggest British bands down the years, including Radiohead, Muse, Arctic Monkeys, Depeche Mode, and Coldplay.

Location 053: about 25 miles southeast of Palm Springs near neighboring Coachella at the Empire Polo Club, 81-800 Avenue 51, Indio, CA 92201

Joshua Tree
Gram Parsons' shrines

Cap Rock is the special place of pilgrimage for fans of country rock pioneer Gram Parsons, who loved the spot in life and visited regularly with, among others, Rolling Stone Keith Richards. Gram was so entranced by the location's atmosphere that, following his untimely death aged 26 in 1973, two friends stole his body en route to the funeral in New Orleans and attempted to cremate Gram's body on Cap Rock. The attempt to fulfil what seemed like Gram's own wishes (as opposed to that of his stepfather's) was badly botched by his friends. The two fled the scene, leaving the body's charred remains, when police gave chase having spotted a gasoline-fueled fire in the distance. The National Park authorities have removed a concrete slab memorial which once marked the spot of the cremation. This hasn't deterred fans from still making Cap Rock a point of pilgrimage to leave messages and mementos on the rocks but the concrete "Gram Safe at Home" memorial has been relocated to the Joshua Tree Inn, the place where Gram died from what turned out to

THE GRAM PARSONS ANTHOLOGY

Gram Parsons' favorite escape destination from Los Angeles was to Joshua Tree, where he would combine his dual pastimes of drug taking and UFO watching

be a lethal cocktail of alcohol and morphine in room #8. The room has the same mirror and picture hanging in it today that were there during Gram's last visit to the Hacienda-style inn.

Locations 054 and 055: Joshua Tree National Park is a three-hour automobile trip east of Los Angeles. The Joshua Tree Inn is at 61259 29 Palms Highway, Joshua Tree, CA 92252. A short journey southeast of the inn takes you to Cap Rock (where there is a parking lot). This boulder-strewn spot favored by hikers is situated in the Joshua Tree National Park at the junction of Park Boulevard and Keys View Road.

❛We were quite taken with the mysterious other worldly beauty there. Joshua Tree's certainly got something – it's why Gram went there❜

Emmylou Harris, for whom Gram Parsons was her self-confessed muse, recalls a trip to Joshua Tree and a stay at the Joshua Tree Inn

California

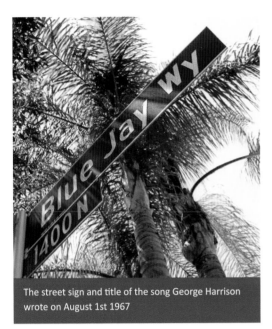

The street sign and title of the song George Harrison wrote on August 1st 1967

Los Angeles
George Harrison's foggy 'Blue Jay Way'

The song 'Blue Jay Way' was written by George Harrison while renting a house on this L.A. street, at the end of a series of winding roads high above Sunset Strip. He was inspired to write The Beatles' 1967 Magical Mystery Tour track when waiting for a visit from the band's press officer, Derek Taylor, who was delayed and lost in the L.A. fog. This scenario became the subject of the song, which Harrison wrote on a little Hammond S-6 organ that his landlord had left in the corner of the room. The song was written as a joke exercise by Harrison to keep himself awake until Taylor arrived. A couple of years later the house was responsible for helping create a second piece of rock history. While renting the place in 1969, Paul Simon and then Art Garfunkel worked on a new song here that became 'Bridge Over Troubled Water,' and recorded the distinctive percussion track for the duo's infectiously catchy track 'Cecilia.'

Location 058: this private house (according to one source, worth a cool $4million) up in the Hollywood Hills is at 1567 Blue Jay Way, L.A., CA 90069

La Honda
Neil Young's Broken Arrow Ranch

In Northern California's Santa Cruz Mountains, off Skyline Boulevard, lies the land Neil Young purchased in 1970 for a reported $350,000 and where he still calls home today. Young, who fell in love with the 140-acre property with its two lakes, two houses, and barn, would go on to buy up more than 1,000 extra acres. Formerly the Lazy Double L Ranch, on account of the two lawyers named Long and Lewis that had the place previously, he renamed the place Broken Arrow Ranch and has been inspired to write, rehearse, and record some of his best music there. 'Old Man,' from his career-changing Harvest album, was written for the ranch's live-in foreman Louis Avila who first showed Young around his new property and stayed on to work for him. Incredulous that someone so young could afford such a beautiful but expensive chunk of real estate, 70+-aged cattleman Avila gave the new owner a guided tour of the woodland, pastures, and ocean views in a blue jeep that inveterate collector Young has kept ever since. The house quadrupled in size after Young's marriage to Pegi in 1978 and disabled son Ben's arrival, necessitating space for Ben's specific medical needs. Around the ranch are dotted objects of obsession to the Canadian-born musician. Aside from the livestock, his model railroad has its own barn, with real railroad rolling stock out back. Then there's his vintage automobile collection, treasured guitar amps, baseball caps, tour jackets, master recording archive barn, recording facility Redwood Studio, and graveyard of scattered, rusty old vehicles waiting to be renovated or stripped of their last remaining useful parts. There are countless photographs of Young at Broken Arrow, and those included on the covers of his prodigious catalog of albums include the front of Old Ways and the back of the Crosby, Stills, Nash & Young release American Dream.

❝I was ready for a change from Los Angeles where I was living and had seen this beautiful area of land from the airplane on my trips to the Bay Area. Looking out the window, I saw rolling hills above the ocean with the grass a wheat color, looking like velvet on the hillsides. In the canyons, redwoods had stood for centuries ❞

Neil Young describes the property that became the Broken Arrow Ranch in his autobiography, Waging Heavy Peace

Location 056: the ranch is off Bear Gulch Road (CA 94062) between Skyline Boulevard to the north and La Honda Road further south. Stretches of the winding Bear Gulch Road near the ranch are privately owned by Neil Young. The town of La Honda is to the southeast

Broken Arrow Ranch was named after the song Neil Young wrote and recorded for the Buffalo Springfield album Buffalo Springfield Again, in 1967. The property provided the perfect landscape photo for the cover of his 1985 country album Old Ways, pictured opposite

Los Angeles
Don Henley's "Deadhead sticker on a Cadillac"

The inspiration for Don Henley's 1984 hit song "Boys of Summer," and more specifically the 'Deadhead sticker' observation in the lyrics, came while driving down Interstate 405. This memorable line is a perfect evocation of driving the California coast in summer, although Henley's enjoyment was interrupted, as he later recalled in an NME interview:

> ❛I was driving down the San Diego freeway and got passed by a $21,000 Cadillac Seville, the status symbol of the right-wing, upper-middle-class American bourgeoisie – all the guys with the blue blazers with the crests and the grey pants – and there was this Grateful Dead 'Deadhead' bumper sticker on it!❜

Location 057: someplace on the San Diego freeway (Interstate 405) through L.A.

Los Angeles/Mid-City
The Ray Charles Library

Opened on September 23rd 2010, on what would have been the legendary musician's 80th birthday, The Ray Charles Memorial Library is both a tribute to his life's work and an inspiration to students. Aside from featuring personal memorabilia in a museum-like setting there is a recording studio where students can begin their own journey to emulate the great man. Divided in to seven galleries, the library is not currently open to the public but reservations for student and corporate group visits can be made in advance by following the instructions on the Ray Charles Memorial Library website. The library's location is an appropriate one, constructed on the site where Ray Charles and his manager Joe Adams ran their operations from 1964.

Location 059: 2107 West Washington Boulevard, Mid-City, LA, CA 90018

California

Los Angeles
The Grammy Museum

What separates this music museum from the rest is its unique
association with the world famous Grammy Awards themselves.
However, the four floors and 30,000 square feet of artefact, film,
and interactive displays are not exclusively about the Grammys,
encompassing intriguing exhibits on subjects as diverse as Studio
Musicians and Session Players, Songwriters, The History of Heavy
Metal, and, of particular interest to readers of this book, Music
Epicenters, mapping America's special music hotspots.

Location 060: in the L.A. Live downtown district surrounded by
theaters, restaurants, studios, and the Staples Center, the Grammy
Museum address is at 800 West Olympic Boulevard, L.A., CA 90015,
but the museum entrance is on Figueroa Street

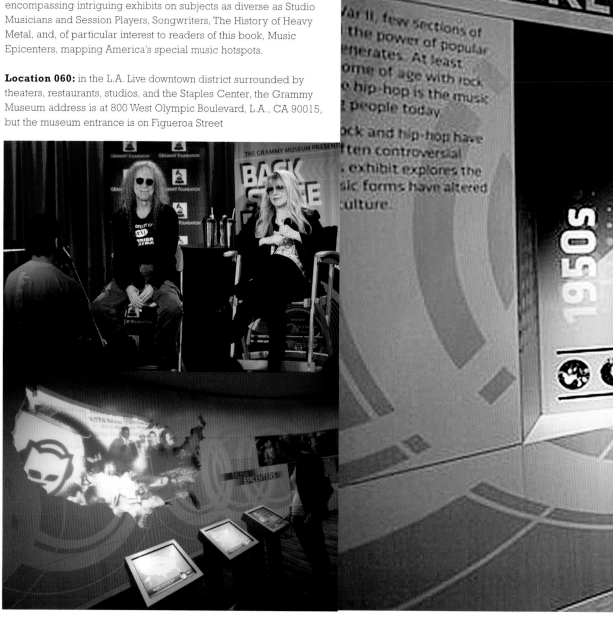

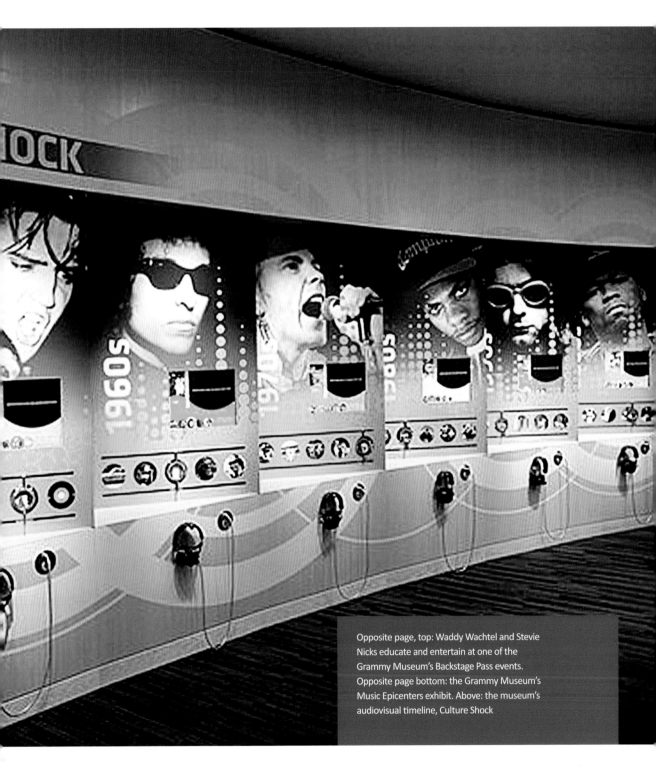

OCK

1960s

1970

Opposite page, top: Waddy Wachtel and Stevie Nicks educate and entertain at one of the Grammy Museum's Backstage Pass events. Opposite page bottom: the Grammy Museum's Music Epicenters exhibit. Above: the museum's audiovisual timeline, Culture Shock

California

Los Angeles/Downtown
Bonnie Raitt takes her time at Union Station

Union Station's Traxx Bar is the setting for the cover photograph on Bonnie Raitt's highly acclaimed 1973 album, Takin' My Time. Raitt is pictured leaning inside the doorway, surrounded by the station's art deco magnificence, with her busker's hat on the floor. Fans can easily reproduce their own version of the cover while admiring Union Station's jaw-droppingly beautiful architecture.

Location 061: the Traxx Bar is in Union Station, which is on the eastern edge of downtown Los Angeles, at 800 North Alameda Street, LA, CA 90012

Michael Dobo's classy cover photo for Bonnie Raitt's third album

Los Angeles/Downtown
U2 on the rooftops and The Million Dollar Hotel

Filming for what turned out to be a Grammy Award-winning video on March 27th 1987, U2 aped The Beatles' famous London rooftop performance when they played on top of a one-story building on the corner of 7th Street and Main Street. U2 performed eight songs including 'Where the Streets Have No Name,' the track for which the Grammy was awarded in 1989, watched by thousands of curious onlookers and nervous-looking policemen, who shut the rooftop gig down. The backdrop to the video is provided by the Million Dollar Hotel sign. This hotel is significant to U2 fans as it's the place that inspired Bono to write a movie script which eventually turned into the 2000 movie Million Dollar Hotel, directed by Wim Wenders.

Locations 062 and 063: in downtown L.A. at 103 East 7th Street, on the corner with Main Street, L.A. CA 90014. The Million Dollar Hotel (Rosslyn Hotel and New Million Dollar Hotel Rosslyn across the street – excitingly connected by an underground tunnel) is at 451 South Main Street, L.A., CA 90013

The U2 photoshoot on the roof of the New Million Dollar Rosslyn Hotel, which sparked Bono into creating a movie. The original Hotel Rosslyn can be seen across the street to the right

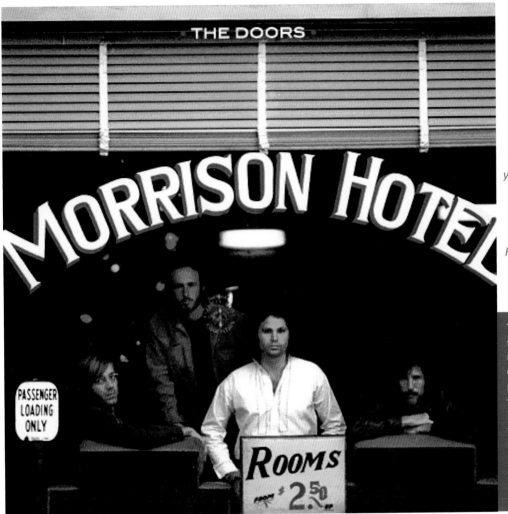

THE DOORS

MORRISON HOTEL

PASSENGER LOADING ONLY

ROOMS FROM $2.50 UP

> *It was the kind of place you could start a religion... ...or plan a murder*
>
> Ray Manzarek

The Doors look surprisingly relaxed considering this photoshoot was achieved in double quick time with no knowledge or permission from the hotel owners

Los Angeles/Downtown
The Morrison Hotel

It was The Doors' Ray Manzarek who spotted it first when out for a drive one Sunday in Downtown Los Angeles. The Morrison Hotel then became the title of the band's next album, connecting The Doors' lead vocalist Jim Morrison to this rather shabby establishment. The keyboards player tipped off photographer Henry Diltz and art director Gary Burden, and the group

photo opportunity inside the Morrison Hotel on South Hope Street became the cover of the 1970 release. The other group shots from the photo session, which appear on the inside and back of the album sleeve, were shot at a now totally demolished bar nearby called the Hard Rock Café, which supposedly gave the founders of the worldwide chain of restaurants the idea for their

new project's brand name.

Location 064: the Morrison Hotel building still stands (spelled out in large letters high up at one end), although the doorway and front window are barely recognizable today at 1246 South Hope Street (near the corner with West Pico Boulevard), Downtown L.A., CA 90015

California

Los Angeles/Alhambra
Phil Spector's Pyrenees Castle

The often dubbed genius record producer Phil Spector lived at Pyrenees Castle from 1998 up to 2003, when he was arrested at his home for the murder of actress Lana Clarkson. His seriously spooky replica French chateau sits on a hilltop in Alhambra and has gained a reputation for being haunted according to reports from owners dating back through nine decades of history. Visitors surviving the

❛I've bought myself a beautiful and enchanting castle in a hick town where there is no place to go that you shouldn't ❜

Phil Spector talking to Esquire about his purchase of Pyrenees Castle

guard dogs would then have to ascend the 88 stone steps to the entrance. Of the weird stories emanating from the place during Spector's time, surely the wackiest was a report that he wandered around his estate every day, in complete darkness, wearing nothing but a Batman costume.

Location 065: 1700 South Grandview Drive, Alhambra, L.A., CA 91803

Los Angeles/Bel Air
Brian Wilson's home studio

Brian Wilson's Spanish-style Bel Air mansion was where he (along with wife Marilyn) lived, created, and recorded albums such as Smiley Smile and Wild Honey. Some of the early recording methods at his Bellagio Road home were less than sophisticated. His large outdoor swimming pool, which had sprung a leak and was empty, was pressed into action as a makeshift recording base for vocals that had just the right amount of echo when a microphone was dropped onto the pool's bottom and the band recorded their harmonies on Smiley Smile. The property also contributed artistically to the next Beach Boys album, Wild Honey, in 1967. The album's stained glass cover image was photographed from a window at the entrance to the house, although the actual window has since been removed and installed in Brian's first wife Marilyn's current home.

Location 068: the house, with swimming pool but sans Wild

The Bellagio Road stained glass window cover was designed and photographed by Arny Geller

Honey stained glass window, is at 10452 Bellagio Road, Bel Air, CA 90077

Los Angeles/Bel Air
The Mamas & The Papas and Sly Stone mansion

From sixties hippie haven to funky seventies party base, this Bel Air home was the luxurious hideaway for the top stars in two diametrically opposite music genres. In his heyday, soul legend Sly Stone lived in a mock English Tudor mansion on Bel Air Road that was once owned by John and Michelle Phillips of The Mamas & The Papas. The hippie couple, who lived in the place from 1967 with their pet French poodle, made the most of the two-acre terraced garden, complete with pool, meditation bench, and hammock. In Sly Stone's time here the décor was all Tiffany lamps and shag pile carpeting. When Sly first took over the house, he inherited John Phillip's attic studio which he put to good use when working on the hugely successful Sly & The Family Stone album, There's a Riot Goin' On, there.

Location 067: the mansion is at 783 Bel Air Road, CA 90077. Visitors are requested to respect the privacy of the current owners

Los Angeles/ Baldwin Hills
Ike & Tina's place

Now this is what I call rock star chic! At the home husband and wife Ike and Tina Turner shared in Baldwin Hills in the sixties and seventies, the front door handles were bronze castings of Tina's hands.

Location 066: around five miles south of Beverly Hills, 4263 Olympiad Drive, Baldwin Hills, CA 90043

Los Angeles / Beverly Hills
'Sounds of Silence' and the Stones in the park

Franklin Canyon Park has been the setting for two high profile 1966 album cover shoots. The Rolling Stones are pictured next to the park's reservoir on the front cover of their 1966 compilation album Big Hits (High Tide and Green Grass). The famous backward-glancing photo of Simon & Garfunkel on one of the park's narrow roads formed the cover of the duo's second album, Sounds of Silence. With its close proximity to Hollywood, the park has conveniently featured in hundreds of movie and TV scenes including On Golden Pond and The Creature from The Black Lagoon.

Locations 069 and 070: Franklin Canyon Park is on the eastern end

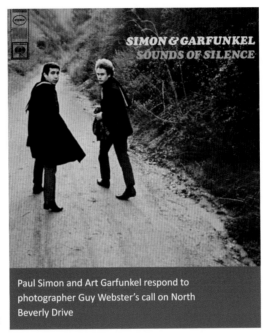

Paul Simon and Art Garfunkel respond to photographer Guy Webster's call on North Beverly Drive

❝That was shot on a dirt road along North Beverly Drive in Franklin Canyon, at a place where the city ended and the country began. It was very beautiful back then. I used to take a lot of rockers back there for shoots❞

Photographer Guy Webster recalls the Simon & Garfunkel cover shoot

of the Santa Monica Mountains. Make for the reservoir (Stones shoot) and North Beverly Drive (Simon & Garfunkel shoot) by accessing the park at 2600 Franklin Canyon Drive, Beverly Hills, L.A., CA 90210

Los Angeles/Beverly Hills and West Hollywood
The Beatles' secret hideaways

It wasn't possible for The Beatles to stay in hotels like other mortal rock stars. Beatlemania dictated that their three trips to L.A. had to be managed securely and as privately as possible. So when The Beatles invaded L.A. for the first time an invasion of the teenage fan kind was what the 'Fab Four''s intended hosts at the Ambassador Hotel feared might happen. The hotel canceled the booking and at short notice John, Paul, George, and Ringo rented British actor Reginald Owen's mansion on St. Pierre Road. Their three-day stay in August 1964 incorporated one famous performance at the Hollywood Bowl and a short vacation ahead of the next gig at Red Rocks in Colorado. While staying at Owen's place (Owen had a minor movie role in Mary Poppins at the time) The

Beatles ventured out to the Whisky a Go-Go, where George Harrison threw a drink at a photographer who was pestering the group but showered a deputy sheriff and actress Mamie Van Doren instead. Ringo Starr also got to meet his idol when invited over to Burt Lancaster's nearby house. On The Beatles' next visit to L.A. in 1965, a luxurious single-story bungalow on Benedict Canyon Drive served as their base. Jimi Hendrix, The Rolling Stones, and Cary Grant have also reportedly stayed at this French country estate once owned by Zsa Zsa Gabor, but presumably not at the same time! Hemmed in by fans camped outside the besieged property, The Beatles are said to have hosted an LSD party here where Joan Baez, The Byrds, and Peter Fonda dropped in. A heated discussion

between Fonda and John Lennon supposedly inspired Lennon to write the Revolver track 'She Said She Said.' On The Beatles' final visit to L.A. (where they played the Dodger Stadium) they stayed at a Beverly Hills house on Curson Terrace. Their short stay was enlivened by a visit from Beach Boys' Brian and Carl Wilson before The Beatles headed north for San Francisco to play what would turn out to be their final concert, at Candlestick Park.

Locations 071, 072, and 073: the 1964 Beatles base was at 365 St. Pierre Road, L.A., CA 90077. In 1965 John, Paul, George, and Ringo stayed at 2850 Benedict Canyon Drive, L.A., CA 90210. Their final stay in L.A. in 1966 was at 7655 Curson Terrace, CA 90046

California

Los Angeles/Beverly Hills
Welcome to the Hotel California

The Beverly Hills Hotel is certainly the building pictured on the cover of the Eagles' mega-selling Hotel California but which place was the subject of the song of the same name? The band weren't that forthcoming but the elegant, opulent, corruption theme of the title track pointed to a bigger picture – the American Dream gone wrong. The Eagles cover brief was for a slightly sinister image of a Hotel California that the band, and particularly Don Henley, had in mind for their 1976 release. British designer Kosh (John Kosh), who already had The Beatles' Abbey Road artwork on his CV, designed the cover and shot photos of the front and centerfold of the band and friends in a nearby flop house called The Lido, which neatly replicated the Hotel California lobby. Aside from the rock and roll fame associated with the Hotel California album cover, The Beverly Hills Hotel has taken care of a who's who of rock legends down the decades. David Bowie's 46-strong entourage once reportedly racked up a $100,000 bill on the RCA tab for a week's stay during their 1972 American tour. The Faces, Fleetwood Mac, Peter Frampton, and The Beatles have all hung out here at the height of their fame, plus just about every A-list Hollywood movie star.

Locations 074 and 075: the Hotel California album front cover depicts The Beverly Hills Hotel by night at 9641 Sunset

Boulevard, Beverly Hills, L.A., CA 90210. The inside picture of the lobby was shot seven miles northeast at The Lido Apartments, 6500 Yucca Street, L.A., CA 90028

The final album cover complete with the Kosh designed and Bob Hickson airbrushed Hotel California logo

❛To get the perfect picture, David and I had perched nervously atop a 60-foot cherry picker dangling over Sunset Boulevard in the rush hour, shooting blindly into the sun❜

Kosh (with the help of photographer David Alexander) risked life and limb to get the perfect Hotel California at sunset shot

Los Angeles/ Beverly Hills
Jan & Dean's 'Dead Man's Curve'

Surfing teen hit single 'Dead Man's Curve' describes a Sting Ray versus Jag drag race across Beverly Hills and Hollywood that ends in "a horrible sight," to quote the lyrics of the song penned by Brian Wilson, Roger Christian, Artie Kornfeld, and Jan Berry and recorded by Jan & Dean in 1963. The exact 'Curve' is easily identified through the song's lyrics: "I flew past LaBrea, Schwab's, and Crescent Heights" locates the fateful bend on Sunset Boulevard. In an almost unbelievable coincidence in 1966, Jan Berry was involved in a real life, almost fatal automobile accident when he crashed his Sting Ray on North Whittier Drive, a short distance from the song's 'Dead Man's Curve.' The story was just too good to pass up for a TV company, who made a movie drama (Dead Man's Curve) based around Jan's accident in 1978.

Location 076: traveling west, the drag race between the song's Sting Ray and Jag ended for the Jag on the sharp right-curving bend shortly after The Maltz Park and the junction of North Whittier Drive on Sunset Boulevard, CA 90010

Los Angeles/Beverly Hills
Jimi Hendrix's summer house

For a few weeks during the 'Summer of Love' in 1967, The Jimi Hendrix Experience lived in the mansion once owned by actor Rudolph Valentino. The Spanish-style house had been called "Falcon Lair" and was built on a clifftop overlooking Benedict Canyon.

Location 079: 1436 Bella Drive, Beverly Hills, L.A., CA 90210

Los Angeles/Beverly Hills
Brian Wilson's 'sand box' home

The Laurel Way home of Brian Wilson was where the pop genius created classic songs 'Surf's Up' and 'Heroes and Villains.' Pretty much housebound, having ceased touring with The Beach Boys in 1965, Wilson still had the urge to write and compose music. At least 10 miles from the nearest beach, he famously used the unorthodox method of replicating a beach vibe in his living room to write. He sectioned off an area of the room with curtains over a specially constructed sand box in which he worked away most nights on his piano, sleeping only during the day.

Location 077 the private hilltop residence is at 1448 Laurel Way, Beverly Hills, L.A., CA 90210

Los Angeles/ Beverly Hills
The Osbournes TV home

The pink house where Ozzy Osbourne and family lived and were regularly filmed for their hugely popular reality TV show is located in, where else? Beverly Hills. Ozzy and family moved into the opulent mansion formerly owned by an African potentate in 1999 and the TV cameras captured day-to-day family life from 2002 to 2005, when the house was put up for sale.

Location 078: a short distance north of Sunset Boulevard at 513 Doheny Road, CA 90210

> ❝A real big sand box, about nine by nine – the piano was in it and Van Dyke Parks used to write with me in it. We put the beach right in my house! It inspired me, created a mood that was unbelievable, magic❞
>
> *Brian Wilson, talking to Mojo in 2009*

Los Angeles/Century City
The Yes skyscrapers

Adorning the cover of Going for the One, the 1977 album by Yes, are the twin, 44-story buildings which form the Century Plaza Towers. According to Hipgnosis album cover designer Storm Thorgerson, his work on the sleeve received some unwanted attention. The gleaming structures and dramatic architecture were forgotten when "the naked man caused a flurry of anti-gay sentiment, or so I heard."

Location 080: just south of Beverly Hills at 2029 Century Park East, L.A., CA 90067

California

Los Angeles/Highland Park
Jackson Browne at the Abbey San Encino

The cover of Jackson Browne's second album depicts the inner courtyard at the Abbey San Encino. The warm, subtle tones of the 1973 cover photograph only hint at a rich history of the neo-Franciscan building. The seated Browne reclines in a rocking chair in the courtyard by a raised lily pond in a knowing, relaxed manner. And he's entitled to. He owned the place at the time of the cover shoot and release of For Everyman, as did his father before him and Browne's extraordinary grandfather, Clyde Browne, who built the place during a 12-year construction period starting in 1915. His grandson made good

use of the abbey's chapel, where he would rehearse songs while playing the 14-pipe organ.

Location 083: the beautiful abbey is still owned by the Browne family and is not open to the public, although it is available for hire as a movie or photoshoot location. The building is set on a hill in an otherwise unremarkable neighborhood in northeast Los Angeles at 6211 Arroyo Glen Street, Highland Park, CA 90042

Brownes have lived at the Abbey San Encino for almost a century

Los Angeles/Griffith Park
The Byrds' Untitled, uncovered

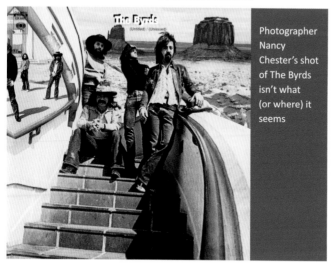

Photographer Nancy Chester's shot of The Byrds isn't what (or where) it seems

The Byrds pose on a staircase on the front cover of their 1970 Untitled album. The steps appear to be rising out of the Arizona landscape of Monument Valley, but the impressive stone staircase is actually at the Griffith Observatory in Griffith Park. (See also the Arizona Rock Atlas USA pages).

Location 082: at 2800 East Observatory Road, CA 90027

Los Angeles/Elysian Park
The Pet Shop Boys' park afterlife

The Pet Shop Boys' 2012 album title, Elysium, came about after Neil Tennant and Chris Lowe went for a stroll in Elysian Park. Famous for its avocado trees and striking rock garden waterfall – why has no enterprising rock band ever shot an album cover here? – L.A.'s' second largest park is named after the concept of the afterlife begun by the ancient Greeks called Elysian Fields or Elysium.

Location 081: in north central L.A. close to Dodger Stadium at 835 Academy Road, L.A., CA 90012

❝We wanted something that said this album's actually quite beautiful. Elysium's a sort of idealized afterlife, and that fits in with some of the songs ❞

Neil Tennant

Los Angeles/ Hollywood
The Capitol Records Tower

One of popular music's most iconic buildings, not least as its image adorned the record sleeves of this famous label, the Capitol Records Tower not only looks great but is practical too, designed prudently to withstand earthquakes. Completed in 1956, the construction proved to be the world's first circular office building and was nicknamed "The House that Nat Built" as a consequence of the huge number of record sales that Capitol artist Nat 'King' Cole had delivered in the period leading up to the tower's creation. Home to offices and recording studios with a unique echo chamber sunk 30-feet into the foundations; the 13-floor-high tower is topped off by a huge spike and a pulsing light which spells out the word "Hollywood" in morse code. Although built as a sign that the music industry was switching influence from East Coast to West Coast in the fifties, the building was sold in 2006. Look out for the Hollywood Walk of Fame pavement stars dedicated to John Lennon and Garth Brooks, positioned outside the building.

Location 084: still functioning as a recording complex, the tower is a dramatic fixture of the Hollywood skyline, situated on the corner of Hollywood Boulevard and Vine Street at 1750 North Vine Street, L.A., CA 90028

Like a beautiful stack of vinyl 45s, the Capitol Records Tower is protected by its listed status on the National Register of Historic Places

California

Los Angeles/Hollywood
'The Wall of Sound' studios

Gold Star Recording Studios was the place where producer Phil Spector recorded most of his famous 'Wall of Sound' recordings featuring The Righteous Brothers, The Ronettes, and The Crystals in the 1960s. Harnessing the perfect echo chamber qualities of Gold Star, Spector produced perhaps the finest example of his 'Wall of Sound' hits when Ike and Tina Turner recorded the epic 'River Deep – Mountain High' there in 1965. That old echo chamber was zealously guarded by Gold Star's owner Stan Ross. He wouldn't let anyone see it. When he sold Gold Star in 1984, Ross contacted Neil Young, who had recorded and mixed his own echoey masterpiece 'Expecting to Fly' there, to see if he would like to buy the chamber. He knew how fond the rock star was of the room, but concerned that moving it would affect the special sound, Young reluctantly declined. The room, which became a meat locker, was eventually demolished along with the rest of the building.

Location 085: before demolition, Gold Star stood at 6252 Santa Monica Boulevard, CA 90038

Los Angeles/Hollywood
Ocean Way studios

Ocean Way comprises four facilities, at Sherman Oaks (Record One), Nashville, St. Barth's, and here in Hollywood, where founder and owner Allen Sides moved his first studio after setting it up on Ocean Way, Santa Monica, in the mid-seventies – which accounts for the name. After a few years operating out of a former garage next to the Pacific Ocean, the operation eventually moved inland to Hollywood, where studios (no longer owned by Sides) still operate today. King of America (1986) by Elvis Costello, Mother's Milk (1989) by Red Hot Chili Peppers, and Hail to the Thief (2003) by Radiohead, were all recorded here.

Location 086: 6050 West Sunset Boulevard, L.A., CA 90028

Los Angeles/Hollywood
Sunset Sound Studios

Sunset Sound started out as a recording studio for Walt Disney's classic movies like 101 Dalmations and Mary Poppins when Walt's director of recording, Tutti Camarata, turned an old automobile repair shop into a recording facility in the late fifties. Opening in 1962, the then music revolution soon made the place the hottest and most convenient recording facility in town for those local musicians hanging out in Laurel Canyon. The Doors' eponymously titled debut album and the band's follow-up, Strange Days, were both recorded at Sunset Sound in 1966/67, as were large parts of The Rolling Stones' Exile on Main St. (1971/72) and The Beach Boys' Pet Sounds (1965/66). Those with a particular fondness for Sunset Sound included The Buffalo Springfield, who recorded some of their best work there in the sixties. Neil Young described the place as pretty much the same in his 2012 autobiography Waging Heavy Peace. With Stephen Stills he recalled parking their Cadillac in the parking lot courtyard by the basketball hoop when making Buffalo Springfield Again. Sunset Studios has grown to include the building next door since Neil and Stephen were regular visitors back in 1967. Neil returned many times down the years to record his debut solo album, Neil Young, After the Goldrush, and On the Beach in "a building constructed so that music would sound good in it," as he put it.

Location 087: the 'Sunset Sound' sign is visible from North Cherokee Avenue, but the address is round the corner at 6650 Sunset Boulevard, LA, CA 90028

Los Angeles/Hollywood
Spirit's motel

The Sunset Highland on Sunset Boulevard is the budget motel on the cover of the second album by local band Spirit. The image on the front of The Family that Plays Together (1968) depicts the band descending the stairs of the motel, which proudly displays its '$6 a night' room tariff.

Location 088: this budget establishment is fittingly now a Budget Inn, still standing at 6830 Sunset Boulevard, L.A. CA 90028

Los Angeles/ Hollywood
Don Henley's 'Sunset Grill'

It should be noted that the Sunset Grill now standing here on West Sunset Boulevard isn't exactly the one that prompted Don Henley to write his 1980s hit song about the characterful, rather ramshackle place that once dished out cheeseburgers to the Laurel Canyon music community back in the sixties. Its fame and popularity was really due to the atmosphere of a place established by Joe and Eva Frolich in 1957. The couple sold up years ago, but what the heck – it still ticks several boxes: there's music memorabilia on the walls, rock music to eat by, and there's a rather special branch of Guitar Center and the RockWalk next door. (See entry below).

Location 089: If you decide to say "let's go down to the Sunset Grill," head for 7439 West Sunset Boulevard, LA, CA 90046

Los Angeles/ Hollywood
The Riot House

Opening as the Gene Autry Hotel in 1963, but renamed the Continental Hyatt House in 1966, the Hyatt on Sunset in 1976, the Hyatt West Hollywood in 1997, and the Andaz West Hollywood in 2009, this hotel was best known to rock fans the world over as "The Riot House." Whether myth, rock legend, or reality, it's worth listing some of the colorful rock and roll incidents that are reported to have taken place here. Residents have included Little Richard (Room 319) and Doors frontman Jim Morrison. Led Zeppelin and entourage commandeered several upper floors in the 70s, which encouraged drummer John 'Bonzo' Bonham to motorcycle up the hallways. The obligatory TV sets have, reportedly, been dropped from windows of rooms occupied by The Rolling Stones' Keith Richards and Who drummer Keith Moon. More creatively,

Rock God Robert Plant surveys the L.A. skyline on the Sunset Boulevard (front side) of The Riot House. Thoughtfully, the rock and roll activity of bands dispatching TVs from windows was performed at the back of the hotel where the roadies had their rooms!

Lemmy is said to have whiled away an evening on his room's balcony strumming an acoustic guitar owned by Roy Wood to compose his song 'Motorhead.' One of the best rock movies, Almost Famous (2000), was filmed around the place but perhaps the hotel's best endorsement as the rock and roll hotel came from the 1984 movie This is Spinal Tap, when the picture's end of tour party was thrown on the roof.

Location 091: the Andaz West Hollywood is at 8401 Sunset Boulevard, West Hollywood, CA 90069

Los Angeles/Hollywood
RockWalk at Guitar Center

A free outdoor sidewalk gallery of handprints made by those musicians who have contributed to the evolution of rock music, RockWalk was the brainchild of the then Guitar Center chairman Ray Scherr back in 1985. RockWalk comprises honored inductees' handprints and plaques of rock gods from AC/DC to ZZ Top and other less obvious rock star figures such as Robert Moog and Harold Steinway. Inductions are fun

ceremonies where the public can see superstars inducting superstars, such as Bruce Willis paying tribute to his good friend and inductee Stephen Stills. Above the sidewalk is a wall of fame featuring posthumously recognized music legends by way of bronze 3D likenesses. These plaques remember performers of the caliber of Elvis Presley, Buddy Rich, and Keith Moon. The Guitar Center also boasts a museum of rock artifacts, with an

abundance of guitars and rock star stage outfits.

Location 090: at the site of the old Oriental Theater which is now Guitar Center Hollywood. Look for the RockWalk awning on the north side of Sunset Boulevard. The hundreds of handprints (which are helpfully mapped on the RockWalk website) are right outside the front door at 7425 Sunset Boulevard, Hollywood, L.A., CA 90046

California

Los Angeles/West Hollywood
The Crosby, Stills & Nash album cover

OK, so there's nothing to see these days, but the location chosen for the eponymously titled Crosby, Stills & Nash album cover shoot is still a place with a tale to tell. When the record company needed a cover to introduce the trio to the record-buying public in 1969, photographer Henry Diltz and designer Gary Burden sourced a funky little white wood-boarded house with an old couch out front as the setting for the perfect group photo. The front cover photo session went well and later that day, joined by Graham Nash's girlfriend Joni Mitchell, they all drove the two-hour journey east up to Big Bear in the snow to shoot the inside album portrait. At the time the trio were still deliberating over a band name, but days later they simply settled on "Crosby, Stills & Nash." Unfortunately, when the photos were processed it transpired that the three were pictured in reverse order as "Nash, Stills & Crosby" – confusing to say the least. So, deciding to do a retake, Gary, Henry, and CS&N all set off for the Palm Avenue house only to discover that since their last visit, just days ago, the property had disappeared and was now just "a pile of timber in the back," as Nash put it. So the wrong order photo ended up on the cover. Confusion reigned immediately after the album was released, until everyone knew who was who, 10 months and two-million sales later.

Location 092: the exact spot of the CS&N cover shoot is a now a small parking lot across the street from the Santa Palm Car Wash entrance on Palm Avenue. It's at the southern-most tip of Palm Avenue, almost at the intersection with Santa Monica Boulevard, L.A., CA 90069

They planned to re-shoot the cover to amend the Nash, Stills & Crosby (left to right) order but Diltz and Burden returned with the trio to find the building gone

Los Angeles/Hollywood
The Lair of the Hollywood Vampires

The Rainbow Bar & Grill is a rock and roll haven for fans, groupies, and the rock stars they worship. In business since 1972 when Elton John had a party thrown for him, the place soon gained a reputation for attracting movie and rock stars, of which a select group were nicknamed 'The Hollywood Vampires'. Up all night and partying to the max were 'vampires' Alice Cooper, Ringo Starr, Keith Moon, Micky Dolenz, and Harry Nilsson. They were just the regular seventies crowd attracted to the mock Tudor British pub-like building on Sunset. They even had a plaque put up in their honor pinpointing the location of "the Lair of the Hollywood Vampires." In the 1980s it was the turn of local heavy metal bands to popularize the place. Members of Mötley Crüe, Poison, and Guns N' Roses were regulars at the Rainbow, which had enjoyed the patronage

❝I got my apartment where it was cos it was close to the Rainbow. I first came here in 1973, the year after it opened ❞

Motörhead's Lemmy: a Rainbow regular for four decades

of Led Zeppelin and Motörhead previously. Perhaps the establishment's most impressive endorsement came when the heavy metal band Rainbow named themselves after the place. Still open today and boasting a huge collection of rock star wall photos, the Rainbow is right next door to another rock landmark, The Roxy Theatre.

Location 094: 9015 Sunset Boulevard, West Hollywood, LA, CA 90069

Los Angeles/Hollywood
The Roxy Theatre

A place to hang out and hear some great music with a reputation for excessive partying, The Roxy Theatre was the venue for John Lennon's so-called "lost weekend" when he infamously convened rock's wildest club with Harry Nilsson, Alice Cooper, and Keith Moon in the upstairs On the Rox bar in the seventies. The intimate atmosphere and acoustics of the former strip club have encouraged Bruce Springsteen, Bob Marley, and Warren Zevon to release live albums recorded here. Punk music got an early kick start when the Flamin' Groovies and Ramones double bill played the Roxy in August 1976. A significant venue for breaking new talent since Neil Young played the opening set in 1973, Adele played one of her earliest and most memorable U.S. gigs here in 2008.

Location 093: the Roxy is at 9009 West Sunset Boulevard, West Hollywood, CA 90069

California

Los Angeles/ Hollywood
The Whisky a Go Go

Beginning life as a Los Angeles discothèque with go-go dancers in the mid-sixties, the Whisky a Go Go soon transformed to establish itself showcasing new bands as rock, heavy metal, punk, new wave, and grunge emerged. Led Zeppelin's first gig in California was at the Whisky in 1968, supported by Alice Cooper. A year earlier Cream had seen their association with the place give them a boost as with many other British bands breaking big on the West Coast. But it was local talent returning regularly that built up the Whisky's reputation. The Doors were the house band and it was a common sight to see movie stars like Steve McQueen dancing the night away. The aura surrounding this

remarkable venue meant that when Black Sabbath hosted a press conference to announce a reunion in 2011 it was the Whisky they chose for the event – 41 years after they made their L.A. debut there.

Above: Huge crowds turn out for a special event to remember the Whisky's house band

Left: Sixties excitement yet to come for the patrons of the Whisky, on the corner of Sunset and San Vicente

Location 095: The Whisky a Go Go is on the corner of Sunset Boulevard and San Vicente (which turns into Clark Street once you head north of Sunset Boulevard) at 8901 West Sunset Boulevard, West Hollywood, L.A., CA 90069

The Hollywood Bowl backdrop includes the equally famous "HOLLYWOOD" sign

Photo courtesy of Los Angeles Philharmonic

Los Angeles/Hollywood Heights
The Hollywood Bowl

This iconic natural amphitheater venue has been hosting classical music events since the 1920s. Perhaps of all the groups that have played the Hollywood Bowl since rock and roll first made its debut here (in 1958 with a Salute to Dick Clark featuring Bobby Darin), it's The Beatles who have made the biggest impression. They played the place three times: once in

❛I don't think there's another place in America that has the heart-shaking impact of the Hollywood Bowl ❜

Bonnie Raitt

August 1964 and twice in August 1965. Following hysterical fan behavior at the 1964 appearance, the Bowl's management wised up to the situation in 1965 and famously hired a Brinks armored truck to transport John, Paul, George, and Ringo to and from their hotel. The Beatles at the Hollywood Bowl album recorded at these concerts wasn't released

until 1977 but due to the scarcity of 'Fab Four' live releases it went straight to the top of the UK chart and hit No.2 in the US. The Hollywood Bowl has its own Hall of Fame and a museum on two floors which has free admission.

Location 096: 2301 North Highland Avenue, Hollywood Heights, L.A., CA 90078

California

Los Angeles/Hollywood
Jackson Browne's surreal cover concept

The cover concept for Jackson Browne's 1974 album, Late for the Sky, was an amalgamation of the American dream and Rene Magritte's surreal painting The Empire of Light. Everything but the sky was the work of photographer Bob Seidemann. He sourced the perfect Hollywood home - with the addition of a chevy out front – to reproduce the Belgian artist's work in South Lucerne Street, close to his own Hancock Park studio. The surreal sky background was from a landscape in New Mexico shot by David Muench.

Location 097: a private residence, the house and stylish street lamp are still there at 215 South Lucerne Boulevard, L.A., CA 90004

Hollywood House, New Mexico for the sky

Los Angeles/Hollywood
Johnny Ramone's cenotaph statue

One of the best rock statues ever created stands in memory of punk rock icon Johnny Ramone (1948-2004) at the Hollywood Forever Cemetery. This extraordinary cemetery, founded in 1899, is "the final resting place to more of Hollywood's stars than anywhere else on Earth," claims its website. A short distance from Johnny's spectacular cenotaph is the gravestone of Ramones bass guitarist Dee Dee Ramone (1951-2002). The black headstone features the Ramones' famous band logo that launched a million T-shirts and a footnote inscription which reads "OK ... I gotta go now."

Location 098: the cemetery is at 6000 Santa Monica Boulevard, L.A., CA 90038. The exact location of Johnny Ramone's grave is Section 8, Lot 2067, Space 1, and Dee Dee is Section 8, Lot 2003, Space 4.

The finished Johnny statue is a popular point of pilgrimage for fans of The Ramones

Sculptor Wayne Toth puts some finishing touches to the Johnny Ramone statue he created for the Ramones guitarist's cenotaph

Where once the Troubadour nurtured folk - rock, these days pretty much anything goes

Los Angeles/West Hollywood
Doug Weston's Troubadour

First opened in 1957 by Doug Weston and relocated in 1961 to its current home, the Troubadour music venue has a rich history of famous debuts, first meetings, and albums recorded at the 300-capacity nightclub. This is where Buffalo Springfield made their live debut in 1966, and members of The Byrds met for the first time – as did future Eagles Don Henley and Glenn Frey, and Carly Simon and James Taylor. The place also had a hand in breaking new British talent, most

memorably when a petrified Elton John, introduced by Neil Diamond, played his highly acclaimed first US gig at the Troubadour in 1970. Live albums recorded here include those released by Donny Hathaway, Miles Davis, Tim Buckley, Elvis Costello, and Neil Diamond's double-platinum-seller Gold. It's always been a great place to witness memorable live collaborations. What a night for the lucky few in 2011 when Cypress Hill, Slash, and System of a Down had a live coming together. Ever

the iconic Los Angeles. place to play, Coldplay, Red Hot Chili Peppers, The Strokes, Prince, and Fleet Foxes have all gigged here in the last decade or so. The hottest bands, some say the hottest waitresses, an intimate vibe, and reasonably priced entrance tickets still make the Troub a must-visit experience.

Location 099: on the busy Santa Monica Boulevard, the Troubadour is at 9081 Santa Monica Boulevard, West Hollywood, L.A., CA 90069

❝I think the start of all the success was the Troubadour thing. It was just amazing. It's an incredibly funky little place, the best club of its kind anywhere, and all it is is some wooden tables and chairs and good acoustics❞

Elton John recalls his Troubadour debut

California

Los Angeles/Laurel Canyon
Frank Zappa's open house

A must-see stop on any tourist trail - the guy who runs the tours now owns the place! It's not so much that this is where Frank Zappa lived, it's rather the catalog of famous rock stars that stayed (Eric Burdon, John Mayall) visited and partied, (The Rolling Stones, Jimi Hendrix, Alice Cooper) in the weirdly-styled place that makes it such a draw. Comprising log cabin and tree house, the property was built in 1915 as a retreat for rich city types to drink, smoke, and generally have a good time. The perfect place, then, for the Laurel Canyon music community to hang out and party in the decade of hippie decadence. And this fascinating abode has history: cowboy movie star Tom Mix and W.C. Fields both lived here fleetingly and Harry Houdini had an equally fascinating place across the street. Although Zappa and family's time was brief too, it was he that really put this spot on the tourist map. With its caves cut into the hillside, trees growing through the 70-foot living room, and a psychedelic bowling alley in the basement, the Baltimore-born avant-garde musician moved into what was already a hippie commune in 1968. It stayed intact until 1981, when the log cabin was virtually destroyed, apart from stonework including the original fireplace and chimney. New owners since then have renovated the grounds and tree house. Rickie Lee Jones, Guns N' Roses, and Stone Temple Pilots have all tapped into the rock history of the property by filming music videos here and,

JULY 20, 1968   THIRTY-FIVE CENTS

Cream's New Record Bombed
The Rolling Stone Interview With Frank Zappa

❝During my 1968 summer vacation in Los Angeles, I spent part of my time living in Frank Zappa's famous Laurel Canyon house. The daily lifestyle there and the parade of eccentric hangers-on became more than enough inspiration for this song, which happened to be the street address❞

John Mayall reveals the story behind '2401', a track on Blues from Laurel Canyon

more recently, music producer Rick Rubin bought the place and lived in it for a while.

Location 100: 2401 Laurel Canyon Boulevard, Laurel Canyon, CA 90046

Frank Zappa peers from inside the mouth of a cave at his Laurel Canyon Boulevard home

Los Angeles/Laurel Canyon
Jim Morrison's 'Love Street'

When The Doors' frontman Jim Morrison lived in Laurel Canyon with girlfriend Pamela Courson, 'Love Street' was the name the couple used to describe their view from the top of their house on Rothdell Trail. From this lofty vantage point, close by Laurel Canyon's Country Store, the couple could observe all the comings and goings of the hippies who populated the neighborhood back in the 1960s. Morrison wrote many songs at the house including 'Love Street,' which appeared on The Doors' third studio album, Waiting for the Sun, in 1968.

Locations 101, 102 and 103: 8021 Rothdell Trail is (the box-like building where Jim Morrison lived) and the Country Store referred to in his lyrics for 'Love Street' - ''this store where the creatures meet''- is next door at 2108 Laurel Canyon Boulevard, CA 90046. In 1966, before moving to Rothdell Trail, Morrison lived up at 8826 Lookout Mountain Avenue, CA 90046. Here he was inspired to write the Doors' classic 'People are Strange.'

Jim Morrison's place next to the Country Store: the hub of all hippie life in Laurel Canyon

David Roberts

Los Angeles/Laurel Canyon
Glenn Frey's 'Kirkwood Casino'

> ❝The first day I got to L.A., I saw David Crosby sitting on the steps of the Country Store in Laurel Canyon, wearing the same hat and green leather bat cape he had on for 'Turn! Turn! Turn!' To me, that was an omen ❞
>
> *Glenn Frey*

None of the original Eagles line-up were native Californians but the band's whole creative force is indelibly linked with the state. When the band's Glenn Frey had the opportunity to move to Laurel Canyon, as part of the second wave of laid-back rock star movers and shakers, he moved into a little hacienda which ended up with the reported nickname "The Kirkwood Casino and Health Club." Just how unwholesome this health club might have been is best left to the imagination but the tall box-like property was certainly party central for a short time in the early 1970s. Like Frey, fellow Eagle Don Henley was another Ridpath Drive resident who had also lived higher up the Canyon on Cole Crest Drive. The house on stilts at Cole Crest had some rock heritage as Roger McGuinn of The Byrds was the previous resident. As the seventies wore on, and the Eagles profile became less Laurel Canyon and more Hollywood, Frey up-sized to movie star homes at Dorothy Lamour's old house (on a hilltop at Trousdale) and James Cagney's one-time hideaway off Coldwater Canyon Drive.

Locations 104 and 105: Glenn Frey's early seventies home is at the corner of Kirkwood Drive and Ridpath Drive (No. 8301), Laurel Canyon, L.A., CA 90046 and the former Cagney home where Frey lived for 16 years is at 1740 La Fontaine Court, Coldwater Canyon, Beverly Hills, L.A., CA 90210

Los Angeles/ Laurel Canyon
Mark Volman's low rent properties

An insight into why so many of the new breed of young musicians were moving into Laurel Canyon in the mid to late 1960s comes courtesy of Mark Volman of The Turtles, who lived in two properties on Lookout Mountain. Apart from the obvious close proximity to recording studios and music venues down on Sunset Strip and in the city, cost was a factor. Volman reckoned that the area was full of cheap rental properties, with a three-bedroom home only costing $195 a month.

Locations 106 and 107: Mark Volman's homes were at first 8530 then 8760 Lookout Mountain Avenue, Laurel Canyon, L.A., CA 90046

California

Los Angeles/Laurel Canyon
Marilyn Manson's White Room

Once the home of movie star Mary Astor, who in 1941 co-starred with Humphrey Bogart in The Maltese Falcon, The Rolling Stones made this place infamous when they lived and filmed some of their unreleased Cocksucker Blues movie here in 1971/72. Denny Doherty (The Mamas & The Papas), Barry McGuire (who had a Billboard No.1 with 'Eve of Destruction'), and, more recently, Marilyn Manson have all called the place home. In Manson's case, he lived here (with white cat Lilly and a portrait of Mary Astor over the mantelpiece) from 1997 to 2004 and created most of his 1998 chart-topping album, Mechanical Animals, in the pool house overlooking Hollywood. The property became a major ingredient in the making of his third studio album. Manson had the pool house room painted completely white in an artistic attempt "to fill that void with songs," as he later revealed to Kerrang! magazine. The album cover follows the same theme and depicts a white, stark-naked Marilyn Manson.

Location 110: at 8803 Appian Way, Laurel Canyon, L.A., CA 90046

Los Angeles/Laurel Canyon
Carole King's 'Tapestry' house

The album Tapestry has sold more than 25 million copies since it was released in 1971 and was marketed by one of the simplest cover shots, depicting singer-songwriter Carole King at home with her pet cat Telemachus.

Locations 108 and 109: the cover of Tapestry was created at Carole King's home on Wonderland Avenue, CA 90046. The nearby, larger, turreted house she owned around the same period in Laurel Canyon was at 8815 Appian Way, CA 90046

❛The photographer Jim McCrary would make our fat feline famous by including him in a photo that would become the cover of a best-selling album. Jim's photo would also immortalize my living room on Wonderland Avenue with its hatch-cover bench and Indian-print curtains. The black Baldwin Acrosonic spinet piano on which so many hit songs had been written was behind Jim and therefore not visible in that photo ❜

Carole King describes the Tapestry cover location
in her memoir A Natural Woman

Los Angeles/Laurel Canyon
Neil Young's 'Witch's Castle'

High up in Laurel Canyon, in what he likened to a witch's castle, is Neil Young's former home. The small rustic pine cabin with curved shingles was part of the property owned by actress, astrologer, and piano teacher Kiyo Hodel. She lived in the house, Doors' drummer John Densmore lived in the equally weird-looking garage down on Utica Drive, and Young rented the cabin which was up an enormous flight of steps. This is the little place where he wrote 'Mr. Soul,' 'Expecting to Fly,' and 'Broken Arrow' for the 1967 Buffalo Springfield album Buffalo Springfield Again. His lifestyle here was not without a little luxury, but only a little. The refrigerator out back contained his bare essential food supply of not much more than pork and beans. The living area was furnished with a llama rug on which Neil and friends would stretch out and listen to the latest sounds in front of his prized KLH record player.

Location 111: the cabin is at 8451 Utica Drive, Laurel Canyon, L.A., CA 90046

Buffalo Springfield at Neil Young's Witch's Castle, photographed by Dennis Hopper

California

Los Angeles/ Laurel Canyon
The Court of Cass

Labeled 'The Queen of L.A. Pop' by Rolling Stone magazine, Mama Cass Elliot, aside from being a fine singer in The Mamas & The Papas, was friend, agony aunt, and host to all the musicians that gravitated to Laurel Canyon in the 1960s. If there was such a thing as a central hub to this laid-back hippie neighborhood of rustic cabins, Cass's home would be it. Her Canyon house, once owned by movie star Natalie Wood and later Ringo Starr, was where she held court to visitors like Eric Clapton and neighbors Joni Mitchell and Micky Dolenz. Cass's hospitality was the catalyst for many creative get-togethers - although Crosby, Stills & Nash have differing opinions on where they first harmonized together.

❛The Hollies were staying at the Knickerbocker hotel in Los Angeles and Cass called me and said I'm going to pick you up in 10 minutes, I want to introduce you to somebody. She drove me up Laurel Canyon to this house ❜

Graham Nash

❛There's this big argument that we first sang at Joni Mitchell's house. No, it was at Cass's, we were at the kitchen table, which was the third room up and outside was the pool ❜

Stephen Stills

Location 113: at 7708 Woodrow Wilson Drive, Laurel Canyon, L.A., CA 90046

Los Angeles/Laurel Canyon
The 'Our House' story

The 'house' referred to in the Crosby, Stills, Nash & Young hit song 'Our House' was the Laurel Canyon home which Joni Mitchell purchased in 1968 and shared with her lover Graham Nash and Hunter the cat. Originally built into the side of a hill by a 1920s jazz pianist, the little knotty-pine cottage was furnished with carvings, antiques, stained-glass windows, and bottles. It was here that Nash wrote 'Our House' in an hour, capturing the spirit of the couple's domestic bliss on a day when, as the lyrics describe, Joni put the flowers in the vase that she bought that day. According to Nash, that cold, gray day began with breakfast on Ventura Boulevard and a visit to an antique store nearby, where a vase in the window caught Joni's

Joni Mitchell at the window of her house and 'Our House' on Lookout Mountain Avenue

❛When the trees spread out, the branches were right at the windows. Birds flew in and nested. It was a charmed little place ❜

Joni Mitchell describes her Laurel Canyon cottage to author Dave Zimmer

eye. Purchasing the vase, they returned home and set about cutting and arranging flowers and lighting the fire, all of which prompted Nash to encapsulate this "ordinary moment," as he put it, in the song he sat down to write at Joni's piano. Depending on who you believe to be correct, the first time Crosby, Stills & Nash harmonized together might well have happened here at Joni Mitchell's place. Crosby and Nash certainly believe so, although Stills recalls the event happening in Mama Cass's kitchen, nearby on Woodrow Wilson Drive. An accomplished artist, the painting Joni Mitchell created of the view from her window at Lookout Mountain Avenue was included on the cover of her Ladies of the Canyon album, released in 1970.

Location 112: now a private residence, Joni Mitchell's former cottage is at 8271 Lookout Mountain Avenue, Laurel Canyon, L.A., CA 90046

Los Angeles/San Fernando Valley
Burrito Manor #2

In 1968, former Byrds men Gram Parsons and Chris Hillman were both in the throws of divorce and rented a three-bedroom ranch-style property in a bid to create and record some new material for a new band and a new album. The results from a hugely productive period together, in the bachelor pad they dubbed "Burrito Manor," would wind up on the cult early country-rock classic The Gilded Palace of Sin. When The Flying Burrito Brothers, comprising Parsons, Hillman, "Sneaky" Pete Kleinow, and Chris Ethridge weren't rehearsing or writing they'd venture out to hang out or play at the plethora of nearby venues like The Palomino Club, the Whisky a Go Go, The Golden Bear, and the tiny Corral Club, which The Rolling Stones made a point of visiting to catch the Burritos' live set when over in Los Angeles to mix their Let it Bleed album. For a time Parsons and the Stones' Keith Richards were big buddies and the Stones were so enamored by the Burritos' new brand of country that a healthy proportion of their repertoire reflected the association.

Locations 116, 117, 118, and 119: the private property that was once Burrito Manor is on De Soto Avenue, Reseda, San Fernando Valley, L.A., CA 91303. The Palomino Club was, until 1995, located at 6907 Lankershim Boulevard, North Hollywood, CA 91605. The Whisky a Go Go has its own Rock Atlas entry, the Golden Bear was, until 1985, at 306 Pacific Coast Highway, Huntington Beach, CA 90740. The Topanga Corral nightclub (twice destroyed by fire) was at 2034 Topanga Canyon Boulevard, Topanga, CA 90265

There are two other properties in and around Los angeles that were dubbed "Burrito Manor."

Locations 120 and 121: in chronological order, Burrito Manor #1 was the place where Gram Parsons and the rest of the members of The International Submarine Band were based for a while. It was ISB bass guitarist Ian Dunlop who first came up with the name of new band The Flying Burrito Brothers before departing the project. This house was on Kirkwood Drive, off Laurel Canyon Boulevard, CA 90046. Burrito Manor #3 was where Gram Parsons, Chris Hillman, and Michael Clarke shared a place after returning from their first Flying Burrito Brothers tour of the U.S. It was at the end of Beverly Glen on the Valley side (off Woodrow Wilson Drive) at 2786 La Castana Drive, Hollywood Hills, CA 90046

Los Angeles/Mid City
Little Richard's home

When Little Richard's fame began to translate to some hefty pay checks he bought a home here, where he lived with his mother. The gay rock 'n' roll legend, who at this time made a lifestyle change by becoming a fundamentalist Christian and abandoning music, moved to Virginia Road, a tree-lined neighborhood of mini mansions in the late fifties, where he married Ernestine Campbell in 1959, a marriage that lasted just six years.

Location 114: west of the center of L.A. and south of West Hollywood at 1710 Virginia Road, CA 90019

Los Angeles/Westlake
Jimmy Webb's MacArthur Park

The epic Jimmy Webb-penned song 'MacArthur Park' was a big hit for Richard Harris in 1968 and Donna Summer ten years later. MacArthur Park was the spot where Webb and Susan Ronstadt (cousin of Linda Ronstadt) dated before their relationship broke down – an event that inspired the song's dramatic feel. Susan Ronstadt worked in an insurance company nearby and the couple would meet for lunch, feed the ducks, and go on paddleboat rides. Even odd lyrics from the song such as "someone left the cake out in the rain" have a basis in fact. Webb observed a children's birthday party in the park which sparked that particular line.

Location 122: MacArthur Park is a mile or so northwest of downtown L.A. in the area called Westlake (which was once the name of the park until it was renamed after General Douglas MacArthur) at 2230 West 6th Street, L.A., CA 90057

Los Angeles/ Mission Hills
Ritchie Valens' gravestone

Along with Buddy Holly and The Big Bopper, Ritchie Valens died in the fateful Iowa plane crash on February 3rd 1959, later dubbed "The Day the Music Died." The 'La Bamba' singing star was buried here at the San Fernando Mission Cemetery, five miles west of Pacoima, where he was born and raised.

Location 115: Ritchie Valens' grave is in the Section marked C of the San Fernando Mission Cemetery, 11160 Stranwood Avenue, in Mission Hills, CA 91345

California

Los Angeles/Studio City
Stills and Stones at Peter Tork's house

Although not strictly speaking located in Laurel Canyon, here's a property that epitomizes the laid-back shabby chic luxury of the area in the late sixties and early seventies. This is no tiny singer-songwriter hideaway in the hills. Although privately shielded by trees, this large house and south-facing pool was where The Monkees' Peter Tork sunk a hefty chunk of his financial fortune when the TV group hit the jackpot in the mid-sixties. With a capacity for large party gatherings the house hosted some of the biggest names in rock once Stephen Stills leased the place from his

friend Tork – who famously got the Monkees job when Stills recommended him following his own audition failure. In mid-August 1969, when Crosby, Stills, Nash & Young needed to practice for their debut as a quartet in Chicago (gig #2 at Woodstock), they moved rehearsals out of the house and onto the property's driveway to get the feel of playing live outdoors. The neighbors didn't appreciate the free show, but when the cops were called the expected aggravation was negligible – a surprise considering the drug consumption that was rife at the

Keith Richards and Mick Jagger study color proofs of the cover of the soon-to-be-released Let it Bleed album, around the pool at Stephen Stills' house at Shady Oak Road

time. Later that same year, when The Rolling Stones were in town, Mick Jagger, Keith Richards, and Mick Taylor all lodged at the property and jammed and rehearsed with Stills, who would also play along with Jimi Hendrix, Rick James, and Buddy Miles when the guitarist, bassist, and drummer convened for lengthy sessions at Shady Oak Road.

Location 123: Studio City is northwest of Laurel Canyon and the house is the last property off a road leading from Viewcrest Road at 3615 Shady Oak Road, Studio City, L.A., CA 91604

Los Angeles/Venice
Rip Cronk's Jim Morrison mural

The Venice beach area was a special place for The Doors. Iconic photos of the group were taken here and the beach was the birthplace of the band, where Jim Morrison and Ray Manzarek first met in 1965. Although Morrison's grave is in Paris, France, L.A. Doors fans can still visit the most visual memorial to him - a 35-foot-high outdoor wall mural. Rip Cronk's acrylic-on-masonry vision of the bare-chested Morrison is a short stroll from the beach.

Location 124: the intersection of 1811 Speedway and 18th Avenue, Venice, West L.A., CA 90291

Rip Cronk's mural of Jim Morrison was painted in 1991

Los Angeles/Westwood
Remembering Roy Orbison and Frank Zappa

Acknowledged as two geniuses (albeit in quite different spheres musically) it seems strange that both Roy Orbison (1936-1988) and Frank Zappa (1940-1993) should be buried in unmarked graves. Their remains lie here at Westwood Memorial Cemetery Park, and despite the absence of any kind of marker, fans still visit to pay their respect at the two plots. Plot number 97 is where Orbison is buried in the grassy space between headstones for movie director Frank Wright Tuttle and Grandma Martha Monroe. Frank Zappa's unmarked grave (plot number 100) is close to a tree and to the right of actor Lew Ayres' headstone.

Location 125: west of central L.A. at Memorial Cemetery Park, 1218 Glendon Avenue, Westwood, CA 90024

California

Los Angeles/Woodland Hills
Captain Beefheart's cabin

The place Captain Beefheart — (real name Don Van Vliet) called home is a cabin in a leafy corner of Woodland Hills. The property's famously eccentric tenant chose a place that has its own eccentric qualities. Looking like a giant children's tree house, the cabin was base camp for Captain Beefheart and His Magic Band's grueling eight-month-long rehearsals of the fiendishly complicated cult classic album Trout Mask Replica. When Don was concerned that his music might be disturbing his two tall eucalyptus trees outside the kitchen door a report suggests that he billed local buddy and Trout Mask Replica producer Frank Zappa for a tree surgeon to tend to them!

Location 126: Woodland Hills is west of central L.A. and Don Van Vliet's former home still stands at 4295 Ensenada Drive, Woodland Hills, CA 91364

Don Van Vliet and his secluded home on Ensenada Drive

Los Olivos
Neverland

When Michael Jackson purchased the 2,600-acre former Sycamore Valley Ranch in 1988 he set about creating his very own Neverland, the fictional destination in J.M. Barrie's book Peter Pan. With a name change to the Neverland Valley Ranch, the King of Pop installed a 10,000-volume library of books, fairground, railroad, fort, indian village, movie theater, fire department (to deal with neighborhood brush fires), and a zoo. For 15 years Jackson lived and worked here. Most of the Dangerous album is reported to have been written by him while perched in his tree house overlooking the property's large lake. When Jackson decided that Neverland had lost its attraction, following the lengthy police investigations into his private life, he instigated plans to sell the place. It took almost two years to find homes for all his exotic pets before a sale was possible. Elephant, giraffe, tiger, chimpanzee, and orang utan were all eventually found acceptable homes. His two alligators were shipped out to the G.W. Exotic Animal Memorial Park in Oklahoma, where the largest was named "M.J." in the singer's honor. A year before his death in 2009 Jackson sold the ranch.

Location 127: 50 miles northwest of Santa Barbara, at 5225 Figueroa Mountain Road, Los Olivos, CA 93441

The sale of Neverland meant the removal of fun fair rides and the zoo's inhabitants - even the gates were put into storage

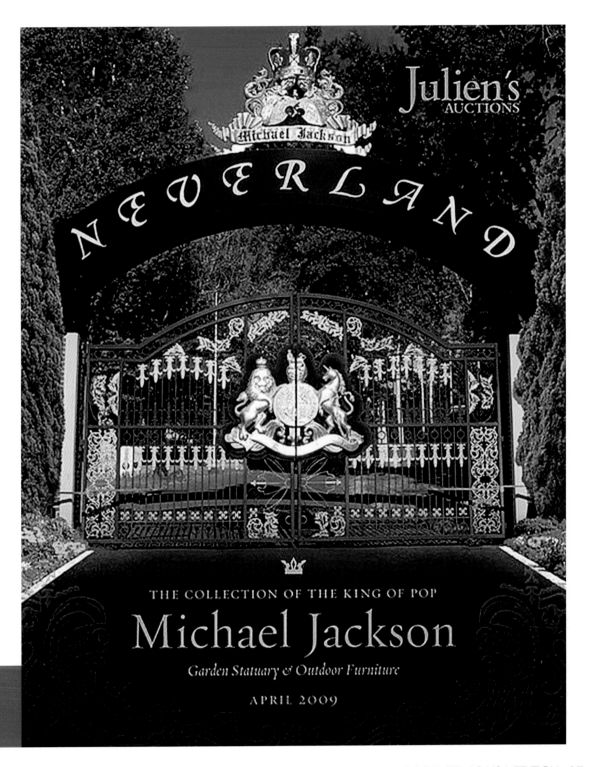

California

Malibu
Bob Dylan's Shangri-La Ranch

When Bob Dylan sold his Woodstock, N.Y., home in 1973 he bought a modest house on Point Dume, Malibu. Soon, all that was left of the original property was a single wall as Dylan, then wife Sara, and architect David Towbin set about creating a sprawling fantasy home which employed more than 50 construction workers and craftsmen over a two-year period. Shangri-La Ranch, with its purpose built recording studio, had a gypsy caravan, guest house, pheasants, chickens and horses, and several outbuildings over 12 acres. In an elevated position, with views of the ocean, the property lies two roads distance from the Pacific. The architecture is quirky but beautiful. Distinctive features include the large Russian-styled copper onion dome on the roof, a remarkable curving red-brick veranda created by John August, and a natural-styled swimming pool with huge artificial mushrooms rising up from the water. The house and recording facilities have been used extensively on Dylan's solo projects and the property was the catalyst for the accidental formation of The Traveling Wilburys. When George Harrison and his producer Jeff Lynne were searching for a place to record a hurriedly needed single B-side, the two contacted Dylan. Invited to Point Dume, the three were then joined by Tom Petty and Roy Orbison in a sequence of events that led to the creation of a new supergroup and, when a old box in Dylan's garage bearing the words "Handle With Care" inspired an impromptu jam, lyrics flowed, creating the song that became The Traveling Wilburys' first single. These days Shangri-La is owned by producer Rick Rubin, who has created albums here with Adele and Black Sabbath.

> *The copper dome is just so that I can recognize it when I come home*
>
> Bob Dylan talking to Playboy magazine in 1978

Location 128: Point Dume is a peninsula near Zuma Beach. Shangri-La Ranch is at 29400 Bluewater Road, Malibu, CA 90265

View of a Poet's Home: Roderick Smith's oil painting of Bob Dylan's Shangri-La was completed on site on a hill a mile away using a telescope

Littlerock
The ZZ Top gas station

Rock's most famous gas station lies in the dusty Antelope Valley, near Palmdale. On this spot in Littlerock, ZZ Top got a career boost in 1983 when the band's mega popular 'Gimme All Your Lovin'' pop video was shot here. Directed by Randy Newman's cousin Tim, the video features the band making their limited acting debut, a young gas station worker, three exceedingly beautiful women, and introduces, for the first time, the iconic red 1933 Ford Hot Rod, which was owned by band member Billy Gibbons. The gas station also makes an appearance in the final scene in the first Terminator movie.

'Gimme All Your Lovin'': the ZZ Top pit-stop

Location 129: ten miles due east of Palmdale at Littlerock, on the corner of 90th Street East and Avenue South at 37202 90th Street, CA 93543

Malibu
Courtney Love's 'Healing Place'

Burning palms and surf boards, Malibu is the subject and the video image for Hole's 1998 hit single 'Malibu' from Courtney Love and co's Celebrity Skin album. The song story goes that Courtney's late husband, Kurt Cobain, had stayed in rehab at a Malibu clinic before his death in 1994. Her lyrics implore him to drive or fly away to Malibu or go and part the sea.

Location 130: Malibu is 30 miles west of L.A., CA 90265

❛The song's about living in a trailer in Malibu with my first boyfriend, Jeff. I was 16. And it's kind of about Kurt, too. It's an empathy song: come to me, I'll save you. I wanted the boy in the song to drive away from Hollywood and the drugs. When I was pregnant, Kurt and I always had this thing about getting out of the basement apartment we lived in with dealers next door and going to live in Malibu. It's a very healing place ❜

Courtney Love talks to Blender magazine

Mount Tamalpais
The first rock festival?

A candidate for what might have been the earliest rock festival was staged on June 10th and 11th 1967 at the Tamalpais Mountain Theater. An unexpectedly large gathering of 36,000 watched the 'Fantasy Fair and Magic Mountain Music Festival' with a bill that introduced some of the West Coast's finest up-and-coming bands. For $2 you could see The Byrds, Jefferson Airplane, Tim Buckley, and Canned Heat, promoted by San Francisco radio station KFRC.

Location 131: Mount Tamalpais is 20 miles northwest of San Francisco. The Cushing Memorial Amphitheater or Mountain Theater where the festival took place is in Mount Tamalpais State Park, 801 Panoramic Highway, Mill Valley, CA 94941

California

Malibu
The Beach Boys' Surfin' Safari cover

When The Beach Boys' debut album was due for release on the Capitol label the record company's experienced photographer, Kenneth Veeder, was dispatched to snap the new group in their natural habitat, the beach and cliffs at Paradise Cove, a mile or so west of central Malibu.

Location 132: Paradise Cove can be reached via 28128 West Pacific Coast Highway, Paradise Cove Road, and Pacific Coast Highway, Malibu, CA 90265

❝Nik Venet [The Beach Boys' producer] saw the guy with the truck on Hollywood Boulevard, pulled him over and asked if he wanted to make $50. He followed us to Paradise Cove with the Capitol photographer, who lined us up and we took a bunch of photos with the hopes that one of them would be used as the album cover❞

Beach Boys guitarist David Marks

In the truck hired for $50, The Beach Boys fake getting ready to surf at Paradise Cove in 1962

Mill Valley
The Huey Lewis album cover

There's a real homegrown feel to Sports, the 1983 No.1 album by Huey Lewis & The News. Recorded exclusively in the Bay Area at the Record Plant, Automatt and Fantasy Studios, the 10 x platinum release carries a picture of Mill Valley's 2am Club on the cover. This is the place where the band hung out in their early days. Look carefully at the cover for the guitar made from a toilet seat displayed above the bar. It's the work of local character Charlie Deal, who made similar distinctive guitars for customers including local musicians Jerry Garcia (Grateful Dead), Marty Balin (Jefferson Airplane), Craig Chaquico (Jefferson Starship), and Huey Lewis himself. The bar gained more recent fame when an L.A. band enjoyed their visits so much they named themselves 2AM Club.

The 2am Club, complete with Charlie Deal's toilet seat guitar above the bar

Location 133: Mill Valley is 11 miles north of San Francisco. The famous 2am Club is on the corner of (380) Miller Avenue and Montford Avenue, Mill Valley, CA 94941

Newhall
Gene Vincent's "Be-Bop-A-Lula" gravestone

Musical notes spell out "Be-Bop-A-Lula" on Gene Vincent's gravestone at the Eternal Valley Memorial Park cemetery. The song, co-written by Vincent and recorded first by him with his band The Blue Caps, was by far his biggest hit on the Billboard pop chart. His popularity outside the US means that just as many fans from Britain and Europe visit this small memorial stone to the Virginia-born rock and roll and rockabilly pioneer. Plagued by injury and ill health for most of his life, he died in California aged just 36 in 1971.

Location 134: north of L.A. and south of Santa Clarita, Eternal Valley Memorial Park is at 23287 Sierra Highway, Newhall, CA 91321

❝In loving memory of husband, son and father, Vincent Eugene Craddock. known as Gene Vincent, recording star Feb. 11. 1935 - Oct. 12. 1971❞

The inscription on Gene Vincent's California gravestone

Northridge
Newport Pop 69

The Newport Pop Festival, held near Newport Beach in Orange County in 1968, wasn't welcomed back in 1969, hence the change of location. The open spaces of a former race track and entertainment event center at Devonshire Downs was the spot where "Newport 69," as it was billed, took place, drawing crowds estimated at 200,000. Steppenwolf, The Byrds, and Eric Burdon (with War) were three of the acts that had played the previous Newport Pop Festival. This time, three days, stretching from Friday 20th to Sunday June 22nd, saw The Jimi Hendrix Experience top the bill. The trio were now so popular – they had recently topped the albums chart for the first time with Electric Ladyland – they commanded a $100,000 fee. This figure, suggested by the band's bass guitarist Noel Redding according to his autobiography, Are You Experienced?, failed to bring the best out of Hendrix, who played with his back to the crowd before redeeming himself with a memorable jam with Eric Burdon during Buddy Miles' appearance on the festival's final day. Newport 69's close proximity to suburbia led to street violence and fans, locals, and police officers needed medical attention. A ban on festivals by local authorities put paid to any future Newports at Devonshire Downs.

Location 135: north of L.A., Devonshire Downs is now a planned residential community in Northridge, developed by the North Campus Development Corporation on behalf of California State University Northridge, CA 91330

'Down on the Corner': CCR at the Duck Kee Market

Oakland
Creedence at the Duck Kee Market

The East Bay area was where Creedence Clearwater Revival recorded down at Fantasy Studios. So, it was convenient when recording their Willy and the Poor Boys album in 1969 to head for a nearby local landmark for pictures to be taken for the LP's cover. CCR and a few street kids assembled outside the Duck Kee Market Chinese food store in Oakland for the photoshoot. The prominent sign above the store, which is clearly seen on the album front cover, went from familiar local landmark to world famous landmark as the record it decorated went on to shift more than 4 million copies. So famously associated was the Duck Kee Market sign with CCR that it promptly disappeared in 1998, stolen, some suspect, by a CCR rock memorabilia collector. Until the store closed and was laid to waste, the owners touchingly kept a copy of the album next to the cash register to reassure CCR fans that they had visited the correct place.

Location 136: Oakland is 12 miles east of San Francisco across the bay. The Duck Kee Market's former location is at the intersection of Peralta Street and 32nd Street, Oakland, CA 94608

California

Oxnard
Willie Nelson's Teatro cover

Willie Nelson's 1998 album Teatro was recorded in the atmospheric old movie theater bearing that name in Oxnard. For three-quarters of a century the Teatro was a popular movie theater until local multiplexes made it redundant. In the 1990s, brief ownership by record producer Daniel Lanois enabled Willie Nelson to record there, with the sessions filmed by movie director Wim Wenders for Willie Nelson at the Teatro.

Location 138: Oxnard is a coastal city 35 miles west of L.A.

The theater still stands in the center of the city at 624 Oxnard Boulevard, CA 93030

The Teatro is currently undergoing a makeover

Oakland
John Lee Hooker's final resting place

There's a dedication plaque to John Lee Hooker (the "King of Boogie") on the third floor of the Garden of Ages at the Chapel of the Chimes columbarium and mausoleum in Oakland. He was buried here in 2001 having performed his final gig some 60 miles north in Santa Rosa, just five days before his death aged 83.

Location 137: Chapel of the Chimes is at 4499 Piedmont Avenue, Oakland, CA 94611

Palm Springs
Sonny Bono's statue

Fans of the singer Sonny Bono may be disappointed when visiting his statue in Palm Springs. The likeness and quality of Emmanuil and Janet Snitkovsky's bronze may be good, but it's modeled on his Palm Springs mayoral role period rather than the iconic look sported during the Sonny and Cher years. More in keeping with the musical side of his life is the "And The Beat Goes On" headstone inscription at his grave in Desert Memorial Park, Cathedral City.

Locations 139, 140, and 141: Palm Springs is approximately 100 miles east of central Los Angeles. The Sonny Bono statue is outside the Mercado Plaza shopping mall at 149 South Palm Canyon Drive, Palm Springs, CA 92262. Sonny Bono's grave is at Desert Memorial Park, 31705 Da Vall Drive, Cathedral City, CA 92234. Interstate 80, north of Palm Springs, has been named the Sonny Bono Memorial Freeway in the former mayor's honor.

Much-loved mayor and one half of Sonny and Cher, Sonny Bono was born in Detroit, Michigan, killed in a skiing accident in 1998, and immortalized by this statue on South Palm Canyon Drive

SIDE ONE:			SIDE TWO:			OTHER CREDITS:
CHRISTINE'S TUNE©		*3:02	WHEELS©		***3:02	PRODUCERS: THE BURRITOS, LARRY MARKS AND HENRY LEWY / ENGINEER: HENRY LEWY / SPECIAL CREDITS: *JON CORNEAL, **EDDIE HOH, ***SAM GOLD-STEIN, ****POPEYE PHILLIPS/ PERSONNEL: GRAM PARSONS—RHYTHM GUITAR, KEY-BOARD INSTRUMENTS; CHRIS HILLMAN—RHYTHM GUITAR, MANDOLIN; CHRIS ETHRIDGE—BASS, PIANO**; SNEEKY PETE —STEEL GUITAR / SPECIAL THANKS TO ART DIRECTOR—TOM WILKES AND THE BOYS IN GRAPHICS / MICHAEL VOSSE / & PHOTOGRAPHER—BARRY FEINSTEIN. Ebel Records, A Division of Demon Records Ltd. Brentford, Middx. Manufactured in England. Manufactured under licence from A&M Records Ltd.
(GRAM PARSONS/CHRIS HILLMAN)			(CHRIS HILLMAN–GRAM PARSONS)			
SIN CITY©		*4:10	JUANITA©		*2:28	
(GRAM PARSONS, CHRIS HILLMAN)			(CHRIS HILLMAN–GRAM PARSONS)			
DO RIGHT WOMAN©		*3:56	HOT BURRITO #1©		****†3:37	
(CHIPS MOMAN–DAN PENN)			(CHRIS ETHRIDGE–GRAM PARSONS)			
DARK END OF THE STREET©		*3:55	HOT BURRITO #2©		****†3:15	
(SPOONER OLDHAM–DAN PENN)			(CHRIS ETHRIDGE–GRAM PARSONS)			
MY UNCLE©		*12:36	DO YOU KNOW HOW IT FEELS©		**2:06	
(GRAM PARSONS/CHRIS HILLMAN)			(GRAM PARSONS–GOLDBERG)			
			HIPPIE BOY*		****4:55	
			(CHRIS HILLMAN–GRAM PARSONS)			

© VOCALS: GRAM PARSONS, CHRIS HILLMAN
† VOCAL: GRAM PARSONS
* BACKGROUND VOCALS: CHRIS HILLMAN, CHRIS ETHRIDGE
○ VOCAL: CHRIS HILLMAN & HOT BURRITO CHORUS

ED CD 191

Pearblossom
The Gilded Palace of Sin

In 1969, The Flying Burrito Brothers released their acclaimed LP The Gilded Palace of Sin, with a cover photographed in the desert at Pearblossom. The group, all decked out in their nudie suits, along with photographer Barry Feinstein, stumbled across a rustic shack on some waste ground where the cover shots were created with two girls seductively stood in the palace/shack doorway. The shoot was an early morning dash out of L.A. and the band don't just appear to have been up all the previous night but engaging in "other enlightening activities" as Chris Hillman put it.

6 *The funny thing about that photo shoot, which I had forgotten about until Michael Vosse reminded me, was that the original shot was set up with the young lady hanging onto my leg. Gram Parsons seeing a shot at stardom slipping through his hands managed to talk Barry and Tom into trying it with him replacing me... I really didn't care having already been on five or six Byrds album cover shoots* 9

Chris Hillman

Location 143: Pearblossom is a 70-mile drive north of L.A. Exact spot in Pearblossom unknown. The town is in the Antelope Valley northeast of L.A., CA 93553

Front cover: this Pearblossom shack was the convenient setting for the Gilded Palace of Sin whorehouse when the band were looking for a suitable location

Back cover: Gram Parsons gets the girl

Palm Springs
Elvis Presley's Honeymoon Hideaway

When Elvis Presley and his bride Priscilla got married in Las Vegas the newlyweds spent their honeymoon on May 1st 1967 in Palm Springs. The striking property, now known as the "Honeymoon Hideaway" was leased by Elvis for a year from September 16th, 1966 for the sum of $21,000. A sucker for tradition, Elvis gathered Priscilla up in his arms and carried her over the threshold and up the stairs of their honeymoon house while crooning the 'Hawaiian Wedding Song' from his movie Blue Hawaii.

Location 142: you can tour and even stay at the estate which is in north Palm Springs at 1350 Ladera Circle, CA 92262

California

The High Sierra Music Festival in full sing in July 2012

Quincy
The High Sierra Music Festival

For two decades the Plumas-Sierra County Fairgrounds in Quincy have staged a July roots music festival, providing opportunities to swim, bike, fish, golf, and hike in the vicinity of this quaint mountain town. A feature of the performance stages is the large scale handmade art created by fans invited by the festival organizers to provide the distinctive backdrops. Stellar musical performances in recent years have come from Ben Harper, The Black Crowes, and My Morning Jacket, but it's the impromptu jam sessions, great value for money, and 21st-century hippie attitude that gives the festival its own distinctive character.

Location 144: nicely remote, about 70 miles northwest of Reno, at the Plumas County Fairgrounds, Quincy, CA 95971

San Anselmo
Van Morrison's St. Dominic's Preview cover

The San Francisco Theological Seminary's Montgomery Chapel steps provided the backdrop to Van Morrison's Saint Dominic's Preview album front cover. The magnificent doors form the entrance to a building that could pass for a fairy castle movie set. The shoot was the work of 27-year-old Manhattan-born photographer Michael Maggid, who took additional pictures for the 1972 release at St. Anselm's Catholic Church, where some of the album was recorded.

of San Anselmo is 25 miles north of San Francisco over the Golden Gate Bridge. The Montgomery Chapel is on Richmond Road at the intersection with Bolinas Road, San Anselmo, CA 94960, and St. Anselm's Catholic Church is a short walk away at 97 Shady Lane, San Anselmo, CA 94960

Michael Maggid's photo of Van Morrison on the Montgomery Chapel steps

❝Van was living in Fairfax, not far from the chapel where we shot the photos. I had worked with him on his previous album's photos, and my wife and I hung out with Van and Janet [Planet] a bit socially. It was certainly a rather casual and unhurried affair, consisting of me, my wife Jillian, and Van with guitar. My recollection is that we had chosen the chapel together, it sort of fit the album title song ❞

Photographer Michael Maggid

Locations 145 and 146: the city

Palo Alto
Pigpen's gravestone

"Pigpen was and is now forever one of the Grateful Dead" reads the highly appropriate inscription on the gravestone of Ronald C. McKernan at Alta Mesa Memorial Park. Pigpen was the multi-instrumentalist and vocalist in the Grateful Dead until his tragic death on March 8th 1973.

Location 147: Palo Alto is about 25 miles south of San Bruno (near San Francisco), where Pigpen was born in 1945. His final resting place is in the Hillview section (16) at the Alta Mesa Memorial Park, 695 Arastradero Road, Palo Alto, CA 94306

San Bernardino
Steve Wozniak's US festivals

Apple Computer co-founder Steve Wozniak was the driving force and sponsor of two huge festivals in 1982 and 1983. The US (you and me as opposed to United States) Festivals were staged at a purpose-built location at Glen Helen Regional Park, which is now the remodeled, vast, 65,000-capacity San Manuel Amphitheater at Devore, which has hosted Ozzy and Sharon Osbourne's Ozzfest. Back in 1982 the US Festival headliners were The Police, Tom Petty & The Heartbreakers, and Fleetwood Mac. The following year's big draws were The Clash, David Bowie, and Van Halen. A massive 375,000, record-breaking single day attendance on Sunday May 29th 1983 witnessed the 'Heavy Metal' bill, which saw Van Halen pocket a reported $1.5 million fee. Although Wozniak's two-festival sponsorship included air-conditioned tented areas exhibiting new computer technology and the hottest bands on the planet, the whole project made a financial loss in 1983 despite setting a Guinness World Record for the largest festival attendance, at 725,000.

Location 148: San Bernardino is due west of Los Angeles. The San Manuel Amphitheater is at 2575 Glen Helen Parkway, San Bernardino, CA 92407

San Fernando and Van Nuys
Wayne's World comes to town

Let's get this straight. The "real" Wayne's World is in Aurora, Illinois! But places you see in the movie are in San Fernando. Cassell's Music is the store where the famous "May I help you?" guitar riff is played by Wayne when out shopping for the white Fender Stratocaster. The 1991 Paramount movie shoot saw actors and crew descend on the store for four days of filming. The movie's exterior location for Garth's house was in nearby Van Nuys.

Locations 149 and 150: San Fernando is 18 miles north of downtown L.A. Cassell's Music is at 901 North Maclay Avenue, San Fernando, CA 91340. Garth's house is about 10 miles west of the store on 7102 Texhoma Avenue, Van Nuys, CA 91406

The store carried a wall sign "NO Stairway to Heaven." Wayne's World starred Mike Myers and Dana Carvey

California

Paige K. Parsons – Treasure Island Music Festival

San Francisco
The Treasure Island Festival in the Bay

Treasure Island Music Festival takes place annually on the artificial island in San Francisco Bay. Traditionally rock music is showcased on the second day of the two–day October festival which has attracted the likes of Fleet Foxes, Grizzly Bear, The Hold Steady and The xx to this breezy but scenic location.

Location 151: if you are heading for the festival it's best to park on the mainland and take a shuttlebus. There is limited parking on the island,which is reached by the Dwight D. Eisenhower Highway 80, Treasure Island, San Francisco, CA 94130

St. Vincent performing at the bright and breezy 2012 Treasure Island Music Festival

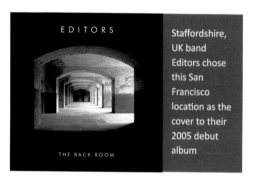

Staffordshire, UK band Editors chose this San Francisco location as the cover to their 2005 debut album

San Francisco
Fort Point attracts Editors

Below the Golden Gate Bridge, inside a fort dating back to the U.S. Civil War, lies the spot where the photo on Editors' debut album cover was taken by Wynn White. Fort Point's arched brick casements form the front cover of The Back Room, the band's 2005 release which eventually peaked at No.2 on the UK albums chart.

Location 152: Fort Point which is a visitor attraction open to the public, is on Long Avenue, San Francisco, CA 94129

2400 Fulton Street:
the mansion and
the album

San Francisco
Jefferson Airplane mansion

Although not unique, there aren't many houses that have had a rock album named after them. But when the house is as spectacularly grand as 2400 Fulton Street perhaps it's not so surprising. This was where Jefferson Airplane were based in the late 1960s, and in recognition of the property's contribution to the band's success 2400 Fulton Street duly became the title of their 1987 'best of' compilation album. Hippie central in 1968, when the band purchased the place, it was at various times home, crash pad, office, and basement rehearsal room before it was eventually put up for sale in the mid-1980s.

Location 153 across the street from the eastern end of Golden Gate Park and a short walk from Haight-Ashbury, 2400 Fulton Street is on the corner with Willard North, San Francisco, CA 94118

San Francisco
Tower of Power Bridge

The funk and soul outfit Tower of Power originated in Oakland. Fitting then that the cover of their 1974 album, Back to Oakland, pictured the Bay Bridge which connects San Francisco with Oakland.

Location 154: the west end of the Bay Bridge from San Francisco to Oakland, CA 94105

San Francisco
Revolution at Buena Vista studio

When rock musicians turned into rock stars at the beginning of the 1970s they invested in mansions such as this one. Graham Nash moved to 737 Buena Vista Avenue West in 1970 but the house, built in 1897, had previous rock history. In 1965, the top floor ballroom was converted into a recording studio and this is where the Grateful Dead recorded their first single, 'Don't Ease Me In,' a year later. They were hard times: the band had to lug their equipment up four flights of steps, then the single on the Scorpio Records label vanished almost without trace due to poor distribution. Unrepresentative of their sound and with little control over the production and mixing the band were not pleased with the results, but it was at least a beginning. Aside from the Grateful Dead recording and rehearsing, the studio also hosted sessions for the soundtrack to the movie Revolution (1968), when the old mansion reverberated to the sound of Quicksilver Messenger Service and the Steve Miller Band.

Location 155: Graham Nash's former home and the Buena Vista studio was at 737 Buena Vista Avenue West, San Francisco, CA 94117

Music for 'The biggest revolution the straight-world has ever seen' was recorded at 737 Buena Vista Avenue West

San Francisco
Wally Heider's Hyde Street Studios

Hyde Street Studios opened for business to capitalize on the local talent that had come to prominence during the 'Summer of Love,' but by the end of the sixties had begun pouring their more organized creative ability into making albums. San Francisco wasn't competing with L.A. studios until Wally Heider helped lure some of the L.A.-based bands north to Hyde Street, San Francisco, with stunning attention to detail and great equipment. First to try out the purpose-built complex, which had been constructed by Dave Mancini (son of Henry the orchestra leader), were Jefferson Airplane. The resulting album, Volunteers (1969), typified the cooperation shown by many bands working in and around the Bay Area at the time. Guesting on Volunteers, both musically and lyrically, were the Grateful Dead's Jerry Garcia plus David Crosby and Stephen Stills. Then when Crosby, Stills, Nash & Young were recording at Heider's, Garcia lent a hand on their Déjà Vu album (1970) by adding the beautiful pedal steel part to 'Teach Your Children.' When the Grateful Dead laid down tracks later that same year for their new album, American Beauty, they hung around to contribute to David Crosby's first solo LP, If I Could Only Remember My Name. And so the cross-pollination continued for a few years until Wally Heider left the studios having fallen out with the corporation who took over the ownership. Studios A, B, C (the Creedence Clearwater Revival album Cosmo's Factory was named for this one), and D still operate sporadically but not quite at the capacity they once did back in the 1970s when The Doobie Brothers, Van Morrison, and Gram Parsons recorded classic albums here.

Location 156: the studio still stands in the Tenderloin neighborhood, a short walk north of downtown San Francisco at 245 Hyde Street, CA 94102

San Francisco
Green Day's Warning cover

The cover of Green Day album Warning: pictures the band walking down Waverly Place in San Francisco. The trio cut their punk teeth at places like 924 Gilman Street in nearby Berkley but this 2000 album was a not entirely unsuccessful attempt at folk-punk with the band said to be heavily into Bob Dylan at the time. Maybe that's what influenced the street scene cover with echoes of Dylan's Freewheelin' cover, shot decades earlier in New York City.

Location 157: the Chinatown area of San Francisco at 133 Waverly Place, San Francisco, CA 94108

Green Day on the streets
of San Francisco

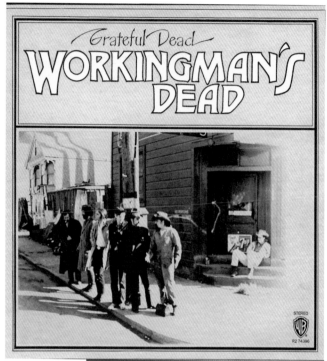

This 1970 album cover photo was shot in the Mission District where Jerry Garcia spent his childhood

San Francisco
Mission District album cover shoot for the Dead

For the cover shot on the Grateful Dead's Workingman's Dead album, artist Alton Kelley brought the band to the Mission District in San Francisco and photographed them with a simple Kodak Brownie camera, which created the desired utilitarian effect.

Location 158: exact location unknown, but in the Mission District, San Francisco, CA 94112

❝They stood on that old street corner somewhere in the Mission District [of San Francisco]. And they were bitching and griping about having to stand out in the street looking like that, getting their picture taken. That's why it came out so well! Billy [drummer Bill Kreutzmann] got so pissed off he just went back and sat in a doorway. We were at a bus stop and he was actually going to get on the next bus! ❞

Alton Kelley

San Francisco
Bill Graham's concert venues

One of rock's legendary promoters, Berlin-born Bill Graham did as much to create the 'San Francisco Sound' as any musician when he began booking bands like Jefferson Airplane in 1966 at The Fillmore Auditorium. When the opportunity presented itself to move a mile or so north to a larger ballroom, Graham took the Fillmore name across town. Between 1968 and 1971 the newly-named Fillmore West attracted an estimated 3 million rock fans and gave birth to the 'San Francisco Sound.' The Saratosa Tribune described the Fillmore West's last night as "a blaring wake that lasted until dawn." The recorded and filmed 'wake,' which saw music from Santana, and the Grateful

Dead and poetry from Allen Ginsberg, wasn't really the end. Though Bill Graham had talked about retiring and taking it easy he actually did no such thing and continued booking bands at the much larger Winterland ballroom. As demand for tickets had grown, the 5,400-capacity ice-skating rink and arena came into its own and became a second home to the Grateful Dead, the venue for Peter Frampton's hugely popular Frampton Comes Alive! recording, and the location of the Sex Pistols and The Band's final concerts – the latter's last stand was perhaps Winterland's finest moment when Martin Scorsese's movie The Last Waltz was filmed there. The early

hours of January 1st 1979 witnessed the crumbling old building's own final moments as a music venue before demolition in 1985. Still operating, The Fillmore lives up to its legendary name by promoting 21st-century rock from outfits like Eels, The Vaccines, Cradle of Filth, Johnny Marr & The Healers and Black Rebel Motorcycle Club.

Locations 159, 160 and 161: Bill Graham died in 1991 but his legacy lingers. The Fillmore is still going strong at 1805 Geary Boulevard, San Francisco, CA 94115 but both the Fillmore West (10 South Van Ness Avenue, CA 94103) and Winterland (2000 Post Street, CA 94115) are no more.

San Francisco
Jerry Garcia's childhood homes

Grateful Dead legend, Jerry Garcia, spent his early days at 121 Amazon Avenue. His eventful childhood was full of trauma. Before the age of five, he had witnessed the drowning of his father on a fishing trip and had a finger chopped off by his brother in a wood-cutting accident. Aged five, Jerry moved a few blocks away to 87 Harrington Street and lived with his grandparents. Harrington Street became the title of an illustrated book Garcia was writing at the time of his death in 1995. In it he described the local, ethnically Italian, Spanish, and Irish communities and the heavy influence of Catholicism.

"When I lived at 87 Harrington St., the neighborhood church was Corpus Christi (body of Christ), located one block northeast of Harrington Street and occupying about one half block of area. It was, when we first moved there, a typical wooden frame, sort of classic little old church-in-the-lane cum here's the church, here's the people, open the doors, etc... kind of deal."

The impressionable Garcia was clearly affected by the close proximity of "God's House" as he called it. "In those days they still had the wonderful Latin Mass with its resonant sonorities and mysterious ritual movements, the incense, the music, choir, organ, bells, candles, the muted light through the stained glass windows."

In his teenage years during the late fifties, his mother moved Jerry north out of the city to Cazadero in Sonoma County, concerned

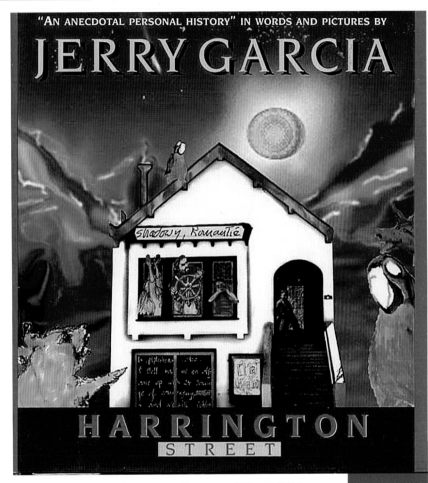

"AN ANECDOTAL PERSONAL HISTORY" IN WORDS AND PICTURES BY

JERRY GARCIA

shadowy, Romantic

HARRINGTON
STREET

that the city had become a dangerous place. The pull of the church had been replaced by different revelations. By this time he'd discovered rock and roll and marijuana.

Locations 162 and 163: Jerry Garcia's childhood homes are located in the Excelsior section of the San Francisco Mission District. Amazon Avenue and Harrington Street are both CA 94112

Jerry's second home, pictured on the front of his childhood autobiography.

6 A lot of fighting, race riots, all that high school shit that was so heavy in the '50s. Gangs go out cruising on a Friday night with other hoodlums, drinking wine and having fights. The tops of the hills in the city weren't built on yet. It was still like going to the country. Trees, ponds, grass, animals. We went up one day and smoked a couple of joints. After that I really got into it. And I wasn't into changing my mood, I was into getting stoned! 9

Jerry Garcia

California

San Francisco
The Beatles' last concert

On August 29th 1966, The Beatles made their final appearance in front of a paying audience at Candlestick Park. The cool, breezy Monday evening signaled the end of their third tour of North America but also their retirement from live touring anywhere. All their creative effort would now be confined to recording studios. The date was certainly not billed as "the last chance to see." Perhaps if it had more tickets might have been shifted. As it was, 25,000 fans turned up at the baseball field that was home to the San Francisco Giants, well below the stadium capacity of 42,500, and organizers were said to have made a financial loss. The evening's entertainment kicked-off with a raft of support acts (Bobby Hebb, The Cyrkle,

The Remains, and The Ronettes) before The Beatles' 11-song, 33-minute set and their final bow to a concert audience after closing with 'Fab Four' favorite 'Long Tall Sally.'

Location 164: the stadium (home to the SF 49ers) has an uncertain future. It's located about five miles south of downtown San Francisco, at 602 Jamestown Avenue, CA 94124

The stadium today and an advert forThe Beatles final live touring appearance

San Francisco
The Dead and Bowie at the Mars Hotel

The real Mars Hotel, which appeared as if dumped on the sc-fi landscape illustrating the cover of the 1974 Grateful Dead From the Mars Hotel album cover, is long gone. A steel and glass building has replaced the old hostelry on the corner of Fourth Street and Howard Street. The Mars Hotel also played a small part in arguably what was the birth of the music video when providing fleeting back drops to David Bowie's street scene in filmmaker and photographer Mick Rock's 'Jean Genie' promo movie in 1972.

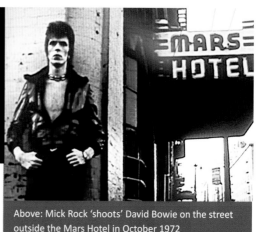

Location 165: The Mars Hotel once stood at 192 4th Street at the corner of Fourth Street and Howard Street, downtown San Francisco, CA 94103

Above: Mick Rock 'shoots' David Bowie on the street outside the Mars Hotel in October 1972

San Francisco
At home with the Grateful Dead

When the 1967 'Summer of Love' was spreading vibrations of peace across the world, the Grateful Dead lived here in Haight-Ashbury, at its epicenter. The beautiful pale purple house lies across the street from what was once the San Francisco Hells Angels chapter HQ. Check out the Grateful Dead pavement art on the sidewalk in front of what was home to the band from 1966 to 1968. The corner of Haight and Ashbury was the most important intersection in the world if you were a 'Flower Power'-loving hippie back in the 1960s. Thousands flocked to the spot from all over America. Their invasion of San Francisco's bohemian quarter was sound-tracked in 1967 by the omni-present 'San Francisco (Be Sure to Wear Some Flowers in Your Hair),' sung by Scott McKenzie. This hit helped popularize the hippie movement and the city across the globe. It made San Francisco a news story and

The Dead force themselves to pose for a 1967 record company press shot

provided another dimension in the city's hunt for tourist dollars.

Locations 166 and 167: the Grateful Dead's former home is at 710 Ashbury Street, San Francisco, CA 94117. The Haight-Ashbury intersection is just where it says it is, a block away from the Grateful Dead House, CA 94117

Jim Marshall

California

San Jose
Birthplace of The Doobie Brothers

The basement of a tiny house on South 12th Street was where a group of musicians became The Doobie Brothers. Here they practiced, honed their skills, and, with a supply of songs from Tom Johnston, developed the driving country-rock that would propel them out of San Jose once 'Listen to the Music' hit big in 1972.

Me, Dino, Little John, Greg - I don't remember if Pat was there - were having breakfast in the 12th Street house. Everybody was sprinkling weed on their toast, in their cereal, smoking joints. So Dino says, "Why don't you call yourselves The Doobie Brothers?

Tom Johnston

Location 168: San Jose is 50 miles south of San Francisco. The Doobie Brothers' house is right behind the Naglee Park Garage at 285 South 12th Street, San Jose, CA 95112

San Luis Obispo
Boo Boo Records makes the Top 30

Rolling Stone magazine listed Boo Boo in a sweep of the 30 best US record stores. Reassuringly little-changed since it began selling vinyl in 1974, Boo Boo Records has simply made its mark by offering a deep catalog (doom metal and dream pop aficionados won't be disappointed, according to one satisfied customer) to choose from in an intimate environment, presided over by friendly helpful staff. San Luis Obispo has been home to Jon Anderson (Yes) and Peter Buck (R.E.M.) in the past.

Location 169: San Luis Obispo is 200 miles northwest of L.A. Boo Boo Records is at 978 Monterey Street, San Luis Obispo, CA 93401

San Quentin
Johnny Cash and Metallica in prison

When Johnny Cash followed up his successful live appearance at Folsom Prison here at San Quentin State Prison it produced his most widely known song. 'A Boy Named Sue' was recorded along with an album's worth of material during this prison live performance on February 24th 1969. The result was Johnny Cash at San Quentin, which gave Cash his biggest hit single and his first Billboard No.1 album. Another acclaimed concert was recorded here in 1990 when B. B. King created his Grammy-winning album Live at San Quentin. But, perhaps San Quentin's most extraordinary rock 'n' roll claim to fame came in 2003 when the video to Metallica's 'St. Anger' single was filmed inside the complex with the band playing in front of inmates in various areas, interspersed with segments of prison life and criminal acts filmed outside the prison. The closing credit of Metallica's 'St. Anger' video, signed by James, Lars, Kirk, and Robert read, "For all the souls impacted by San Quentin, your spirit will forever be a part of Metallica."

Location 170: California's oldest prison is bordered by San Francisco Bay to the south and west, and by Interstate 580 to the north and east, and sits on Point San Quentin near the northern terminus of the Richmond - San Rafael Bridge. The 275-acre site has its own ZIP code, CA 94974, and nearby San Quentin Village is at CA 94964

Santa Monica
'Free coffee for all' at McCabe's Guitar Shop

"The largest selection of stringed things to make music within California" and "free coffee for all" is the invitation on McCabe's website. You get the impression nothing is too much trouble at this place if you want to listen, learn, play, or buy a guitar, banjo, mandolin, or violin. The roll call of well-known musicians that have visited and played at McCabe's in over half a century is astonishing: The Bangles, Bernie Leadon, Tom Waits, P.J. Harvey, and The Incredible String Band to name but five.

Location 171: Santa Monica is the beachfront city west of L.A. and McCabe's Guitar Shop is at 3101 Pico Boulevard, Santa Monica, CA 90405

The Record Plant Sausalito: "the building is resting," as Mick Fleetwood put it in 2009, supporting a campaign to preserve a place "wanting to be helped"

Below: Fleetwood Mac in all their glorious disharmony

Sausalito
Rumours at the Record Plant

When entrepreneur Chris Stone and recording engineer Gary Kellgren founded their Record Plant studio in New York back in 1968, the success of their joint venture led to Record Plants springing up in Los Angeles and then Sausalito in 1972. The latter was a getaway from big city recording and its rustic-looking frontage disguised the fact that this was a place where rock star extravagance was well catered for. A jacuzzi, speed boat moored ready for action, overnight accommodation, and catering to pamper the most particular rock star's requirements made the Record Plant a draw for bands with big enough budgets. One room (a converted office) had its own bed surrounded by velvet drapes with a control booth sunk into the floor nicknamed "Sly Stone's Pit." It was here that the funk legend spent most of his time while making the 1971 Sly & The Family Stone album There's a Riot Goin' On. Famously breaking up with each other during the making of their classic album Rumours, Fleetwood Mac spent an astonishing 35 consecutive 12-hour days here before cocaine addiction and a scheduled tour interrupted their time at the Record Plant. More recent Billboard 200 chart-toppers recorded exclusively here before the place was mothballed and sold off include Load (1996) and Reload (1997) by Metallica and Before These Crowded Streets (1998) by Dave Matthews Band.

Location 172: Sausalito is a small city in the San Francisco Bay area, The Record Plant (the building is currently slated to be partly reinvented as a yoga and dance center) is at 2200 Marinship Way, Sausalito, CA 94965

❛I can't deny there was a lot of lunacy in the studio. But Stevie [Nicks] and I rented a condominium in Sausalito to get away from all that. It was the boys who all stayed at the Record Plant house. So that's where all the madness was happening ❜

Fleetwood Mac's Christine McVie talking to Mojo about Rumours at the Record Plant

California

Sausalito
Written on the dock of the bay!

Otis Redding's only No.1 single was written on a houseboat at Waldo Point. The 'bay' in '(Sittin' on) the Dock of the Bay' was the San Francisco Bay where Otis watched the ships he wrote about in the lyrics of the song. At the time, in 1967, he was performing locally at the Fillmore West in San Francisco when promoter Bill Graham offered Otis the use of the houseboat instead of the usual hotel. The song was co-written by Steve Cropper, who added guitar fills, arrangement, and the line "I left my home in Georgia" (which he literally did) to complete the song which Otis never got to hear a completely finished version of. He died on December 10th 1967 and three months later

the record hit the top of the Billboard Hot 100 on March 16th 1968, where it remained for four weeks. The houseboat provided other well-known musicians with a place to stay. Neil Young had reason to recall his stay on the watery accommodation following a later conversation with Steve Cropper. '(Sittin' on) the Dock of the Bay' was a favorite of Young who would often play it live when closing his set. He felt especially connected to the song when Cropper revealed to him where

and when it had been born. It transpired that Young had stayed on the very same houseboat a week after Otis' brief stay in 1967.

Location 173: Sausalito is north of San Francisco Bay. The exact spot where Otis sat on the dock of the bay is the subject of argument. The two most likely places are each worth a visit. Take a walk between both along the waterside beyond Marin County Heliport to the Issaquah Dock in the Waldo Point Harbor, Waldo Point, Sausalito, CA 94965

Santa Ynez
A Brown Dirt Cowboy at the Roundup Ranch

As teenagers, Elton John and his long-time lyricist Bernie Taupin always had a love bordering on obsession for America's Old West. The English duo spelt out that love clearly on album titles like Captain Fantastic and the Brown Dirt Cowboy and the themes expressed in their songs on Tumbleweed Connection. No surprise, then, in 1993 when Taupin bought his very own ranch in the Santa Ynez Valley. Aside from songwriting, Taupin has proved to be a gifted horseman, raising and showing cutting horses and pursuing his passion for the extreme sport of bullriding. The 2006 Elton John album The Captain & the Kid continued the duo's biographical themes explored on the earlier Captain Fantastic and The Brown Dirt Cowboy release from 1975. The cover of the later album pictures Elton and Bernie down on Taupin's Roundup Valley Ranch.

Location 174: northeast of Santa Ynez and east of Highway 154, Roundup Valley Ranch is at 2905 Roundup Road, Santa Ynez, CA 93460-9558

Cowboy and lyricist Bernie Taupin sits astride Neal, one of his favorite horses at the Roundup Valley Ranch

Westlake Village
'Remember' Harry Nilsson and Karen Carpenter

Singer-songwriter Harry Nilsson's final resting place is marked by a photographic portrait of the man who wrote the classic songs 'Without You' and 'Everybody's Talkin'.' His headstone also carries the word "Remember," the title of one of his less well-known songs. Nilsson lived predominantly on the West Coast and died at his Agoura Hills home in 1994 aged 52. In 2003, the remains of singing star and drummer Karen Carpenter (1952-83) were moved here from her original interment in Forest Lawn Cypress Cemetery to the impressive Carpenter family crypt.

Location 177: Westlake Village is very close to Santa Monica. The cemetery is Pierce Brothers Valley Oaks Memorial Park, 5600 Lindero Canyon Road, Westlake Village, CA 91362

Born in New York and remembered in Westlake Village

The music was strictly New Orleans but the cover shoot was Californian

Vernon
Dr. John's Gumbo wall

The cover of Dr. John's 1972 album Gumbo pictures the good doctor pausing in front of the giant-sized rural mural outside The Farmer John Company in Vernon.

Location 176: the extremely long mural is five miles south of downtown Los Angeles and extends along Soto Street and East Vernon Avenue, Vernon, CA 90058. Discovering which bit of it Dr. John 'borrowed' for his cover shoot is the problem

Twentynine Palms
Robert Plant's desert love song

The Mojave Desert oasis that is Twentynine Palms was immortalized in song by Robert Plant. A love song to the desert city and someone the writer associates with the place, '29 Palms' was a track (and hit single release) from the Led Zeppelin singer's 1993 solo album Fate of Nations.

Location 175: Twentynine Palms is about 50 miles northeast of Palm Springs, CA 92277

Colorado

Aspen
The John Denver Sanctuary

The John Denver Sanctuary near Rio Grande Park features a memorial stone to the singer who died in a light aircraft crash in 1997. Fans gather here on the anniversary of his October 12th death to remember the man who penned songs 'Rocky Mountain High,' 'Annie's Song,' 'Country Roads,' and 'Windsong,' the lyrics of which are engraved in the large boulders surrounding his headstone. During the most successful years of his music career, John lived with wife Annie in the Starwood area of Aspen.

Location 178: across the park from the Rio Grande Place Visitor Center, 130 South Galena Street, north of East Main Street, Aspen, CO 81611

❝John loved Colorado. It changed his life. He had the ability to put into words I think things that we all felt. He wrote 'Rocky Mountain High' on a trip to Williams Lake during the Perseid meteor showers when we were backpacking and camping up there ❞

Annie Denver, at the Sanctuary dedication day

This 1994 album featured Billboard Hot Dance Club Play chart-topper 'God is a DJ'

Denver
The Bluebird theater starring Faithless

Apart from being an extremely interesting century-old building and a popular concert venue since 1994, Denver's Bluebird theater is featured on the cover of Sunday 8PM, the 1998 album by Faithless. The British dance music act's name and album title are neatly displayed on the front of a building which was listed on the National Register of Historic Places in 1997.

Location 179: the Bluebird theater is near the center of Denver at 3317 East Colfax Avenue, Denver, CO 80206

Denver
Led Zeppelin's US debut - sponsored by Vanilla Fudge

First impressions were very encouraging when Led Zeppelin plugged in and played their first US gig. They were a late support act addition to an already sold-out show featuring Vanilla Fudge and Spirit on December 26th 1968. Zeppelin only got the gig when Vanilla Fudge cut their own $750 fee for the date to enable the band, unknown outside the UK to all but a few US musicians, to get the concert booking break they needed. The lines were jammed to local rock radio station KLZ the next day from inquisitive listeners excited by the British outfit's impact on a bill where they threatened to blow the two US bands off the

❝You didn't have to be a genius to know that Led Zeppelin was going to be a smash. Oh my god. People were going crazy! ❞

Denver promoter Barry Fey

in-the-round Denver Auditorium stage. The venue's promoter, Barry Fey, rushed an unreleased copy of the quartet's debut album over to KLZ, who proceeded to play the LP repeatedly that day as Led Zeppelin headed east through a blizzard to snowy

Seattle for their second booking.

Location 180: Downtown Denver. The old Denver Auditorium was at 1245 Champa Street (now the remodelled Temple Hoyne Buell Theater) at 14th Street and Curtis Street, Denver, CO 80204

Led Zep's U.S. debut: The Rocky Mountain News music critic was intrigued by Jimmy Page's use of a violin bow on his guitar strings

Denver
The Twist & Shout Record Store

Said to be the largest independently owned record collection in Denver, the Twist & Shout record store holds 250,000 new and used records in its 12,000-square-foot floor space. Aside from the amazing choice of vinyl and CDs the place sells music and movie related toys and gifts and has enticing mystery grab bags of assorted vinyl or CDs which customers take and open at home, to their obvious delight if shoppers' feedback is anything to go by.

Location 181: close to the center of Denver, Twist & Shout is at 2508 East Colfax Avenue, Denver, CO 80206

Colorado

Morrison
Red Rocks Amphitheater

The possibilities presented by the rock formations in this part of Colorado for a dramatic natural outdoor amphitheater were realised by Jefferson County businessman John Brisben Walker in 1906. Beginning with a brass band concert, Brisben Walker's vision has changed little now that Red Rocks attracts some of rock's biggest names to the venue's capacity of 9,450. They don't come much bigger than The Beatles, who played Red Rocks on August 26 1964. Still relatively unfamiliar with outdoor performances, John, Paul, George, Ringo, manager Brian Epstein, and producer George Martin were, in the wake of almost constant death threats to the band, seriously concerned about the ease with which a sniper might take a shot at the stage from high up in the rocks. The Beatles were also unaccustomed to the high altitude at Red Rocks, and for moments when short of breath oxygen canisters were placed side of stage for their use. Despite breaking the then outdoor concert record attendance with a crowd of 7,000, unusually for The Beatles 2,000 of the tickets for this appearance remained unsold. The amphitheater has seen its fair share of controversy, particularly around the late sixties and early seventies when Aretha Franklin's no-show due to a contract dispute sparked rioting and the destruction of a piano. Then there was the tear-gassing of rioting crowds at the Denver Pop Festival in 1969 and the same police action at a Jethro Tull gig in 1971. Many Red Rocks concerts have made it on to record and film. U2 did both in 1983 when their Live at Red Rocks: Under a Blood Red Sky was released as a movie and two tracks from the band's memorable performance during the War Tour found their way onto the live album, Under a Blood Red Sky. And the photogenic venue continues to attract bands who want to be filmed in the breath-taking geological landscape. Mumford & Sons, like U2 before them, had reached a similarly high point with their popularity when their The Road to Red Rocks live concert DVD was released in 2012. Previous to that, in 2010, Widespread Panic overtook the Grateful Dead as the band with the most performances at Red Rocks. In June of that year they achieved their 35th sold-out concert.

Location 182: Morrison is about 15 miles west of the center of Denver. The Red Rocks Park & Amphitheater Visitor Center is at 18300 West Alameda Parkway, Morrison, CO 80465

> Right: where the Great Plains meet the Rocky Mountains - rock at Red Rocks
> Below: one of many to benefit from the Red Rocks experience were the Dave Matthews Band, whose Live at Red Rocks 8.15.95 album was certified double-platinum after peaking at #3 on the Billboard 200

Morrison

Colorado

Nederland
The Caribou Ranch recording studios

Music producer James Guercio created the perfect secluded recording facility when he purchased a 4,000-acre piece of land with ranch in the Rocky Mountains in 1971, at a time when rock music was entering its extravagant heyday. A year later his converted barn would become the recording studio that would attract some of the biggest names in rock to this remote location on the road to the nearby ghost town of Caribou. The ranch-based studio has a track record of rescue missions which began in 1972 when former James Gang guitarist Joe Walsh began recording his solo project Barnstorm with Bill Szymczyk at his home studio in Nederland. Disaster struck on day one of the recording when a mixer blew out. Aware of Guercio's plans to create his ranch style studio in the neighborhood, Szymczyk switched the project to Caribou, where the Barnstorm album was completed in the as yet unfinished building. Mission accomplished, the recording work began to flood in and, in addition to bands recording in the idyllic surroundings, many album covers were photographed outside in the Rocky Mountain landscape. Among those making music that used a picture of their stay on the front cover of an album release were Supertramp (Even in the Quietest Moments), America (Hideaway), Earth Wind & Fire (Eyes and Ears) and Amy Grant's Christmas album. Most famous of all though were the Elton John albums Rock of the Westies and

Caribou. The latter was another Caribou Ranch-to-the-rescue mission when Elton and band flew in for an enormously pressurized week-and-a-half in January 1974 to write and record Caribou in the short time available before jetting off on a scheduled tour of Japan. That same year Elton and John Lennon recorded a cover of the Beatles song 'Lucy in the Sky with Diamonds' at Caribou. Other

Barn-front view of Caribou Ranch shot by Tom Likes, who was assistant engineer and assistant maintenance engineer from 1975 to 1980

rock legends to have sampled the mountain hospitality, before fire destroyed and shut down the studio control room in March 1985, were Rod Stewart, Stephen Stills, Billy Joel, Waylon Jennings, Carole King, The Beach Boys, and Chicago. "Elton would write a whole album in one week and cut it in one week. No distractions, you're set up. That was the whole concept." Producer James Guercio recalls the making of Caribou in January 1974.

Location 183: the ranch is no longer a recording studio but well worth a visit for the hiking trails around the ranch and nearby picnic tables, open apart from April, May and June, to protect the wildlife. To find the place head north out of Nederland on Highway 72, turn off left onto County Road 126, and then look out for the "Caribou Ranch Open Space" sign, Nederland, CO 80466

> ❝You could sing an octave higher. The sounds were different at that elevation and I never knew that. We didn't understand this. The engineers all had theories . . . [Producer] Tommy Dowd, great guy, he was an atomic scientist. He'd tell me what I'm telling you. He called and said, 'I gotta bring Rod [Stewart] up, he can't hit these notes.' He came up and we put Rod and Britt Ekland in a cabin . . . 'If You Leave Me Now,' Chicago, they had to come up here. Could never hit the notes [at sea level] ❞
>
> *James Guercio describes the unique location almost 9,000 feet up in the Rockies*

Rollinsville
The Stephen Stills album cover

In the early 1970s Stephen Stills' safe haven away from the pressures of Crosby, Stills, Nash & Young was his Rollinsville cabin up in the Rocky Mountains. No rock star recluse, Stills volunteered as a local auxiliary firefighter for the Rocky Mountain rescue unit and would sometimes get up on stage and play at bars in an area populated by fellow muso acquaintances Richie Furay, Chris Hillman, and Joe Walsh. According to photographer Henry Diltz, his mountain home was the setting for a spontaneous but memorable photo session a day after Stills got a call on the cabin phone to tell him that his guitar sparring partner and friend Jimi Hendrix was dead. Stills reacted to the sad news by heading outside to clamber up the mountain and weep for a couple of hours. After a long night of story-telling, mourning the great guitarist, dawn broke revealing a fresh blanket of snow outside the cabin. This would turn out to be the setting for the snow scene captured by Diltz which made the cover of Stills' solo debut album in 1970, an LP on which Hendrix guested and which Stills dedicated to "James

Halfway through the photoshoot, Stills jumped up and ran back into his cabin to fetch the pink giraffe - a gift from girlfriend Rita Coolige - that appeared in the chosen picture shot by Henry Diltz

Marshall Hendrix." This part of the country also served as the backdrop to the band photograph of Stills' supergroup Manassas that appeared on the cover of the outfit's second album, Down the Road, in 1973.

Location 184: Rollinsville is 20 miles southwest of Boulder, Rollinsville CO 80474

❝When I was growing up in the Southeast I hated the humidity and was totally addicted to air-conditioning all the time. I discovered that in Colorado there was air-conditioning all the time and I loved it❞

Stephen Stills

Trinidad
Ronnie Lane's gravestone

East Londoner Ronnie Lane is buried at the Masonic Cemetery in Trinidad, his last hometown after relocating to the US in 1984. The ex-Small Faces and Faces band member and frontman for his own band, Slim Chance, first left Britain for Houston then Austin, Texas, before settling in Trinidad with his third wife Susan Gallegos, the granddaughter of an Apache Chief. Lane was suffering from multiple sclerosis when he died aged 51 in

1997. The simple but striking headstone for the Plaistow-born bass guitarist, nicknamed "Plonk," bears the inscription "LANE – "God Bless Us All."

Location 185: the cemetery at Trinidad, Las Animas County, is in southern Colorado, about one mile north of Downtown Trinidad, his final home, CO 81082

RockAtlasUSA

Connecticut

Danbury
Lauro Nyro's 'Mother's Spiritual' home

A bucolic cottage surrounded by trees and fields in Danbury was home and work place to Laura Nyro. The Bronx-born singer-songwriter recorded her 1978 album Nested there in a mobile facility and spent more than $150,000 on a permanent home studio for the recording of Mother's Spiritual in 1983. Danbury is also her final resting place. Friends buried her ashes outside her bedroom window beneath a Japanese maple tree, a spot where the ashes of her dog Ember were also buried.

Location 186: a private residence, the cottage is on Zinn Road, Danbury, CT 06811

One of the Laura Nyro albums recorded in Danbury

New Haven
The Rolling Stones at Toad's Place

Toad's Place was first a restaurant when rented by Michael Spoerndle in 1975. A year later and the premises began ringing to the sounds of bluesmen Muddy Waters and John Lee Hooker as the place became a much-loved, dumpy little nightclub and live concert venue. Small it may be, but the list of major rock performers that have played here is mighty, a fact advertized by the walls of Toad's, where the names

David Bowie, Bob Dylan, Radiohead, Little Richard, U2, and many more are proudly displayed. Arguably the biggest night in the club's history came on August 12th 1989 when The Rolling Stones played for an hour here as a thankyou for Connecticut's hospitality to them. They had just spent eight weeks rehearsing the Steel Wheels tour at Wykeham Rise, a former girls' boarding school in the nearby rural town of

Washington. That unannounced gig in front of 700 Toad's Place patrons set the mold for bands like The Black Crowes to warm up for tours in similar fashion.

Location 187: New Haven is in south Connecticut. Toad's Place is near the campus of Yale University in downtown New Haven at 300 York Street, New Haven, CT 06511

Westport
Wishbone Ash head west

When UK rock band Wishbone Ash relocated to the U.S. (reportedly to avoid what they felt were crippling tax issues, and to break the American rock scene) they settled in Connecticut. They even called their 1976 album New England, such was their successful acclimatization when working on their seventh studio album. The record was created in the basement of lead vocalist, bass guitarist, and songwriter Martin Turner's Laureledge home with the aid of a mobile recording truck parked outside. When they weren't at work the band could frequently be found down at the beach or catching some live music at Westport's Players Tavern. This small club hosted performances from artists of the caliber of Muddy Waters and Patti Smith and was a real draw for music fans in the 1970s. Although Wishbone Ash's stay in Connecticut only lasted three years, guitarist Andy Powell still calls this beautiful rural spot home, having lived in Westport, then nearby Weston and Redding, since the 1970s. Among other creative types to favor the area were REO Speedwagon, whose

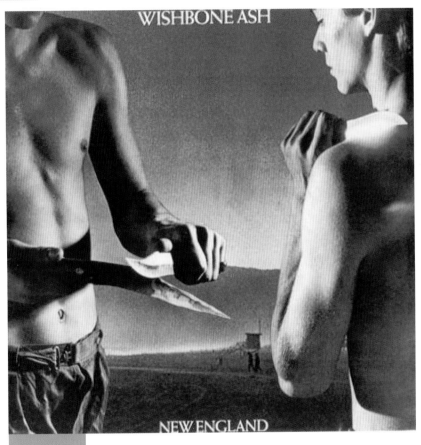

British rock, made in New England

1971 debut album track '157 Riverside Avenue' namechecks Westport.

Location 189: Westport is a coastal town 47 miles northeast of New York City. The Players Tavern is no more. These days it is the dressing room area for the Westport County Playhouse at 25 Powers Court, Westport, CT 06880

Redding
Mary Travers' gravestone

A member of the folk trio Peter, Paul & Mary, Mary Travers was born in Louisville, Kentucky, but settled in her 18th-century home in the small town of Redding, where she was buried following her death, aged 72, in 2009. Her gravestone in the local cemetery serves as a brief biography which reads "Mother, Wife, Friend, Activist" and "Voice of a generation that echoes through the ages."

Location 188: Redding is 10 miles south of Danbury. The Mary Travers gravestone is at Umpawaug Cemetery, 149 Umpawaug Road, Redding, CT 06896

RockAtlasUSA

Delaware

Wilmington
George Thorogood's 'Delaware Slide'

Wilmington's own rock star isn't nearly as 'Bad to the Bone' as the lyrics of his best-known song would have you believe

'Delaware Slide' is a song by George Thorogood & The Destroyers ("the Delaware Destroyers" to be geographical) which appeared on the band's self-titled debut album in 1977. It's a superb slide guitar reproduction of the old blues staple, 'Rollin' and Tumblin'' which Thorogood turned into a song about trying and failing to mend a broken relationship and hitting Highway 95 to do so. Fans of Thorogogood might also like to know about the Riverfront Blues Festival, which takes place every August in Wilmington's Tubman-Garrett Riverfront Park.

Location 190: Wilmington is 30 miles southwest of Philadelphia, PA. The song's Highway 95 runs right in and out of Wilmington. Naamans Manor on Wilmington's outskirts is where George Thorogood grew up, DE 19810

Wilmington
Bob Marley on the 'Night Shift'

Before introducing reggae to a wider American audience, Wilmington is where reggae legend Bob Marley operated a forklift truck and learned a trade, welding, while working in a factory in 1966. Many believe his 1976 song 'Night Shift' (a track on his Rastaman Vibration album with The Wailers) is based on his work experience at this time. During this period he lived with his mother Cedella, a Wilmington resident, and was later joined by wife Rita, who he had recently married. Craving independence, and after little financial reward as a musician in Jamaica, Marley was determined to start his own record label. He flew to the US and worked at the Chrysler automobile plant to save up the necessary funds. By the time he'd earned $700 he had enough to form the small Wail'n Soul'm record label back home. This still less than lucrative operation, which included a record store, kept Marley involved in music but it would be another decade before his own genre-busting breakthrough would hit the US and the wider world. Cedella Marley ran her own local record store called Roots in Wilmington, on Market Street. Cedella's enterprising business operated until 1976 (about the time her son's career had reached a high point). Marley's Delaware legacy lives on in the annual Peoples' Festival, a tribute to Bob Marley, usually celebrated in July at Tubman-Garrett Riverfront Park in Wilmington.

Locations 191, 192, 193, and 194: Wilmington is 30 miles southwest of Philadelphia, PA. Bob Marley worked at the Chrysler plant in Newark (15 miles west of Wilmington) and at DuPont at 1007 North Market Street, Wilmington, DE 19898. The former location of Roots record shop was also on North Market Street. The annual Bob Marley tribute at the Peoples' Festival is staged at Riverfront Park, Rosa Parks Drive, Wilmington, DE 19801. The riverfront also hosts the Riverfront Blues Festival in August and you should head for Rodney Square in the city center if jazz is your bag. Here the Clifford Brown Jazz Festival kicks off every June.

Florida

Bronson and Gainesville
Bo Diddley's gravestone and plaza

Ellas Otha Bates was born in McComb, Mississippi, raised in Chicago, lived in Florida towns Archer and Hawthorne, buried here in Bronson, and is known worldwide as Bo Diddley. The bluesman (whose songwriting credits read 'Ellas McDaniel' or 'E. McDaniel'), influenced a new generation of blues-rock performers in the early sixties, most famously The Rolling Stones. Bo Diddley has a memorial stone standing five feet tall at Bronson's Rosemary Hill Cemetery, which features the image of the signature rectangular guitar he designed himself. Officials in nearby Gainesville unveiled a mural and named a local downtown spot 'Bo Diddley Community Plaza' after his death in 2009.

Locations 195 and 196:
Bronson is 25 miles southwest of Gainesville. The cemetery is at the junction of East Thrasher Drive and Marshburn Drive, Bronson, FL 32621. Bo Diddley Community Plaza is located at 111 East University Avenue on the corner of South East 1st Street and East University Avenue, Gainesville, FL 32601

Bo Diddley Road Runner The Chess Masters: 1959-1960

CHESS
RECORD CORP

CH-104
(CH-104-A)
Arc Music, Inc.
BMI
A Division of Sugar Hill Record, Ltd., 96 West Street, Englewood New Jersey, 07631
45 RPM
Time: 2:24
BO DIDDLEY
(E. McDaniel)
BO DIDDLEY

'Hey Bo Diddley' and 'Bo Diddley' were two songs he wrote for himself as "E. McDaniel." Virtually everything else you need to know about this great man is written on his gravestone

Florida

Greenville
Ray Charles' statue and childhood home

It comes as a surprise to many that Ray Charles was raised in Florida. Although born in Albany, Georgia, the small north Florida town of Greenville is where Ray Charles grew up and called home. Here he spent his childhood from a month old until he began his music career aged just 15. Greenville was where he became totally blind by the time he was seven years old, a disability that only added to the aura of one of America's most iconic figures. His huge contribution to popular music is remembered by the local community through the life-size bronze statue erected in his honor. The town also preserved his tiny childhood home as a museum, dedicating it on the day that would have been Ray's 79th birthday, in 2006. The driving force behind the project was Ray's childhood friend and future Greenville Mayor Elesta Pritchett.

Location 197: Greenville is about 40 miles west of

Justina Cone

Still attracting the ladies: Visiting the Ray Charles Childhood Home are, left to right: Miss Emerald Coast USA, Jami Daniels, Mayor Elesta Pritchett, Miss Northwest Florida, Morgan Mount, Brandi Purves, and Robin Mount

Tallahassee. The Ray Charles statue is on the south side of U.S. Highway 90, downtown Greenville, in Haffye Hays Park, Greenville, FL 32331. Ray Charles' childhood home is at 443 South West Ray Charles Avenue, Greenville, FL 32331

❝No one knew where Greenville was. No one before I got started trying to preserve the legacy of Ray Charles here in Greenville ❞

Greenville Mayor Elesta Pritchett

Jacksonville
The Lynyrd Skynyrd memorials

Jacksonville has at least three locations where Lynyrd Skynyrd fans can pay their respects and remember Ronnie Van Zant, the band's original lead singer. Born and raised in Jacksonville, Van Zant was a victim of the 1977 air crash that killed him and also wiped out guitarist and songwriter Steve Gaines, guitarist Cassie Gaines, and assistant road manager Dean Kilpatrick. Ronnie Van Zant is now securely buried in a vault at the riverside Memorial Park in Jacksonville, in the family plot. Previously his remains, along with those of Steve Gaines, had been desecrated at their original resting places in Orange Park. Vandals were reported to have removed Van Zant's ashes and scattered them. Both rock stars' Orange Park mausoleums have nevertheless

been retained to allow fans to continue to visit. A positive legacy in Van Zant's name is the Ronnie Van Zant Memorial Park south of Jacksonville at Lake Asbury. Funded by band associates and fans, this recreational facility was created in 1992 and features nature trails, sports fields, and sporting equipment.

Locations 198, 199 and 200: the riverside Memorial Park cemetery is at 7242 Normandy Boulevard, Jacksonville, FL 32205. Jacksonville Memory Gardens, Orange Park cemetery is at 111 Blanding Boulevard, Orange Park, FL 32073. The Ronnie Van Zant Memorial Park is just south of Jacksonville at 2760 Sandridge Road, Lake Asbury, FL 32043

Miami
Eric Clapton's 461 Ocean Boulevard

The cover of Eric Clapton's 1974 album, 461 Ocean Boulevard, pictures him relaxing and strumming a guitar at his rented home base during the recording of the album at Criteria Studios, six miles away. Clapton barely spent a month at No. 461 but pilgrims from as far away as Japan still flock to see this address on Ocean Boulevard. The Bee Gees and the Eagles have also rented the property while creating some of their best work, but the photoshoot for Clapton's second solo album is what has connected this address so indelibly to the British guitar hero.

Location 202: a private residence, 461 Ocean Boulevard backs onto the ocean at Golden Beach, Miami, FL 33160

> *We hoped that by renting the very same house, some of the magic would rub off on us, and we'd make a great record too*
>
> *Don Felder of the Eagles, who rented 461 during the making of Hotel California at Criteria*

Eric Clapton poses front, back, and inside #461, the property rented for him by manager Robert Stigwood

Live Oak
The Spirit of the Suwannee Music Park

On the banks of the famous Suwannee River in north central Florida, the Spirit of the Suwannee Music Park hosts some highly rated annual events and festivals. The Wanee Music Festival kicks off in April, regularly hosted by The Allman Brothers, and The Suwannee River Jam follows a month later, attracting high profile artists such as Sheryl Crow and claiming to be the largest country jam in the South. You can even experience one of the most famous river song stories here first-hand by heading 'Way Down upon the Suwannee River' trail alongside all the other nature or sporting activities that this park has to offer. The song that carries that enduring line, 'Old Folks at Home,' is an old Christy's Minstrels tune from 1851 which is Florida's official song.

Location 201: Live Oak is 70 miles northwest of Gainesville at 3076 95th Drive, Live Oak, FL 32060

Florida

Miami
The Beatles take a TV break

In February 1964, The Beatles spent a 10-day break in Miami escaping the gloom of a British winter and performing in front of millions for a second time on American coast-to-coast TV. The Deauville resort hotel's Napoleon Ballroom was borrowed for the band to rehearse ahead of the recording of what would be The Beatles' second appearance on The Ed Sullivan Show. On February 16th 1964 they capitalized on their earlier record-breaking New York TV appearance with the follow-up taped in front of 2,600 ticket holders in the hotel's Mau Mau Club and beamed to 70 million watching Americans. The excitement generated by their presence in Miami meant that they were virtual prisoners in the hotel, inside (rumour has it) Deauville rooms 1112 and 1113. John, Paul, George, and Ringo did 'escape' the claustrophobia of Beatlemania at times during their stay. In between photoshoots and meet and greets they managed nights at the Mau Mau Lounge, being entertained by comedians and singers, dancing "The Mashed Potato," and watching a Coasters concert. The visit to Miami also coincided

with the headline-grabbing boxer Cassius Clay's stay. The future Muhammad Ali was in training for his world heavyweight title fight with Sonny Liston at the 5th Street Gym and the inevitable mock sparring session and photo opportunity took place here between the boxer and The Beatles, making newspaper headlines around the world. Away from their hotel The Beatles did manage a degree of privacy as guests at a couple of the resort's large beachfront mansions and tried - without much success, it has to be noted - water-skiing, power-boating, and fishing. The pictures taken at the time by Deso Hoffmann of the 'Fab Four' paddling in the surf show four skinny pale-skinned English boys enjoying the novelty of warm sunshine in February, their highlight of the American experience to date, as Ringo Starr remarked in the band's numerous interviews.

Location 204: you can still live like a Beatle at the Deauville Beach Resort, 6701 Collins Avenue, Miami Beach, FL 33141

Miami
Classic album recordings at Criteria Studios

Now owned by the New York recording studio organization The Hit Factory, from 1958 until 1999 these studios were simply Criteria Studios, creating some of rock's best-known classic albums. Derek & The Dominos' Layla and Other Assorted Love Songs (1970), Eric Clapton's 461 Ocean Boulevard (1974), the Eagles' Hotel California (1976) and Bob Dylan's Time out of Mind (1997) were all recorded here. A large part of R.E.M. album Automatic for the People was recorded at Criteria and the band

used part of a sign on the nearby Sinbad Motel at Biscayne Boulevard for the 1992 release's cover image.

Location 203: three miles inland from the ocean at 1755 Northeast 149th Street, North Miami, FL 33181

A view from the ceiling at Criteria back in the 70s shows Stephen Stills, (right) Chris Hillman (center), and the rest of Manassas recording in Miami

Miami
The Ultra Music Festival

Straying from the rock path a touch but the Ultra Music Festival is a great diversion for those who like great electronic music in a spectacular outdoor setting. This festival is now staged every March in Downtown Miami's Bayfront Park and has lately begun attracting daily attendances of 50,000 plus. Kraftwerk, The Prodigy, The Black Eyed Peas, Orbital, and Underworld have all graced the event in its relatively short history, which has also seen Ultra Music Festivals in Argentina, Brazil, Croatia, Chile, Spain, and South Korea.

Location 205: the festival is staged at 301 Biscayne Boulevard, Bayfront Park, FL 33132

St. Petersburg
The Bananas Music store

With three million items in stock, St. Petersburg's Banana Music warehouse is clearly not a brief diversion for the traveling vinyl junkie. It resembles another kind of records office (public records and archives rather than the vinyl variety) with avenues of boxes on two large floors. Opened as a book store in 1977, the owners only added a single shelf of vinyl when a personal purchase of one specific album from a local garage sale could not be bought without buying the seller's entire stack. Owners Doug and Michelle Allen did just that and apparently every one of the records sold minus the one owner Michelle had already kept back for herself. Surprised and encouraged by this the couple gradually turned the place into a record store and sold off the book stock. Today they operate the warehouse and a second store which offers more variety of products including movies and CDs. Def Leppard, Jimmy Buffett, and Sonic Youth have all been among the customers attracted by Bananas Music in this vacation city.

Locations 206 and 207: St. Petersburg is on the peninsula west of Tampa. The Bananas Music vinyl warehouse is at 2226 16th Avenue North, St. Petersburg, FL 33713,

and the CD, vinyl, and movie shop is a mile northwest at 2887 22nd Avenue North, St. Petersburg, FL 33713

Doug and Michelle Allen with their 3 million stock items

❛One Japanese customer who visited said in Japan there was a map of all the big record stores: a couple in London, Paris, Tokyo, New York, L.A., and little St. Petersburg, Florida. That was nice to know ❜

Michelle Allen

Tampa
A Who world record at the Ford Amphitheatre

Guinness World Records lists the shortest music concert as being a gig by The Who that ended after just 13 seconds, here at the Tampa Amphitheatre. On March 13th 2007 the band's appearance on stage was cut short at this early point when lead vocalist Roger Daltrey quickly realized that, due to a worsening bout of bronchitis, he couldn't sing. The concert, attended by 9,000 fans, was rescheduled for March 25th, with Daltrey in fine form that night, and passed without further incident. Coincidentally, The Who once held the record for the loudest concert at Charlton Athletic's football ground in the UK, not a feat they could easily replicate here. Bands have to obey a special decibel limit at this Florida venue due to the close proximity of a residential area.

Location 208: Tampa is on the Florida west coast. The Ford Amphitheatre (now MidFlorida Credit Union Amphitheatre) is at the Florida State Fairgrounds, where Interstate Highway 4 and U.S. Highway 301 meet, Tampa, FL 33610

Georgia

The striking riverside plaza dedicated to Albany-born Ray Charles

Albany
Birthplace of Ray Charles

Although he lived here barely a month, Albany is famous as the birthplace of Ray Charles, who was born on September 23rd 1930 in a pecan grove in the Flower City region south of Albany, on Highway 300. Ray Charles Plaza in Albany is the closest you can get to the memory of the great man, who died in 2004. Here in the center of the city the blind musical legend is immortalized in a statue by sculptor Andy Davis. Here he sits at a baby grand piano with waterfalls trickling around him as recordings of his music broadcast through the plaza speakers. A miniature version of the sculpture with braille inscriptions has thoughtfully been included nearby at a touchable height. Students from the Georgia Academy for the Blind were involved in the design of this sizable project.

Location 209: Albany is 100 miles south of Macon. The Ray Charles Plaza and statue is by Riverfront Park in Downtown Albany, off South Front Street across from the Hilton Garden Inn, Albany, GA 31701

❝Ray Charles was an ordinary man with extraordinary talents and dreams. Not only did he have a dream but believed it was real and reachable. So I called his birth town of Albany and got together a board to help raise the funds to create the Ray Charles Plaza ❞

Artist Andy Davis

Athens
R.E.M. debut at St. Mary's

All that remains these days of the church where R.E.M. rehearsed and made their performance debut, and where the band's Michael Stipe and Peter Buck called home for a while, is the crumbling church tower. This oddly isolated structure was once part of the church where the band played their first gig on April 5th 1980, while called The Twisted Kites. They played to 350 expectant fans that night inside St. Mary's Episcopal Church on Oconee Street and the tall red tower still attracts visits from fans of the band, though some who grab chunks of masonry as souvenirs might be jeopardizing the long term existence of the building.

Location 210: Athens is 75 miles east of Atlanta. St. Mary's Episcopal Church steeple is at 394 Oconee Street, Athens, GA 30601

Athens
R.E.M.'s Murmur cover

Unsurprisingly for a band so linked to their Athens roots, the cover of R.E.M.'s 1983 debut album Murmur feature images of their local surroundings. The front cover landscape, strangled by the invasive Japanese vegetation kudzu, was photographed by R.E.M. singer Michael Stipe's college friend Sandra-Lee Phipps on a railroad embankment in Athens. Also shot by Phipps, the back cover depicts the 1880s wooden trestle structure that bridges Trail Creek in the city's Dudley Park. This area was once part of the railroad line in and out of Athens and is being preserved as an historic corridor.

Locations 211 and 212: the Murmur front cover location is on the railroad embankment at the junction of Chattooga Avenue and Hiawassee Avenue, a mile or so north of Downtown Athens, GA 30601. The now-

famous trestle is at Dudley Park, a mile east of downtown Athens. Access Dudley Park from East Broad Street and take the road under the trestle, or make for the end of the structure on the west side of South Poplar Street near the intersection with Oak Street, Athens, GA 30601

The extraordinarily famous trestle that still draws R.E.M. fans to Dudley Park

John A. Porcellino www.king-cat.net

Athens and Decatur
The Wuxtry Records stores

Some record stores attract some cool customers. Wuxtry Records can boast some cool employees. Both Peter Buck (R.E.M.) and Danger Mouse are reported to have worked behind the counter of Wuxtry Records in Athens, which first opened for business in 1976. Such was its success, a second Wuxtry Records store was added two years later in Decatur. "A walk-in museum of the greatest music" claims the Wuxtry website and there really is a museum annex with a growing number of rock-related Athens artefacts for you to peruse while buying (or indeed selling your own) records. Rolling Stone magazine's praise for the stores owned by Dan Wall extends to the "terrific comics shop upstairs" at the Athens store. Think Hi Fidelity the movie (as one customer pointed out) and you get an idea of this place's look and feel.

Locations 213 and 214: Wuxtry Records store in Athens is at 197 East Clayton Street, Athens, GA 30601. The second store is 65 miles east of Athens in the city of Decatur (an intown suburb of Atlanta), at 2096 North Decatur Road, Decatur, GA 30033

Georgia

Atlanta
Paul McCartney's Run Devil Run cover

The cover of Paul McCartney's 1999 return to his rock and roll roots album, Run Devil Run, has a picture of a drug store in Downtown Atlanta on the front. It was a store McCartney visited and, fascinated by the weird and wonderful potions and remedies on sale, purchased Run Devil Run bath salts. The Run Devil Run brand name inspired him to write the album's title track, name the album, and quickly take some photos of the store front. Sometime after his visit, at the former Beatle's request, a professional photographer was dispatched to shoot the eventual cover picture.

Location 215: Miller's Rexall Drugs is the Run Devil Run store, still open for business at 87 Broad Street, Atlanta, GA 30303

The store where Paul McCartney bought his bottle of Run Devil Run bath salts

❝ I was in Atlanta recently with one of my kids and we went down to the funky area of town and found this shop that sold various kinds of potions to stop evil ❞

Paul McCartney describes his visit to the Atlanta emporium

Atlanta and Douglasville
Elton John's Peachtree Road

Peachtree Road in Buckhead is where Elton John has a home and it is the thoroughfare that he chose as the title of his 2004 album of that name. Surprisingly, the album's cover image (snapped by photographer and movie director Sam Taylor-Wood) is of a railroad crossing 35 miles west near Douglasville, as Peachtree Road presented too busy a location for the mellow vibe of the album.

Location 217: Elton John's home is at North West Peachtree Road, Buckhead, GA 30309. The cover was shot 35 miles west of Buckhead near Douglasville, GA 30134

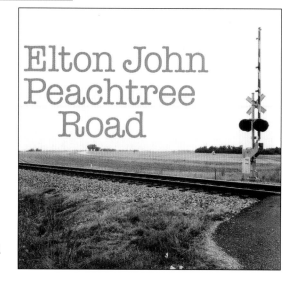

Atlanta
The Music Midtown festival

Atlanta's Music Midtown festival began in 1994, ended its annual run in 2006 but is now back in good health and attracting some of rock's biggest hitters. Foo Fighters and Pearl Jam headlined the sold-out two-day event in September 2012.

Location 216: Midtown is now held in 10th Street Meadow at Piedmont Park, Atlanta, GA

Augusta
The James Brown statue

The "Godfather of Soul," James Brown, has a life-size bronze statue in his honor in Augusta, the place he called home from the age of six. The statue was unveiled by Brown himself in 2005, at a spot a mile from the once poverty-stricken neighborhood where he grew up. Here, he was raised by his aunt Honey in his childhood home on Twiggs Street.

Location 218: Augusta lies about 75 miles southwest of Columbia. The statue stands on James Brown Boulevard, in the middle of Broad Street (No. 854), between 8th and 9th Streets, GA 30901. The now demolished childhood home was at 944 Twiggs Street, No. 938 being the nearest plot to where the house, a former brothel, was located.

Jennifer Yang

Augusta's James Brown statue is the work of sculptor John Savage

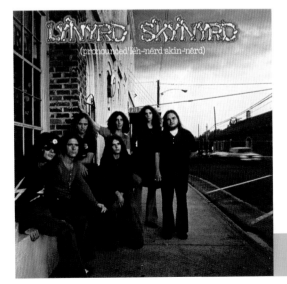

The debut album photocall in Jonesboro

Jonesboro
Lynyrd Skynyrd: down at the depot

Down by the train depot on Main Street is where the band members of Lynyrd Skynryd assembled to have their picture taken for the cover of their Pronounced 'leh-'nérd 'skin-'nérd album in 1973. The single-story depot, seen in the picture's background, still stands but the building the band were standing and sitting against has been demolished and replaced.

Location 219: Jonesboro is 17 miles south of Atlanta. The Lynyrd Skynyrd photoshoot took place at the corner of West Mill Street and South Main Street, Jonesboro, GA 30236

Georgia

Ren Davis and davisguides.com

Macon
Otis Redding's Georgia

The Otis Redding statue in Macon captures a San Francisco Bay song-writing moment

He may have been born in nearby Dawson, but Macon is the city most associated with Otis Redding. It's the place where he grew up from the age of five and where his funeral took place in 1967, attended by 4,500 at the City Auditorium. The city remembers Otis with a statue that reproduces the moment, shortly before he died, when he wrote 'Dock of the Bay' hundreds of miles away in San Francisco Bay. The bronze image, unveiled in 2002, depicts the soul singer-songwriter sittin' on the dock of the bay on an elevated spot overlooking the Ocmulgee River at Gateway Park. In a nice touch, sculptors Bradley Cooley and Bradley Cooper Jr., have included Otis' notebook, displaying the lyrics of his most popular song. Close by the statue is the Otis Redding Memorial Bridge, dedicated in 1974 by Macon City Council and complete with a plaque to prove it. The dedication took place on December 10th 1974, the seventh anniversary of the singer's tragic death in a Wisconsin plane crash. Otis Redding's grave is at the 300-acre estate at Round Oak, which he bought in 1965. The place he named the Big O Ranch is today

managed by his widow Zelma Redding. For the story of how Otis Redding wrote and recorded '(Sittin' on) the Dock of the Bay' check out the Rock Atlas entry for Sausalito, California.

Locations 220, 221, 222, 223, and 224: at the northwest corner where Riverside Drive meets Martin Luther King Jr. Boulevard, the Otis statue is in Charles H. Jones Gateway Park, Macon, GA 31201. The Otis Redding Memorial Bridge is next to the park on Martin Luther King Jr. Boulevard, spanning the river. The location for his funeral at the City Auditorium is at 1st Street, Macon, GA 31201. Otis was born in Dawson, GA 39842, about 100 miles southwest of Macon, where he grew up. The Big O Ranch and Otis' impressive, large, stone grave are private but that doesn't stop many fans turning up at the estate (20 miles northwest of Macon). From Round Oak, it's off Jackson Road, and leads to the winding, unmarked Otis Redding Road which eventually takes you to the 'Big O Ranch' sign with stone columns and a steel gate, at Round Oak, GA 31038

Macon
The Allman Brothers

Although formed in Jacksonville, Florida, when The Allman Brothers Band were offered a recording contract by Capricorn Records in 1969, their home base switched to Macon, Georgia. The band's bass guitarist Berry Oakley and his wife Linda moved into an old English Tudor-style house on Vineville Avenue, northwest

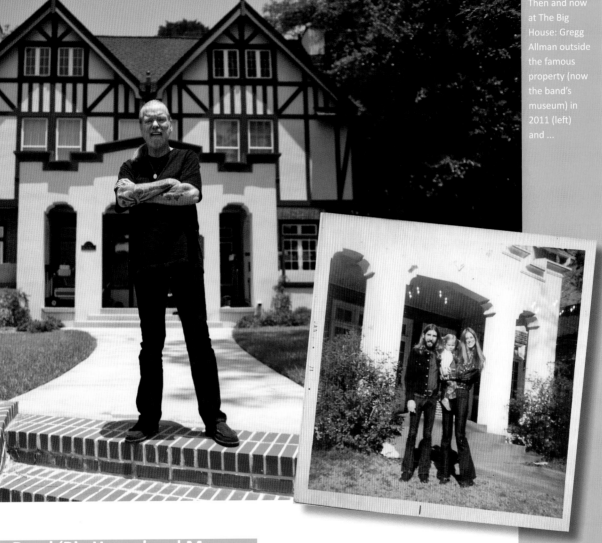

David Plakke Media NYC

Then and now at The Big House: Gregg Allman outside the famous property (now the band's museum) in 2011 (left) and …

Photo by Candace Oakley

Band 'Big House' and Museum

of Downtown Macon, and were joined soon after by Duane and Gregg Allman, who shared the $225 monthly rent. "The Big House," as the property became known, was the hub of most band activities from 1970 until 1973 and is now fittingly open to everyone who wants to visit it as The Allman Brothers Band Museum. The

five-bedroom, three-story house, which once accommodated band members, girlfriends and wives, children, and roadies, now displays a large stash of accumulated memorabilia, gold records, instruments, and stage clothing, along with hi-tech interactive exhibits. Many of the band's trail-blazing southern

rock songs were created at The Big House: Dickey Betts wrote 'Blue Sky' in the living room and 'Ramblin' Man' in the kitchen.

Location 225: less than two miles northwest of Downtown Macon, The Allman Brothers Band Museum is at 2321 Vineville Avenue, Macon, GA 31204

… The Allman Brothers' bass player Berry Oakley, with partner Linda and daughter Brittany (above)

Georgia

Macon
The Allman Brothers' street, bridge, and boulevard

Before The Allman Brothers Band set up their Macon home base at The Big House on Vineville Avenue, they rented two bedrooms in a property on College Street which roadie Twiggs Lyndon found for them. College Street was the location of their photoshoot for the cover of their 1969 debut LP. The front picture was taken next door at The Bell House, listed on the National Register of Historic Places. The album's back cover was snapped

at the nearby Rose Hill Cemetery, a spot frequently visited by the band as a special place of inspiration. It is also where band members Duane Allman (1946-1971) and Berry Oakley (1948-1972) are buried. Both were killed in motorcycle accidents and both were honored in the dedicating of local landmarks in 2001.

Locations 226, 227, 228, 229, and 230: the band's first house in Macon is 309

College Street and the 1969 album cover shoot took place at The Bell House, 315 College Street, Macon, GA 31201, and at the Bond Tomb at Rose Hill Cemetery located at 1091 Riverside Drive, Macon, GA 31201. Duane Allman Boulevard is the portion of State Highway 19 between Holt Avenue and College Street, Macon, GA 31201, and Raymond Berry Oakley III Bridge is at the same state highway as it spans Interstate 75, Macon, GA 31201

Hawaii

Kauai/Kappa
A private Beatles museum

The Kauai Country Inn claims to have the only private Beatles museum in the United States. Not open to the public then, but if you're a guest you can see a wide range of Beatles memorabilia including a Beatles Mini Cooper S once owned by their manager Brian Epstein.

Location 231: on the east coast of the island of Kauai, 6440 Olohena Road, Kapaa, Kauai, HI 96746

Maui/Makawao
Jimi Hendrix's final US gig

Ryan Ozawa

A breezy, exposed field on the island of Maui proved to be the location of Jimi Hendrix's final gig on American soil. Less than a month after this performance on July 30th 1970, he died in London, aged just 27. The filmed performance in front of several hundred sun-baked hippies is often described as the Haleakala Crater Concert as the Haleakala volcano forms most of the land mass of Maui.

Location 232: close to the Seabury Hall school, Olinda Road, just outside Makawao, Maui, HI 96768

Oahu/Honolulu
The Elvis Presley statue

The "World's First Satellite TV Concert" was broadcast from International Center Honolulu on January 14th 1973. No doubt a big deal in technology circles, the event is remembered more for the subject of the transmission. "Aloha from Hawaii" was the historic concert by Elvis Presley. The event was also extremely convenient for Elvis and manager Colonel Tom Parker. Never happy to tour Elvis around the world, Parker had the perfect opportunity to get his star on stage, live in front of millions around the globe without leaving the USA. In addition to the 8,000 crowded inside Honolulu's

The life-size, 1,100-pound, Elvis Presley statue created to commemorate not only the "World's First Satellite TV Concert" but also Elvis's 1961 benefit gig and his movie Blue Hawaii

International Center, the audience watching 'The King' live that day was estimated at between 1.1 and 1.5 billion, including the staggering statistic that 98 percent of all Japan's TV viewers were watching. The venue for the concert (now renamed the Neal S. Blaisdell Center) still stands and to remember the day history was made a bronze statue of Elvis has been erected outside.

Location 233: south on the island of Oahu, the statue is on the walkway in front of the Neal S. Blaisdell Center at 777 Ward Avenue, Honolulu, Oahu, HI 96814

Hawaii

Oahu and Kauai
Elvis's Blue Hawaii

You can take a great tour of Elvis Presley locations if your love of 'The King' extends to his movies. The top of Mount Tantalus is the vantage point where Elvis and girlfriend enjoyed the view and a picnic in the1961 movie Blue Hawaii. Here you can look down on many of the island settings for Blue Hawaii, Girls!, Girls!, Girls!, and Paradise Hawaiian-Style. Hanauma Bay is where the beach scenes were mostly shot for Blue Hawaii and where Elvis returned in 1965 for the Paradise, Hawaiian Style helicopter rescue scene. The extinct volcano Diamond Head can also be seen prominently in Blue Hawaii. It stands behind Waikiki Beach. Scenes were shot near Diamond Head Lighthouse on Diamond Head Road at the far eastern end of Waikiki. What looks to be the best Elvis movie location of all to visit is the Polynesian Cultural Centre on the west coast of Oahu. Here you can relive the drama of the locals' drum ceremony, visit the fabulous waterfall finale location, and even enter the thatched hut that Elvis used as a changing room in Paradise, Hawaiian Style. If you are visiting Elvis locations in Hawaii, you can stay at two hotels he used. If you book yourself in on the 22nd floor of The Ilikai you'll be in the perfect place to recreate 'The King''s visits, and similarly on the top floor of the Hilton Hawaiian Village or Room 14A, where he stayed on his first visit to Hawaii in 1957. Why stop there? The island of Kauai is where the Coco Palms Resort played host to Elvis and more scenes from Blue Hawaii.

Locations 234, 235, 236, 237, 238, 239, and 240: the Oahu island locations begin with Mount Tantalus, best accessed by Puu Ualakaa Park Honolulu, Oahu, HI 96822. Hanauma Bay is about 15 miles east of Honolulu,

ECSTATIC ROMANCE...EXOTIC DANCES...EXCITING MUSIC IN THE WORLD'S LUSHEST PARADISE OF SONG!

ELVIS PRESLEY RIDES THE CREST OF THE WAVE IN BLUE HAWAII

A HAL WALLIS PRODUCTION

TECHNICOLOR® AND IN PANAVISION®

14 TERRIFIC SONGS!

CO-STARRING JOAN BLACKMAN · ANGELA LANSBURY · NANCY WALTERS · DIRECTED BY NORMAN TAUROG · SCREENPLAY BY HAL KANTER
A PARAMOUNT RELEASE

HI 96825. Diamond Head and Waikiki Beach are at Honolulu, HI 96815. The Polynesian Cultural Center is north of the island at 55-370 Kamehameha Highway, Laie, HI 96762. The Ilikai Hotel & Suites is at Waikiki Beach front, 1777 Ala Moana Boulevard, Honolulu, HI 96815. The Hilton Hawaiian Village Waikiki Beach Resort complex is also at Waikiki Beach front, 2005 Kalia Road, Honolulu, HI 96815. The Coco Palms Resort on the island of Kauai is currently closed due to the devastation and damage sustained during hurricane Iniki in 1992. It is located at Kuhio Highway, Kapaa, HI 96746

Idaho

Idaho
The B-52s' 'Private Idaho' and Joey Ramone's 'Danny Says'

'Private Idaho' is a single by The B-52s and a track included on their 1980 hit album Wild Planet. The song inspired the title, if not the movie, My Own Private Idaho, which starred River Phoenix and Keanu Reeves and was

directed by Gus Van Sant. The state was also name checked by The Ramones in one memorable lyric. "Gotta go to Idaho" says the line in 'Danny Says,' a favorite song of Joey Ramone's which he wrote for The Ramones' 1980 album End

of the Century. Ramones manager Danny Field is the subject of the song which has been covered by Foo Fighters and Tom Waits.

Location 241: the entire state!

Pocatello
The first date of Fleetwood Mac's Tusk Tour

The MiniDome in Pocatello was the unlikely starting point for Fleetwood Mac's Tusk Tour in 1979. October 26th that year saw this modest-sized city (the fifth biggest in the state) host, arguably, the world's biggest band at the beginning of one of rock's most self-indulgent tours. Although popular, the band

was not in great shape mentally, physically, or financially at the time. One of America's oldest enclosed stadiums and now renamed the Holt Arena, this Pocatello venue has witnessed many other gigs where the place has been bursting at the seams. Local music fan Don Furu rated The Moody Blues'

Pocatello gig as his all-time favorite and was lucky enough to have seen Garth Brooks at the Holt Arena when 17,000 squeezed inside. Garth fans began camping out in wind and rain a week before tickets went on sale for his 1993 concert. But it is the wild Fleetwood Mac gig that most sticks in ▶

The MiniDome, complete with the perfect roof for sliding down on your butt, as Fleetwood Mac fan Alison Jordan recommends over the page

Idaho

▶ the mind of fans who descended on little old Pocatello's MiniDome in this entertainment-starved area. In particular, rock goddess Stevie Nicks made quite an impression on her Idaho fans that night.

❝Stevie Nicks walked over to the front of the stage. It appeared as though she wanted to fly off it. Then she was gone. From where I was standing I couldn't tell if she jumped or if she fell. All I know is that she disappeared for several minutes❞

16-year-old sophomore at Idaho Falls High School, J.C. Brown

❝My first memory of the dome was shortly after it was constructed in 1970. A friend that lived near the dome and I climbed to the top and slid down on our butts. Although the bolts that helped give our feet purchase on the way up did a number on our butts and "pants" on the way down. I was one year out of high school when I attended the Fleetwood Mac concert at the MiniDome. As I recall it seemed as if Stevie Nicks changed her dress many times throughout the show. Also, fans were blowing on her so her hair and dress were flowing❞

Pocatello Fleetwood Mac fan Alison Jordan

❝I do remember Stevie Nicks! She was not herself that night, she looked f****d up. I remember her stumbling around and forgetting her lyrics. They had to stop and restart songs many times❞

Ed Scott, a high school junior back in 1979

❝It was my first concert. I was very excited. I thought it was a fantastic show and Stevie Nicks seemed to be having a great time. I remember she had this beautiful white handkerchief dress and she seemed to be a little intoxicated. It was a packed house, and it was a big deal for little old Pocatello❞

19-year-old Pocatello girl Wendy Anderson

❝Stevie Nicks had a good buzz going. During one of the songs she stepped from the mic and went to the front edge of the stage where we guys were and leaned over and said, "Do you want to f**k me?" Well do you?" And we all yelled, "Hell yes!" That got me a smack alongside my head from my eight months pregnant wife Mari❞

Powers Candy warehouseman, John Powers

Location 242: Pocatello is 230 miles east of Boise. The Holt Arena (formerly the MiniDome) is close to the center of Pocatello at 550 Memorial Drive, Idaho State University, Pocatello, ID 83201

The always lovely and diaphanous Stevie Nicks was floating on air in Pocatello

Illinois

Alsip
Muddy Waters' gravestone

Legendary bluesman Muddy Waters was born McKinley Morganfield on April 4th 1915 in Mississippi and died in Westmont, Illinois, on April 30th 1983, six months after playing his final performance at an Eric Clapton concert in Florida. His gravestone here at the Restvale Cemetery is easy to find despite no "Muddy Waters" inscription. His birth name, guitar, and the line "The Mojo is Gone" are enough to identify one of popular music's leading lights on an otherwise small, rather insignificant gravestone. And Muddy Waters is not alone. As the state of Illinois contributed so much to the history of the blues, it's not surprising that also buried in this cemetery are musicians Luther Tucker, Hound Dog Taylor, St. Louis Jimmy Oden, Kansas Joe McCoy, Papa Charlie McCoy, Magic Sam Maghett, Big Walter Horton, John Henry Barbee, Jazz Gillum, Valerie Wellington, and Earl Hooker.

Location 243: Alsip is 20 miles to the south of downtown Chicago. Muddy Waters' grave marker is three graves from the cemetery office door at Restvale Cemetery, 11700 South Laramie Street, Alsip, IL 60803

Alsip
Willie Dixon's gravestone

Two miles south of Muddy Waters' grave is where songwriter, musician, and boxer Willie Dixon (1915-1992) is buried in Burr Oak Cemetery. Born in Mississippi, he died in California after a life playing and composing blues standards 'Spoonful,' 'Little Red Rooster,' 'Hoochie Coochie Man,' and 'I Just Want to Make Love to You.' His grave marker is inscribed with an image of a double bass, his favorite instrument. Other significant musicians buried at Burr Oak Cemetery include Dinah Washington, Otis Spann, James Kokomo Arnold and Barbara Acklin.

Location 244: The Burr Oak Cemetery is at 4400 West 127th Street, Alsip, IL 60803

Chicago
40,000 pieces of vinyl at Dave's Records

Don't mention CDs around this emporium, it's vinyl all the way at Dave's Records. "No CDs – never had 'em, never will!" is Dave's admirable slogan. You can sift through 40,000 discs on any given day, served by a man who quite obviously was born to run a record store.

> ❝The first store I shopped in was Swollen Head Records in La Grange. It had waterbeds in the basement and black light posters and a logo of a giant green head. My mother was always afraid to shop there for my Christmas presents. I gave her my list and hoped she'd find The Who's Quadrophenia and Neil Young's Decade without too much trouble. I hope we continue that link to the cool record stores of the past ❞

Dave's model for his own Chicago-based store

Location 245: Dave's Records can be found at 2604 North Clark Street, Chicago, IL 60614

Chicago
Lollapalooza in 'Chicago's front yard'

Jane's Addiction singer Perry Farrell conceived the Lollapalooza music festival when setting up a farewell tour for the band. Then Farrell's vision of a musical roadshow across the U.S. became reality, naming the whole thing upon hearing the word "Lollapalooza" used in an old movie by comedy trio The Three Stooges. What began in 1991 broadened out as a popular touring festival, losing momentum at the turn of the century until finding an annual home since 2005 at Grant Park, Chicago, and the introduction of international Lollapaloozas in South America. Since establishing a permanent home in the park, the accent has remained heavily on rock's weird and wonderful. A glance through the 2012 bill listed performers Trampled by Turtles, Bear in Heaven and Yellow Ostrich, joined by heavyweights Black Sabbath, Red Hot Chili Peppers, and Jack White.

Location 246: Grant Park is a large, 319-acre green space on the waterfront, often referred to as "Chicago's front yard," Chicago, IL 60605

Illinois

Chicago

One of the great record labels, Chess helped shape rock and roll music through its signing of Muddy Waters, Howlin' Wolf, Chuck Berry, and Bo Diddley, performers who set down the template for (in particular) British bands The Beatles, The Rolling Stones, and Led Zeppelin to copy, embellish, and establish rock. Chess has moved Chicago locations a few times since Aristocrat Records (based at 71st Street and Phillips) was bought by brothers Leonard and Phil Chess in 1947. Three years later the enterprising duo changed the company name to their own, relocating to Chicago's 49th Street, then a block north of 48th Street and Cottage Grove in 1954. Here Chess built its first rehearsal studio, but sub-standard results forced the company to continue relying on Universal, which it had used in the past for recording production. When the business moved yet again to South Michigan Avenue, Chess fans The Rolling Stones paid a visit to the studios in June 1964 to record at the place where so many of their musical heroes had done so before. The result was the band's UK 'Five by Five' EP (extended play) release, which included an instrumental, '2120 South Michigan Avenue,' the Chess address. The recordings would later form the

basis of the Stones' second US LP, 12 X 5, which helped propel the band on their route to huge success when the album shot to number 3 on the Billboard chart. The famous address of the Chess studio also cropped up as the title of George Thorogood and The Destroyers 2011 album on which they covered the same Stones instrumental, although as far back as 1966 Chess had moved to larger premises on East 21st Street. This is where the building still stands as a second monument to this popular and hugely influential label.

Locations 247 and 248: the most important Chess Records base was at 2120 South Michigan Avenue, Chicago, IL 60616. The location is happily now Willie Dixon's Blues Garden and the HQ for Willie Dixon's Blues Heaven Foundation. Tours of this landmark building have been a feature of the operation in the past, although the current situation is uncertain. The final home of Chess Records is a couple of blocks away, east of the South Michigan location at 320 East 21st Street, Chicago, IL 60616

In the footsteps of their heroes: The Rolling Stones pictured on the cover of their UK chart-topping EP recorded at Chess Records

Chicago
Wilco loft and the Yankee Hotel Foxtrot cover

The Marina City building in downtown Chicago is the subject of the striking image on the cover of Yankee Hotel Foxtrot, the 2002 album by Wilco. The Chicago-based band recorded their most commercially successful album seven miles north of the Marina City towers at the Wilco Loft, a third-story studio space purchased in 1999 which houses an Aladdin's cave of guitars and other gear the band have collected over the years.

Locations 249 and 250: the Marina City towers are sandwiched between North State Street to the east and North Dearborn Street to the west, Chicago, IL 60654. The Wilco Loft is near North Kedzie Avenue and West Irving Park Road, Chicago, IL 60618

Wilco's most successful album, featuring the Marina City towers in downtown Chicago

Chicago
Billy Corgan's tea shop

Madame ZuZu's tea shop is an art-deco-inspired establishment owned by Smashing Pumpkins founder and frontman Billy Corgan. Although it's unlikely that Corgan will serve you with a cup of lemon berry tea every day, he did play two acoustic sets at the place on opening night, in 2012.

Location 251: Madame ZuZu's is in the Highland Park suburb of

Chicago at 582 Roger Williams Avenue, Highland Park, IL 60035

❝I'm a tea guy and living in Highland Park since 2003, I've always wanted to open a salon like this for everyone to enjoy ❞

Billy Corgan

Blending tea-drinking with the arts: Billy Corgan at Madame ZuZu's

Chicago
Laurie's Planet of Sound

This is a record store where it's hard to describe any of the contents for sale without ending a sentence with an exclamation mark! Laurie's Planet of Sound is a popular place for vinyl hunters but they cater for all genres and types of record collector and that, apparently, includes audio cassette collectors! Handwritten staff reviews, cult horror movies, Frank Zappa shorts, and wacky toys add to the mix and it's in the hippest spot to shop in Chicago.

Location 252: North of Downtown Chicago, 4639 North Lincoln Avenue, Chicago, IL 60625

Illinois

Chicago
Graham Nash's 'Chicago Seven' song story

'Chicago/We Can Change the World' is a protest song written and released by Graham Nash which tells the background story to the conspiracy charges leveled at a group of anti-war protesters known as the 'Chicago Seven.' When one of the seven, Bobby Seale, was bound, gagged, and chained to a chair in a Chicago courtroom Nash used the incident in the lyrics of the hit single, taken from his 1971 solo debut album, Songs for Beginners.

❝Hugh Romney (Wavy Gravy) called David [Crosby] and invited CSNY to go and play at a benefit for the Chicago Seven. David and I wanted to do it, Neil [Young] and Stephen [Stills] didn't, for whatever reason. Anyway, I wrote this song to Neil and Stephen and to everybody that I thought might want to hear about the fact that what was happening to the Chicago Seven wasn't fair ❞

Graham Nash

Location 253: the late sixties protests and subsequent riots that Graham Nash wrote about occurred all along the lakefront parks and in the street in front of the Conrad Hilton hotel HQ, the location for the presidential campaigns that were taking place at the time. 521 North Rush Street, Chicago, IL 60611

Chicago
The Blues Brothers get the freedom of the city

The Blues Brothers music-related movies were based on a band created by blues-loving duo Dan Aykroyd and John Belushi back in the early seventies in Toronto, Canada. Successful TV exposure via Saturday Night Live and a Billboard No.1 album followed before the duo's Blues Brothers movie debut in 1980. Filmed on location in and around Chicago, the movie met with an unusually high level of cooperation from the local authorities. Director John Landis was fortunate that Chicago Mayor Jane Byrne was more helpful than her famous predecessor, Mayor Richard J. Daley, who had put a stop on the city granting permission for movie location filming until his death in 1976. Daley's legacy would linger on in the movie, though. When the co-stars' Bluesmobile plows into a building after an epic automobile chase under Chicago's iconic elevated train track, it's ironically the Richard J. Daley Center's large glass frontage that it crashes through when pursued by police and the army. A large proportion of the $27million it cost to make the movie must have been allocated to pay the many personal assistants stationed on street corners throughout Chicago. This army of facilitators with walkie-talkies cleared the streets to film scenes in the early morning on weekends back in 1979. But enough of the logistics, let's get back to the music. Blues Brothers' fans of the original 1980 movie starring Aykroyd and Belushi and its follow-up in 2000 can visit a number of

❝We got a full tank of gas, half a pack of cigarettes, it's dark, and we're wearing sunglasses. Hit it! ❞

❝The mission was to reacquaint people or acquaint people for the first time with this tremendous form of American music ❞

Dan Aykroyd

iconic locations featured in both releases.

Location 254: the movie's opening sequence sees John Belushi's character Jake released from prison and met by brother Elwood, played by Dan Aykroyd. The vast, faux, castle-like Joliet Correctional Center is the setting which can be visited (but not entered obviously!) about 30 miles southeast of Chicago city center. The Joliet Correctional Center is at 1127-1299 Collins Street, Joliet, IL 60432

Location 255: the Bluesmobile's spectacular leap over the fast opening river drawbridge was filmed about 15 miles south of the city. You can find the spot close to the shoreline of Lake Michigan at Calumet Harbor. Take East 95th Street and head due east for Calumet Park and you will cross the (preferably closed and open for traffic!) bridge over the Calumet River, IL 60617

Location 256: the external movie location for the Triple Rock Baptist Church, where soul legend James Brown struts his stuff as Reverend Cleophus James, can be found at the Pilgrim Baptist Church just north of the Calumet River Bridge location, again about 15 miles south of the city center on the corner of East 91st Street and South Burley Avenue. The exact address is the Pilgrim Baptist Church, 9114 South Burley Avenue, South Chicago, IL 60617

Location 257: when searching out

former band members, including a guitarist (played by Steve Cropper) and bass player (Donald "Duck" Dunn), the Blues Brothers pay a call on a red-brick boarding house run by Mrs. Tarantino. The house they visit is at an address on 51st Court (between West 16th and West 18th streets) about seven miles west of the city Center, 1623 51st Court, Cicero, IL 60804

Location 258: although the Soul Food Café where Aretha Franklin sang and served, and John Lee Hooker busked outside, has long since gone, you can still visit the site of the fictional musical instrument shop run by Ray Charles (Ray's Music Exchange). Look out for the colorful outside wall music mural seen in the movie which still remains. These days the

building at the intersection of East 47th Street South Prairie Avenue, about three miles south of central Chicago, is Shelly's Loan Co. The Shelly's Loan Company address is 300 East 47th Street, South Prairie Avenue, IL 60653

Location 259: the Palace Ballroom where the band play the memorable second (but first successful) gig of the movie takes place in reality inside the Hollywood Hotel, Los Angeles, and not in Chicago at all, as with many of the movie's interior scenes. However, the impressive exterior of the Palace Ballroom is 'played' by the South Shore Cultural Center at the corner of South Shore Drive and East 71st Street, seven miles south along the shoreline. South Shore Cultural Center is situated

on 7059 South Shore Drive, IL 60649

Location 260: the climax of the Blues Brothers' car chase happens at Daley Plaza, where the 162-ton, 50-foot high, untitled Picasso sculpture and the Richard J. Daley Center's glass-fronted entrance both feature prominently in the movie. This city center location involving a cast of hundreds of stuntmen and women, cops, soldiers, and pedestrians is best approached from West Washington Street. The Richard J. Daley Center occupies the city block bound by Randolph, Clark, Washington, and Dearborn Streets. The address is 50 West Washington and the Plaza and Picasso sculpture are on the opposite side of West Washington Street, IL 60602

The Blues Brothers: Jake (John Belushi) and Elwood (Dan Aykroyd) on the streets of Chicago

Illinois

Hillside
Howlin' Wolf's gravestone

Chester Arthur Burnett is the name you need to search for if you are visiting Oakridge Cemetery to pay your respects to Howlin' Wolf. Look for the gravestone with his birth name and featuring engravings of the bluesman's guitar and harmonica. Born in West Point, Mississippi, on June 10th 1910, the writer of influential blues classics such as 'Smokestack Lightnin'' died just three miles from his final Hillside resting place in hospital at Hines, Illinois, on January 10th, 1976.

Location 261: Hillside is 15 miles west of downtown Chicago. The gravesite is near the road at Oakridge Cemetery, 4301 West Roosevelt Road, Hillside, IL 60162

Johnsburg
Tom Waits' love song

This village in McHenry County, north of Chicago, is where musician and artist Kathleen Brennan was born and grew up on a farm, a fact written into the lyrics of 'Johnsburg, Illinois'' a track on Tom Waits' 1983 album Swordfishtrombones. The track is a touching love song to Kathleen Brennan, who Waits married on August 10th 1980, after the couple met while both working on the Francis Ford Coppola movie One from the Heart earlier that year.

Location 262: Johnsburg is 60 miles north of Chicago, IL 60051

Rockford
On the Waterfront

More than 100 charitable groups generated millions of dollars for community advancement at Rockford's annual late-August/ early September On the Waterfront festival. One of Illinois' largest music festivals, it stretched over 80 blocks in the city center, showcasing 80 performers on five stages, and claim to be "the best street festival in the Midwest." In 2012 you could have seen bands as satisfyingly different as The Offspring and Leon Russell, but currently the possibility of future festivals looks uncertain.

Location 263: the city of Rockford is 90 miles northwest of Chicago, Rockford, IL 61101

Rock Island
From Lead Belly to Lonnie: the 'Rock Island Line'

'Rock Island Line' is a song first recorded in 1934 and later popularized by Lead Belly. When Scottish-born Lonnie Donegan recorded it in 1955 the song became the focus of the British skiffle movement which helped launch rock and roll in Britain. The lyrics to the song describe the railroad connecting Rock Island on the Mississippi with Chicago, built in the mid-1800s. The railroad connection was an important progression for industry, and in a similar way the song also connected country blues through to skiffle and ultimately created The Beatles.

Location 265: connecting the Mississippi and Illinois Rivers.

The cover artwork of this critically acclaimed album was featured on Rockford's vehicle registration stickers in 2007

Rockford
Birthplace of Cheap Trick

Rockford is the place where Cheap Trick incubated their distinctive power pop-rock sound and emerged, as some misguided observers called them, as "the American Beatles." Guitarist and songwriter Rick Nielsen formed the band in 1972 in Rockford with Tom Petersson. Both are natives of Rockford and few bands have stronger ties to the city than this Illinois outfit. The local authorities recognized the fact in 2007 when the band enjoyed the honor of having local vehicle registration stickers feature the cover artwork from their 2006 album Rockford. Rick Nielsen was the subject of a temporary exhibition in 2012/13 at Rockford's Burpee Museum of Natural History. The stylishly put-together, 5,900-square-foot exhibition featured his iconic guitars and a vast amount of memorabilia, all housed under the title 'Rick's Picks: Rick Nielsen's Lifelong Affair with Guitars & Music.'

Location 264: the city of Rockford is 90 miles northwest of Chicago. Rockford, IL 61101

Rock Island
The Blues Brothers statues

Life-size statues of Jake and Elwood Blues – The Blues Brothers – decorate a street corner in downtown Rock Island. The town is the fictional home of the characters played by Dan Aykroyd and John Belushi from the Blues Brothers' movies.

Location 266: Rock Island is 170 miles west of Chicago. The Blues Brothers statues are a block south of the Mississippi River on the sidewalk corner of 18th Street and 2nd Avenue, IL 61201

Indiana

Belmont
John Cougar Mellencamp country

The farming community around Belmont is John Cougar Mellencamp country. The Seymour, Indiana-born singer-songwriter had strong, passionate opinions when it came to supporting hard-hit Midwest farming families back in the 1980s. There's no better example of this passion than on his 'Rain on the Scarecrow' song from his 1985 Scarecrow album. The raw lyrics are matched by the song's depiction of the harsh circumstances endured by farming families, who appear in the video shot in and around the neighborhood where he lives and where Scarecrow was recorded at his rustic Belmont Mall studio in the woods. The 'Rain on the Scarecrow' video has Mellencamp in a variety of local locations, most notably the tiny Belmont Church of Christ. A hit single from the album, 'Lonely Ol' Night,' sees him captured on that video on

a nearby front porch playing guitar. His home is a few miles from both Belmont and Bloomington on the shores of Lake Monroe. The sense of place in Mellencamp's songs began as early as his debut album Chestnut Street Incident. There's two tracks name-checking the street which you can find in nearby Smithville.

Locations 267 and 268:
Belmont is a hamlet about 11 miles east of downtown Bloomington. The Belmont Church of Christ is at 1295 North Sewell Road, Belmont, IN 47408. Chestnut Street is in nearby Smithville, IN 47401

The Belmont church featured in John Cougar Mellencamp's 'Rain on the Scarecrow' video and the album which peaked at No. 2 on the Billboard 200 chart

Hammond
Roy Orbison's big songwriting break

Roy Orbison's big break as a songwriter came in 1958 when he made a support appearance with The Everly Brothers in Hammond. Although 'The Big O' had already seen some of his songs picked up and recorded it was a chance enquiry from Phil and Don Everly that proved to be a major turning point in his career. "As I was leaving the dressing room, they asked if I had any material. I sang them 'Claudette,' a song dedicated to my wife. They liked it, so I wrote it on the back of a cardboard box and later they recorded it in Nashville. It was a number one hit."

Location 269: Hammond is in Lake County, a few miles south of downtown Chicago, IN 46324

Indiana

Shane Warfel

Gary
The Jacksons' family home

There's no problem finding the former home to America's famous musical family: the streets are named after them. At one time all 11 members of the Jackson family lived in this tiny two-bedroom house in Gary, until Motown Records funded a new home for them in Los Angeles in 1969. The property has become even more of a shrine to the musical family since Michael Jackson passed away. After the 'King of Pop''s death, a marble memorial depicting the singer's signature Moonwalk pose was added to the garden out front where he played as a child. Just inside the front gate is a granite plaque embedded in the paved walkway that leads up to this beautifully preserved single-story home. This plaque, laid in

recognition of Michael Jackson's achievements by the Gary Mayor's office, is likely to be only the first of many personal tributes from the many hundreds of fans who now make the pilgrimage to this small town.

❝You could take five steps from the front door and you'd be out the back. It was really no bigger than a garage ❞

Michael Jackson describes his childhood home, where five brothers shared a triple-decker bunk bed

Location 270: Gary is 25 miles south of Chicago. The Jackson family home, from 1949 to 1969, is on the corner of Jackson Street and Jackson Family Boulevard at 2300 Jackson Street, Gary, IN 46407

The much-visited tiny Jackson family home on 2300 Jackson Street, Gary, Indiana

New Albany
The Darrell Sweet memorial plaque

Nazareth drummer Darrell Sweet has a plaque to remember him at New Albany's Riverfront Amphitheater. It was here on April 30th 1999 where the English-born rock star suffered a cardiac arrest before a Nazareth gig, dying shortly afterward at the city's Floyd Memorial Hospital. The plaque is positioned right next to

the Amphitheater's dressing room door.

Location 272: New Albany is a bridge ride or walk across the Ohio River from Louisville, Kentucky. The New Albany Riverfront Amphitheatre is at 201 East Water Street, New Albany, IN 47150

Indiana
R. Dean Taylor's song of murder and misery

'Indiana Wants Me' is the state's most famous namecheck in song and the biggest hit of R. Dean Taylor's career. The Canadian singer-songwriter wrote what turned out to be a Billboard Hot 100 No. 5 smash hit after watching the 1967 movie Bonnie and Clyde. The 1970 single's lyrics describe a man who committed a crime of passion on the run as a fugitive from the Indiana police. The original recording contained police siren sound effects that had to be removed due to some drivers hearing the song on radio and pulling over in the belief that the Indiana police wanted them!

Location 271: the whole state of Indiana!

Only make believe: R. Dean Taylor proves he wasn't a fugitive from the Indiana police after all

Noblesville
Depeche Mode's 'Debauchery' tour

In the mid-1990s, Depeche Mode were, famously, the band that took a psychiatrist on tour with them. Despite their huge popularity they were always an accident waiting to happen. That accident happened in Indiana in 1994, during what Q magazine dubbed "the most debauched tour ever." Depeche Mode played the Deer Creek Music Center with incredibly painful consequences for the band's singer Dave Gahan. Their tour-ending gig on July 8th had an element of danger early on when support band Primal Scream finished their set and let off steam by firing bottle rockets while Depeche Mode played. The Deer Creek security men were soon in action to avoid a major incident and returned to deal with more trouble as the show drew to an even more dramatic close. At the end of 'A Question of Time'

Gahan launched himself off the stage head-first into what he hoped would be his adoring public below. It meant a 12-foot jump across the barriers, but sadly Gahan was so drunk he ended up slamming shoulder-first into seats fixed to the concrete floor. Fortunately security managed to protect him from being mobbed by the excitable crowd and get him on to a stretcher for the journey to the local St. Vincent Hospital. Hemorrhaging from the inside with two broken ribs, his recovery was long and painful but at least he lived to tell the tale.

Location 273: Noblesville is 27 miles northwest of Indianapolis. The Deer Creek Music Center, now renamed the Klipsch Music Center, is six miles west of Noblesville at 12880 East 146th Street, Noblesville, IN 46060

They wanted me to stay in hospital a while. I said, "Look, I don't want to go into one of those places, I'd rather do this on my own." So I got a little cabin up in Lake Tahoe and just kind of disappeared. I was all strapped up for three weeks

Dave Gahan

Terre Haute
The KISS crazy town

This is the story of one of rock's most famous fanclubs. It all began when Terre Haute radio station WVTS were stubbornly resistant to the powers of glam rock titans KISS. In 1975 the band's local fanbase decided to act. Angry letters and phone calls bombarded the station, all demanding that their favorite band get some airtime. News of the thousands of calls blocking the WVTS switchboard made news across the States and the entire city (only previously musically famous due to its huge record plant being the first in the US to manufacture CDs) went KISS crazy. The band got to hear about the big fuss made by fans and urged on by local US Army personnel and the newly formed and fast-growing KISS Army they agreed

I walked out and [KISS] gave me this plaque with my name on it. Ace put his arm around me, Waring Abbot [photographer] shot a picture, and that was it. It was just one shock after another. At the end of the show, management gave me an address where the after-concert party was going to be held. Ten rooms on the 4th floor of the Sheraton had been reserved and I would get to see the band without their make-up. I'll never forget sitting at the back of this room when KISS made their appearance without their make-up on and it was somewhat of a bizarre disappointment

Bill Starkey, co-founder of the KISS ARMY, recalls the 1975 Terre Haute concert in a Deuce News interview

to play a gig in Terre Haute. The excitement was literally snowballing by this point and, braving the sub-zero November temperatures, a crowd of fans welcomed the band at the airport and 10,000 fans squeezed into the Hulman Center for an extraordinary concert. Exactly 35 years later, on November 21st 2010, the Mayor of Terre Haute declared the day "Kiss Army Day," and in celebration founding Army member Bill Starkey DJ'd an entire day of KISS tracks on Terre Haute radio station 105.5 The River.

Location 274: Terre Haute is north of Interstate 70, west of Indianapolis. The Hulman Center is at 200 North 8th Street, Terre Haute, IN 47809

Iowa

Arnolds Park
The Iowa Rock 'n' Roll Hall of Fame Museum

Open Tuesday through Saturday every week, the Iowa rock 'n' roll Music Association Museum gives visitors an in-depth look at Iowa's rock and roots through informative exhibits that contain band, musician, and radio personality memorabilia from around the state. Their annual Hall of Fame inductee lists include stars like The Everly Brothers and treasured historic locations such as Nob Hill Ballroom.

Location 275: Arnolds Park is 200 miles north of Des Moines. The museum is at 91 Lake Street, Arnolds Park, IA 51331

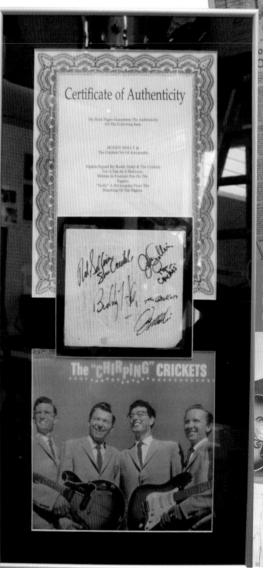

Treasures from the museum: the Slipknot drum kit from the Famous Drummers of Iowa exhibit and a Crickets signed napkin

'The Day the Music Died' and a signed photo of Buddy Holly tuning his guitar on the freezer at the Electric Park Ballroom in Waterloo

Des Moines
The 80/35 music festival

80/35 is a music festival that takes its name from interstate highways that converge in Des Moines. If you want a decent size festival attracting north of 30,000 fans that hosts well known bands but not something that overwhelms with the sheer weight of numbers, then this is for you. Featuring progressive, indie, and jam, it's run on a not-for-profit basis by the good people of the Greater Des Moines Music Coalition and takes place every July 4th weekend. The Flaming Lips, Ben Harper and Relentless7, Modest Mouse, and Death Cab for Cutie have all played here over the last decade.

Location 276: Des Moines is about 200 miles north of Kansas City and 200 miles south of Minneapolis. The 80/35 music festival is in downtown Des Moines at Western Gateway Park, Des Moines, IA 50309

Downtown Des Moines prepares to rock at the 80/35 music festival

Iowa

Clear Lake
'The Day the Music Died'

Clear Lake is a place name associated with one of the saddest events in popular music history. Referred to famously in Don McLean's 1972 epic song 'American Pie' the event is "The Day the Music Died" when after an All-Star Winter Dance Party at Clear Lake's Surf Ballroom, Buddy Holly, Ritchie Valens, "The Big Bopper," and 21-year-old aircraft pilot Roger Peterson were fatally injured in a plane crash. The four were headed through bad weather to reach the next leg of a difficult tour at Moorhead, Minnesota. The Winter Dance Party at the Surf Ballroom was part of a tour plagued by transportation difficulties, freezing temperatures, and illness. The flu which spread among the party of musicians was the least of Buddy Holly's drummer Carl Bunch's problems. Early in the tour he was hospitalized with frostbitten feet, when traveling in a tour bus whose

heater had broken down. The group of musicians struggled on through the tour in a replacement bus, but by the time the party reached Clear Lake on February 2nd 1959, Buddy Holly had had enough and decided to charter a plane out in the early hours of the following morning, accompanied by three of his fellow musicians. Within six miles of take-off, the plane crashed in farmland, a spot marked today by a monument to the rock and roll stars killed that wintry morning. Other reminders of the tragic event include a giant-size replica of Buddy Holly's trademark black-framed glasses as a symbolic sign post to the crash site memorial, a second memorial added to remember the pilot, and the naming of a road near the Surf Ballroom as "Buddy Holly Place". The Surf Ballroom is in a 1950s Rock and Roll time warp. The building, stage, and even the Winter Dance Party all still exist and a museum of memorabilia

has been added to the site to remember the bands ranging from Buddy Holly to The Doobie Brothers who have played the venue.

Locations 277, 278, 279 and 280: Clear Lake is 115 miles north of Des Moines. The Surf Ballroom and museum is at 460 North Shore Drive, Clear Lake, IA 50428. Buddy Holly Place is the road heading north from North Shore Drive near the ballroom, IA 50428. The Mason City Municipal Airport, from which the plane carrying Buddy Holly took off, is just a mile or two east of the Surf Ballroom in Clear Lake at 9184 265th Street, Clear Lake, IA 50428. The crash site memorial, featuring three metal disks and a metal guitar, is on farmland a few minutes' walk west of the intersection of 315th Street and Gull Avenue, five miles north of Clear Lake. It's signposted by the giant Buddy Holly glasses, Clear Lake, IA 50428

Five miles north of Clear Lake is the crash-site memorial to Buddy Holly, Ritchie Valens, and The Big Bopper

Clear Lake

DEL–FI
DONNA

Rodney White

Iowa

Shenandoah
Childhood home of The Everly Brothers

Although The Everly Brothers weren't actually born in Iowa (Don was born in Brownie, Kentucky, in 1937 and Phil in Chicago, Illinois, in 1939), their formative years were spent in the family home in Shenandoah. Their first real exposure to music certainly came here at a time when musician father Ike, mother Margaret, and the young Don and Phil sang on Shenandoah local radio station KMA in the 1940s. The Everly family lived in a tiny white house on Shenandoah's Sixth Avenue, but bizarrely the property has been lifted up and moved to a new, more accessible and prominent place outside Shenandoah's Historical Museum, which exhibits Everly Brothers-related items. Inside the house there are historic photos, a jukebox and an Everly's childhood bunk bed. There is also a guitar signed by the brothers when they reunited for a concert in Shenandoah in 1986. The house is opened for special events like Shenfest. This late-September event features a parade, live music concerts held in front of the house, and a 1950s and 60s automobile show on the adjacent street.

Location 281: Shenandoah is 66 miles southeast of Omaha, Nebraska, and 145 miles southwest of Des Moines. The Everly family home is outside the Shenandoah Historical Museum on the corner of Sheridan Avenue and Railroad Street, Shenandoah, IA 51601

The Everly family home now transported to this spot outside the city museum in Shenandoah

All that harmonizing Phil and Don Everly practiced with their parents in Shenandoah paid off when 'Bye Bye, Love' gave the brothers their chart debut in 1957

BYE BYE, LOVE

By FELICE BRYANT and BOUDLEAUX BRYANT

RECORDED BY THE EVERLY BROTHERS FOR CADENCE RECORDS

PUBLISHED BY
Acuff-Rose PUBLICATIONS

Kansas

Country fun at the Country Stampede, where Travis Tritt, Toby Keith, and Luke Bryan all strutted their stuff in 2012

Manhattan
The Country Stampede music festival

This late-June event is the largest annual music festival in Kansas, attracting mostly country but a good dose of rock too as Kansas (naturally), Lynyrd Skynyrd, Steve Miller, Styx, and ZZ Top have all performed here. Up to 50,000 fans a day attend four early summer days of music, food, and fun complete with a Swinging Saloon.

Location 282: about 120 miles west of Kansas City. Country Stampede is at Tuttle Creek Lake, seven miles north of Manhattan, River Pond Road, KS 66502

Topeka
The band named Kansas from Kansas

This garage band with British prog-rock beginnings were formed in Topeka. The town also supplied a fair proportion of the extensive road crew required to keep these classic rockers on tour in a career dating back to the early seventies. In 2011, former students of Topeka West High School, Phil Ehart, Dave Hope, Kerry Livgren, and Richard Williams, were inducted into the school's Hall of Fame in recognition of their global success as band members in Kansas. A section of the vast mural titled 'Tragic Prelude' in the Kansas Statehouse (aka the Kansas State Capitol) in Topeka was featured on the cover of the debut album by Kansas in 1974. It depicts the abolitionist and liberal John Brown in a work by local Kansas artist John Steuart Curry.

Locations 283 and 284: northeast in the state, Topeka is the capital city of Kansas. The school where it all started and where the band Kansas once played a school assembly is West High School, 2001 South West Fairlawn Road, KS 66604. The album cover mural can be found in the rotunda 2nd floor, east wing of the Kansas Statehouse, 300 South West 10th Avenue, Topeka, KS 66612

John Brown's body appears on the Kansas debut album cover

RockAtlasUSA

Kentucky

Butcher Hollow
Loretta Lynn's childhood home

Country singing star Loretta Lynn (real name Loretta Webb) was born and raised in the coal-mining community of Butcher Hollow, which accounts for the title and sentiments in the song most associated with her. 'Coal Miner's Daughter,' which she wrote and then recorded in 1969, namechecks "Butcher Holler" (as she calls it) and inspired the Academy Award-winning movie Coal Miner's Daughter (1980), which starred Sissy Spacek. The song also provided the title for Lynn's autobiography. Fans can still visit the cabin she grew up in along with younger sister and country singer Crystal Gayle. The Webb family still preserve the place and you can experience $5 guided tours by brother of Loretta and Crystal, Herman Webb, who runs the local store near Van Lear. The property is stuffed with memorabilia including Loretta's first guitar, which you'll find on her bed. Then there's the Loretta Lynn Coal Miner's Daughter Museum at her Tennessee ranch in Hurricane Mills, where you can visit a copy of her cabin at Butcher Hollow.

Locations 285 and 286: the far eastern side of Kentucky, Butcher Hollow is a tiny community close to the former coal-mining town of Van Lear. Loretta Lynn's cabin home is at Butcher Hollow, KY 41265. It's best to head for Webb's Grocery store (to get the guided tour) just off State Highway 302 at 1917 Millers Creek Road, near Van Lear, KY 41265. The Loretta Lynn Ranch (a day's drive and west of Nashville) is open to the public and is at 8000 Highway, 13 South, Hurricane Mills, Tennessee 37078

Louisville
Beatles on the river

The annual Beatles festival, Abbey Road on the River, began in Cleveland, Ohio, in 2002. What the organizers claim is the largest US Beatles festival now takes place in Louisville, attracting 30,000 fans and 60 tribute acts over five days in late May.

Location 287: Abbey Road on the River is held at Belvedere Festival Park, 485 West Main Street, Louisville, KT 40202

Perfect posing: one of the 60 tribute acts that entertain the Abbey Road on the River festival

Abbey Road, Louisville, Kentucky; Birdseye Photography

Kentucky

Louisville
Wilson Pickett's final resting place

Born in Prattville, Alabama, in 1941, died in Reston, Virginia, in 2006, soul singer Wilson Pickett is buried in a mausoleum here in Louisville, a city where he lived for a time with his once violent mother. Among those friends attending the funeral was Little Richard, who preached at the service.

Location 288: the Evergreen Cemetery is about five miles south of downtown Louisville at 4623 Preston Highway, Louisville, KY 40213

The hit-maker Wilson Pickett, responsible for classic soul cuts 'In the Midnight Hour' and 'Mustang Sally,' is buried in Louisville alongside this bronze likeness and a copy of The Lord's Prayer

Louisville
Music and ecology at the Forecastle Festival

Wilco at work at the Forecastle Festival, July 2012

2012 · Susan Keller, Forecastle Archival Team

The Forecastle Festival had modest beginnings in Louisville's Tyler Park back in 2002. More than a decade later the festival attracts fans and the biggest bands from across North America to Waterfront Park. The Black Crowes, The Black Keys, Smashing Pumpkins, Wilco, The Flaming Lips, and local Louisville band made good, My Morning Jacket, have all graced this July event. Aside from the music the festival has an eco-friendly conscience. Forecastle (now a registered trademark) has launched an international non-profit environmental foundation, "The Forecastle Foundation," set up to preserve the final remaining areas of extreme biodiversity that are among the most threatened on the planet. A grand festival with grand ideals.

Location 289: Waterfront Park is on the south bank of the Ohio River, River Road, Louisville, KY 40206

❝The Forecastle is a superstructure at the bow of a ship where the crew is housed. Hard at work in the unruly sea, it's a place workers gather to unwind after a hard day of labor. In other words, Forecastle is a place to come together with your friends and family to have one whale of a good time ❞

The Forecastle Festival describes itself

Renfro Valley
The Kentucky Music Hall of Fame and Museum

Unsurprisingly, great Kentucky musicians like Patty Loveless, Dwight Yoakam and Skeeter Davis are to the fore here at the Kentucky Music Hall of Fame and Museum, but all forms of music are honored and exhibited, not just country. You can touch, play, and record using the museum's instrument room and recording booth. All kinds of memorabilia are displayed, conveying just how varied and distinctive Kentucky music can be.

Location 290: Renfro Valley is 130 miles southeast of Louisville. The museum is at 2590 Richmond Street, Renfro Valley, KY 40473

Louisiana

Metairie
The final resting place of Gram Parsons

Gram Parsons was the subject of a horribly botched cremation at Joshua Tree, featured in the California chapter of Rock Atlas. A feature of his gravestone at his final resting place here in Metairie is the inscription from the lyrics of 'In My Hour of Darkness,' a track from his Grievous Angel album posthumously released in 1974. "Some say he was a star but he was just a country boy" reads a line, which somehow reverses the reality of his short life in which he formed The International Submarine Band, and The Flying Burrito Brothers, was a member of The Byrds, recorded solo, and set a path for all country-rock bands to follow. In death he's a star to countless members of the country-rock fraternity.

Location 291: Metairie is to the northwest of New Orleans and the Garden of Memories cemetery is eight miles from downtown New Orleans off Highway 61 at 4900 Airline Drive, Metairie, LA 70001

Lee Pullen

GRAM PARSONS
Nov. 7, 1946 - Sept. 19, 1973

Gram's gravestone carries this illustration of the man and the 'In My Hour of Darkness' lyrics are beneath it

The cover of Gram Parsons' posthumously-released Grievous Angel album

Mooringsport
Lead Belly's birth and burial place

Lead Belly (real name Huddie William Ledbetter) was born on the Jeter Plantation near Mooringsport in 1888 or 1889 and died in 1949, buried at Mooringsport's Shiloh Baptist Church cemetery. "A Louisiana legend" proclaims the simple, black and white gravestone. He was much more than that – a fact now appreciated by anyone who has ever picked up a guitar.

Location 292: The grave is behind the Shiloh Baptist Church, eight miles west of Blanchard and eight miles south of Mooringsport, at 10395 Blanchard-Latex Road, Mooringsport, LA 71060

Louisiana

New Orleans
Robbie Robertson's Storyville

The New Orleans district of Storyville gave its name to the second solo album by Bob Dylan cohort and member of The Band, Robbie Robertson. The Canadian's fascination for New Orleans dates back to his early teens when he played in Toronto band Little Caesar and The Consuls and was first introduced to the exotic jazz sound of New Orleans. The music and the city became a lifelong interest, influencing greatly his release of Storyville in 1991. The album cover photograph of Robertson was shot under the arches of The Cabildo, New Orleans' old colonial government building.

> 6I've always wanted to do an album that was just dripping with the spices of New Orleans 9

> *Robbie Robertson, interviewed by Bomb after the release of Storyville*

Location 293: The Cabildo is located on the northern edge of Jackson Square, 701 Chartres Street, New Orleans, LA 70130

Robbie Robertson at The Cabildo in New Orleans, a few blocks from the heart of the old Storyville district

New Orleans
'The House of the Rising Sun'

Some claim that the origins of the song 'The House of the Rising Sun' date back as far as the 16th century and might even have come originally from Great Britain. However, there's no doubting where the song was set in the versions covered most famously by Bob Dylan in 1962 and The Animals in 1964. "There is a house in New Orleans," the song begins, and most assume it's not a healthy place to visit, being a jailhouse, gambling den, brothel, or all three. But if you want to seek out the 'real' 'House of the Rising Sun' you'll need a weekend and the ability to do some detective work. Does it actually exist at all? Well, there have been enough establishments named as such according to New Orleans historical records. And there are countless theories. New York folk singer Dave Van Ronk, who introduced Bob Dylan to the song in the first place, had a notion that the old Orleans Parish women's Prison was the place, decorated as it was with a rising sun emblem at the entrance. Then there's the hotel burned to the ground in 1922 in the French Quarter on Conti Street (The Rising Sun Hotel), which by the name alone has a strong claim to be 'the house.' Personally this author's favorite (but not proven), suggestions are by people more closely associated with the story in recent times. In the 1980s Record Ron, owner of Record Ron's Good & Plenty Records store, was told without any shred of definite evidence that his business occupied the space on Decatur Street where 'the house' once stood. But the last word on 'the house' myth lies appropriately with

Animals vocalist Eric Burdon, who helped give the song its international fame. A former bordello run by Madam Marianne LeSoleil Levant on St. Louis Street now houses a respectable real estate company whose owners, through internal excavation, unearthed enough opulent decor and a large gold rising sun ceiling mural to stake a claim. Eric Burdon visited the owners and gave the property on St. Louis Street his seal of approval (without any proof) that this was 'The House of the Rising Sun.'

❝It was all I'd dreamt it would be, a palace in the New Orleans heat. It was a wondrous feeling learning that the place I'd fantasized about for thirty years wasn't some run-down shack but was in fact a place of beauty ❞

Eric Burdon writes in his autobiography, Don't Let Me Be Misunderstood

Locations 294, 295, 296, and 297: The Rising Sun Hotel was at 535 Conti Street, New Orleans, LA 70130. Record Ron's was at 1129 Decatur Street, New Orleans, LA 70116. 'The House of the Rising Sun' Eric Burdon refers to is 826-830 St. Louis Street, New Orleans, LA 70112. To search for these locations, and a few more in the local guidebooks, where better to stay than at the House of the Rising Sun bed and breakfast establishment in New Orleans? You'll find it just across the Mississippi River from the French Quarter on the free ferry at 335 Pelican Avenue, New Orleans, LA 70114. The owners have a wealth of knowledge on the subject but categorically deny that their handily placed accommodation is 'the House'!

"There is a house in New Orleans..." But is it this one? Eric Burdon likes to think so. The St. Louis Street 'House of the Rising Sun'

Louisiana

New Orleans
Louis Armstrong Park

Legendary jazz musician, trumpeter, and singer Louis Armstrong was born in New Orleans on August 4th 1901. The park named for him after his death in New York in 1971 has a statue of the popular musician and scat singer, and in the 32-acre park's southwest corner lies Congo Square, a spiritual gathering place for all musicians who sense its cultural history. This is the fabled area where African slaves once gathered on a Sunday to socialize, sell crops, dance, and perform - the only place they were permitted to do so openly in the urban South.

Location 298: Louis Armstrong Park, close to downtown New Orleans is bordered on its south side by North Rampart Street. The statue of Armstrong and a bust of another jazz great, Sidney Bechet, are located in the park, New Orleans, LA 70116

New Orleans
The pink and "cosy" Euclid Records

The vinyl-hunting visitor to New Orleans has plenty of stores to choose from – head for Jim Russell's Records (1837 Magazine Street) or Domino Sound Record Shack (2557 Bayou Road) and you are unlikely to be disappointed – but Euclid Records gets a special mention here because it's new... and pink! Okay, the color of the outside of this establishment which opened in 2010 doesn't guarantee a perfect browsing experience inside but it does look great. The Bywater neighborhood this distinctive store operates in is said to be "happenin'" and "cosy" according to the owners, whose St. Louis store has been trading since 1981.

Location 302: in the Bywater district, a couple of miles east of downtown New Orleans on the corner of Chartres Street and Desire Street, at 3401 Chartres Street, New Orleans, LA 70117

New Orleans
Little Richard's 'Tutti Frutti' at J&M Studios

A defining moment in rock and roll's timeline occurred on September 14th 1955, at J&M Recording Studio, when Little Richard created one of popular music's most influential songs, 'Tutti Frutti.' Filling in time at the end of a session, he let rip on the studio piano with his own fiery composition and producer Robert 'Bumps' Blackwell was so impressed by the tune's exciting potential he enlisted the help of songwriter Dorothy LaBostrie to work on the song and come up with some rather less risqué lyrics. As a measure of the volatility of the song, when Richard was prompted to repeat his wild performance in front of LaBostrie, he turned away and played it to her while facing the studio wall. At this time, J&M Recording Studio had already been in business for a decade, launched by 18-year-old Cosimo Matassa in the back of his family's grocery store in Rampart Street. In 1955, the young owner, producer, and sound engineer moved his set-up to larger premises under the name Cosimo Recording Studio and created what many

regard as a "New Orleans" rock and pop sound. Matassa's final working studio was Jazz City, which saw the end of his career in the mid-sixties, still producing hits including Lee Dorsey's 'Working in a Coal Mine.' But the old Rampart Street J&M studio retains its iconic status to this day. The building has been recognized as an historic landmark by the Rock and Roll Hall of Fame Museum and carries a plaque as a reminder that 'Tutti Frutti,' 'Honey Hush' by Big Joe Turner, 'I Hear You Knocking' by Smiley Lewis, and 'My Blue Heaven' by Fats Domino were all recorded here.

Locations 299, 300, and 301: still standing with a plaque outside, the old J&M Recording Studio building is on the corner of North Rampart and Dumaine Streets at 838-840 North Rampart Street, New Orleans, LA 70116. The Cosimo Recording Studio once did business at 525 Governor Nicholls Street, New Orleans, LA 70116. Jazz City operated out of 748 Camp Street, New Orleans, LA 70130

Shreveport
The Elvis Presley and James Burton statues

In 2004, to mark the 50th anniversary of Elvis' Presley's first broadcast on the Louisiana Hayride radio and TV shows in Shreveport, a statue of 'The King' was placed at the foot of the steps of the city's Municipal Auditorium. On Elvis' left is a statue added a year later of guitarist and Shreveport native James Burton, who played in Elvis's bands. The impressive art deco-designed venue has a Stage of Stars & Legends Museum where you can learn more about the history of the Louisiana Hayride broadcasts – a show on which Elvis made his first of 50 appearances, on October 16th 1954.

Elvis has left the building

Louisiana Hayride producer Horace Logan was the man who invented the phrase first used in an attempt to calm hysterical fans after a concert at Shreveport's Hirsch Memorial Coliseum

Wes Aldridge

Paul Ridenour

Locations 304 and 305: Shreveport is in the northeast corner of Louisiana. The statues are at the Municipal Auditorium in downtown Shreveport, 705 Elvis Presley Avenue, Shreveport, LA 71101. The Hirsch Memorial Coliseum Stadium is a few miles west of the center of Shreveport, LA 71109

The Elvis and James Burton statues stand side by side on Elvis Presley Avenue

New Orleans
The Voodoo Experience

The Voodoo Music + Arts Experience is an early November annual festival staged to coincide with Halloween. In its short life since 1999, this festival has survived Hurricane Katrina and operated with free tickets for those affected by the area's resulting devastation, relocated to Memphis, and now found a home for an audience of around 100,000 at New Orleans' City Park. Top hip-hop and rock acts are mingled on bills that have included Metallica, Eminem, Blink-182, Snoop Dogg, Muse, and Drake.

Location 303: north of downtown, City Park, 1 Palm Drive, New Orleans, LA 70124

Shreveport
The Lead Belly statue

Born and buried near Mooringsport, Louisiana, the inspirational and innovative country-blues musician Lead Belly has a statue a few miles away in Shreveport.

Location 306: Lead Belly's statue is on the sidewalk out front of the Shreve Memorial Library, 424 Texas Street, Shreveport, LA 71101

Ville Platte
The 'swamp pop capital of the world'

Ville Platte is the "swamp pop capital of the world," claims the Louisiana Swamp Pop Museum & Ville Platte City Museum. This little-known genre had its heyday around the late fifties and early sixties and created minor stars but local legends out of Louisiana talent such as Joe Barry, The Boogie Kings, and Tommy McLain. The museum has all the history and memorabilia on a subject that may be obscure to most but fascinating to locals and a surprisingly large number of fans from outside the USA. Ville Platte also claims to be the "smoked meat capital of the world"!

Location 307: Ville Platte is 80 miles west of Baton Rouge. The museum is north of Main Street at 205 North West Railroad Avenue, Ville Platte, LA 70586

Maine

Lewiston
Jimi Hendrix turns up the volume at the Armory

Lewiston Armory might seem like an unlikely venue for rock music but its sheer size and capacity meant that it was able to attract some top bands to Maine in the 1960s and 1970s. One of the biggest, if not the biggest gig at the 1920s-building constructed as a National Guard battalion HQ and fallout shelter, occurred when The Jimi Hendrix Experience came to play. Supported by Soft Machine, the trio, organizers had imagined, would attract a capacity crowd of 4,000 fans. As it turned out, nearer to 7,000 turned up and although there were no reports of anyone being crushed, all those attending were tightly packed in and forced

to stand. The gig on March 16th 1968 was around the time that more and more amplifiers were being stacked up with volume levels reaching extraordinarily high levels. One eyewitness (or perhaps that should be 'earwitness') heading for the gig in his car to pick up his teenage daughter claimed he could hear Jimi Hendrix half a mile from the Armory. Excitement, and no doubt volume levels, were turned up to 11 again in 1975 when Queen and their Sheer Heart Attack Tour rolled into Lewiston on February 19th for an appearance at the Armory, which historically coincided with their Billboard Hot 100 chart debut when the band's

View of the Armory, Lewiston, Maine — D-6

The Jimi Hendrix single that made its Billboard chart debut on the day of his gig at Lewiston Armory

single 'Killer Queen' was released.

Location 308: Lewiston is about 30 miles north of Portland. Lewiston Armory is a short distance east of downtown Lewiston at 65 Central Avenue, Lewiston, ME 04240

Rockland
The North Atlantic Blues Festival

Bluegrass, folk, and jazz maybe Maine's most popular music genres – and there's some fine festivals associated with all three to be had – but that doesn't mean you can't get a dose of the blues this far northeast. Rockland's annual North Atlantic Blues Festival stages performances by big-name internationally known blues musicians and the festival spills out onto Main Street on Saturday night, where your festival wristband can admit you to the bars and restaurants featuring some fine regional

blues performers. Paul Benjamin and Jamie Isaacson are the men behind bringing the blues 1,500 miles north east from Mississippi. Aside from their festival initiatives, the duo were also behind the extraordinary honor accorded Rockland, which can now boast the USA's most northerly-positioned Blues Trail marker.

Locations 309 and 310: Rockland is 185 miles north of Boston, MA. The North Atlantic Blues Festival site overlooks the harbor at Public Landing,

275 Main Street, Rockland, Maine, ME 04841. The Blues Trail marker is close by the festival site on the edge of Harbor Park, ME 04841

Rockland got a Blues Trail marker in 2010, acknowledging the history of visiting Mississippi blues musicians to this northern extremity

THE BLUES TRAIL:
MISSISSIPPI TO MAINE

As blues has spread from Mississippi to the far corners of the country and the world, the state of Maine has assumed an active role in the presentation and promotion of the music to appreciative local audiences ever since Mississippi-born blues giants Muddy Waters and B.B. King began coming here in the 1970s. The presence of the blues in Maine was solidified in 1994 with the formation of the North Atlantic Blues Festival, a premier annual event that has featured many Mississippi artists.

Maryland

Baltimore
Frank Zappa's hometown bust

In keeping with a brilliantly eccentric career, Frank Zappa is honored by a bust likeness in Vilnius, Lithuania. The devotion of his fans in the European country's capital city stemmed from their interpretation of Zappa as a symbol of freedom during Soviet occupation, back in the musician's heyday. Despite the fact that Zappa never actually visited Lithuania, these avant garde fans' enthusiasm didn't end there. In 2010 they funded a replica bust to be erected in his home city of Baltimore, close to the 4500 block of Park Heights Avenue where he once lived. The bust is the work of sculptor Konstantinas Bogdanas and was approved by the Baltimore Public Art Commission and sanctioned by Zappa's family.

Location 311: the bust is 12 feet above the street in the Highlandtown district of the city, outside the front entrance of the Southeast Anchor Branch of the Enoch Pratt Free Library, 3601 Eastern Avenue, (at the junction with South Conkling Street), MD 21224

Unveiling Frank Zappa's bust in Baltimore: Zappa's widow Gail and three of his children pose for a family picture outside the Enoch Pratt Free Library on September 19th 2010

Baltimore
The Sound Garden record store

There are two equally good Sound Garden record stores. There's the Syracuse, New York, branch and this one on Thames Street in Baltimore. The store was opened by Bryan Burkett in 1994 and has excellent ties to the Baltimore and wider music community. The store encourages a large amount of in-store gigs – quite a few by high-profile bands. A good place to hang out and browse 10,000 square feet of titles, Sound Garden is helped by its near waterfront location, which draws tourists to the many pubs, clubs, and the restaurants in the area known as Fell's Point.

Location 312: close to the waterfront, east of downtown Baltimore, 1616 Thames Street, Baltimore, MD 21231

Maryland

Baltimore's bronze statue honoring Billie Holiday was created by sculptor James Earl Reid

Baltimore
Billie Holiday's statue

Although born in Philadelphia, singer Billie Holiday grew up in Baltimore. The location of the statue on Pennsylvania Avenue matches the spot nearby where the Royal theater once stood, and where Holiday and many other jazz greats performed almost a century ago.

Locations 313 and 314:
The statue is at the junction of Pennsylvania Avenue and Lafayette Avenue, Baltimore, MD 21217. There's a monument to the Royal theater across the street at 1300 Pennsylvania Avenue. Both are located a couple of miles northeast of downtown Baltimore

Baltimore
The Beatles come to Baltimore

Sunday September 13th 1964 was the day The Beatles played Baltimore. They performed two sold-out shows attracting 14,000 screaming fans to each (4pm and 8.30pm) before leaving the Civic Center and staying overnight at the Holiday Inn across the street. Outside mounted police were required to halt fans intent on storming their hotel, where they ate dinner in the revolving restaurant on the top floor. Almost every rock legend, including The Rolling Stones, Bob Dylan, U2, and Bruce Springsteen, have played Baltimore's largest indoor entertainment venue since the 'Fab Four''s visit.

Locations 315 and 316: in downtown Baltimore, the Civic Center is now the 1st Mariner Arena at 201 West Baltimore Street, Baltimore, MD 21201. The Holiday Inn where The Beatles stayed is a short walk from the venue they played, at 301 West Lombard Street, Baltimore, MD 21201

Baltimore
Maryland Deathfest

Death metal, grindcore, doom, thrash, hardcore, black metal, and experimental metal that hasn't even been properly categorized yet are the bedrock of what makes Maryland Deathfest the premier metal festival in the U.S. It takes place every May and in 2013 the organizers announced plans to use two venues in the same area of the city.

Locations 317 and 318: downtown Baltimore, at the former Sonar compound, 407 East Saratoga Street, Baltimore, MD 21202. A second venue for 2013 was added at Baltimore Soundstage. It is a separate venue located half a mile south of the former Sonar compound at 124 Market Place, Baltimore, MD 21202

Jo Bench of UK quintet Bolt Thrower wows the fans down at Baltimore's Maryland Deathfest

returntothepit.com

Massachusetts

Boston
Aerosmith HQ

Commonwealth Avenue, in the Boston neighborhood of Allston, was where Aerosmith made their 1970s headquarters – a crash pad and rehearsal basement where they wrote a number of their earliest songs. On November 5th 2012 the band returned to the important roots of their success to play a promotional gig for their forthcoming album, Music from Another Dimension! On a flatbed truck outside their former home base the live gig drew thousands of fans across the railroad tracks to the spot where a commemorative plaque was also unveiled at the apartment where the band once lived. Before departing the scene of so much band history, vocalist Steven Tyler, guitarist Joe Perry, guitarist Brad Whitford, bass guitarist Tom Hamilton, and drummer Joey Kramer immersed their hands in cement, to make permanent prints to be laid in the Commonwealth Avenue sidewalk.

Location 319: Allston is four miles west of downtown Boston. The former Aerosmith home, plaque, and band members hand prints are at 1325 Commonwealth Avenue, Allston, MA 02134

Aerosmith return to their former Boston HQ at 1325 Commonwealth Avenue for a free outdoor gig attracting thousands in 2012

Jamie Hull / jamiehull.com

Massachusetts

Boston
The Beatles at Suffolk Downs

The Boston Garden at North Station on Causeway Street was the setting for The Beatles' first visit to Boston on September 12th 1964. Sadly that venue, where 13,909 fans greeted the 'Fab Four,' is no more but the Suffolk Downs race track where they returned to perform two years later on August 18th 1966 still thrives. This second and final gig attracted a 25,000 crowd in the stands across from the actual horse racing track where the stage had been erected. Each Beatle arrived at the stage in his own limo driven up the track, an area patrolled by mounted police, who intercepted those fans determined to try and make a dash for their idols on stage.

Location 320: Suffolk Downs race track is about 5 miles northeast of downtown Boston at 525 McClellan Highway, East Boston, MA 02128

Great Barrington
The real 'Alice's Restaurant'

The real-life restaurant in Arlo Guthrie's famous Vietnam draft protest song 'Alice's Restaurant' is actually two different places owned by Alice Brock, a friend of Guthrie. The 18-minute and 34-second-long track first appeared as side one of Guthrie's 1967 debut album, also titled 'Alice's Restaurant.' The first of Alice's two 'restaurants' mentioned in the lyrics wasn't a restaurant at all. When Guthrie refers to the song's Thanksgiving Day dinner incident, these dinners were held in Alice and husband Ray's home, a deconsecrated church in the small ski resort vacation town of Great Barrington. Alice did go on to set up a restaurant in Stockbridge nearby and author Alice's Restaurant Cookbook, published in 1969. What made 'Alice's Restaurant' even more internationally famous was the movie of that same name, also released in 1969, which starred Guthrie as himself with Pat Quinn playing Alice Brock and James Broderick taking the role of husband Ray. Alice also makes at least three cameo appearances in the movie as an extra.

Locations 321 and 322: Great Barrington is in the far west side of Massachusetts. The former church (purchased by Arlo Guthrie in 1991 and now the Guthrie Center) is at 4 Van Deusenville Road, Great Barrington, MA 01230. The Stockbridge Alice's Restaurant (now Theresa's Stockbridge Café but still decorated with Arlo Guthrie album covers and photos of Arlo and Alice) is six miles north of Great Barrington at 40 Main Street, by the General Store, Stockbridge, MA 01262

North Brookfield
The Stones down on the farm

Long View Farm Studios were founded by Clark University professor Gil Markle on his property north of North Brookfield. Over the years this bucolic spot has played host to Aerosmith, Cat Stevens, the J. Geils Band, and Stevie Wonder. But it was the arrival of The Rolling Stones that really put this rural Massachusetts farm on the rock and roll map. In 1981, following a scouting mission by so-called "Sixth Stone" Ian Stewart, accompanied by the band's administration man Alan Dunn, Long View Farm Studios were selected as the perfect spot for the Stones to prepare for their upcoming Tattoo You Tour of the U.S. The suitability of the place was further tested by Keith Richards soon after Stewart and Dunn had visited. Keith even laid down a few tracks to test the acoustics. The converted farm buildings got the Stones' seal of approval, but before the band arrived to rehearse and record a stage was hurriedly constructed as the final requirement before their stay became reality. When they arrived, these world-famous rock stars became local curiosities – Mick Jagger and Keith Richards were even spotted playing tennis at North Brookfield High School. Back at rehearsals, the security was tight but that didn't prevent hundreds of local kids from hearing and occasionally seeing the Stones for free as they watched from a hillside overlooking the farm. Although the farm was the perfect rehearsal

Left: 'Ticket to Ride' for the Boston Beatles
Right: Arlo Guthrie in a scene from the movie at Alice's

hideaway the Stones needed a proper concert to get their act together before the Tattoo You show opener in front of 90,000 at Philadelphia's JFK Stadium. See the Rock Atlas entry for Worcester where they played a memorable warm-up gig for a fortunate 350 locals.

Once they (The Rolling Stones) had left the farm, I had people stopping me on the street and countless newspaper reporters calling me on the phone, asking if I thought that The Rolling Stones were living gods.
"Did they even use the toilets?" I would hear from several of these people.
"Yes, they used the toilets," I remember myself saying. "They were nice guys, a lot of fun, and very talented, but they did use the toilets."
"Oh," they would say, disappointment writ large across their faces, or their voices in a lower register on the telephone

Gil Markle (owner and founder of Long View Farm Studios)

Location 323: North Brookfield is in central Massachusetts, 70 miles west of Boston. The private Long View Farm Studios are on Stoddard Road in North Brookfield, MA 01535

The Stones in North Brookfield: Ronnie Wood breathes in that country air and Mick Jagger takes to the saddle at Long View Farm

Brian Aris

Brian Aris

Massachusetts

Plymouth

Bob Dylan's Rolling Thunder Revue debut

Under the title "Rolling Thunder Revue," Bob Dylan's traveling show, with an assortment of rock and folk legends, made its first appearance at the War Memorial Auditorium, Plymouth, on October 30th 1975. The posters and make-up – at times Dylan wore white face powder and sometimes a mask – created an authentic, old-style traveling variety show vibe with advertized guest stars that included Joan Baez, Ramblin' Jack Elliott, and Bob Neuwirth. Unadvertized guests at the two consecutive night concerts in Plymouth included Mick Ronson and T-Bone Burnett. Dylan was also

accompanied on the tour by his pet beagle as the extensive entourage traveled from city to city in a bus Dylan rented from Frank Zappa. Promoting the opening two dates in Plymouth was a low-key affair. One local fan even remembers only learning about the concert when chancing upon an 8x10 index card advert taped to the door of a local eatery a few days before. The significance of Plymouth as the tour's debut was not lost on Dylan. The historic spot where the Pilgrim Fathers made landfall in America was the subject of a bizarre re-enactment by Dylan and his entourage when they came ashore in a wooden dinghy

(representing the Mayflower) to visit the Plymouth Rock landmark. Other sightseeing trips included a visit to the replica 1920-style Pilgrim Village for a Halloween party and some time spent aboard the replica Mayflower sailing ship. The party's hotel for these early dates of the tour was Falmouth's Sea Crest Beach Hotel.

Locations 324, 325, 326, and 327: Plymouth is 40 miles south of Boston. The War Memorial Auditorium (now named the Plymouth Memorial Hall), is at 83 Court Street, Plymouth, MA 02360. The Mayflower II (the replica ship built in Devon, England and sailed

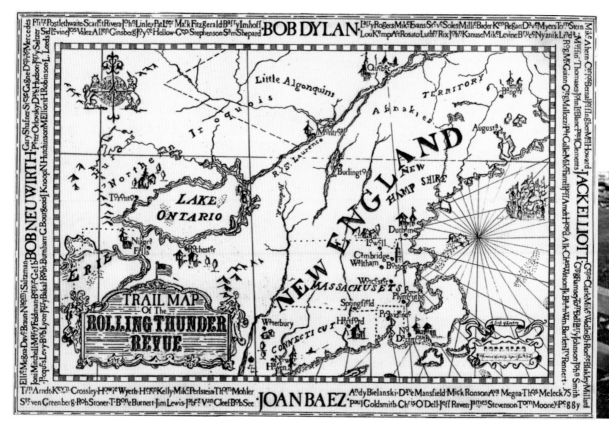

to Plymouth in 1957) is in Plymouth Harbor at State Pier, MA 02361. The Plymouth Rock landmark is on the beach off Water Street, Plymouth, MA 02360. The Sea Crest Beach Hotel is 30 miles south of Plymouth at 350 Quaker Road, Old Silver Beach, Cape Cod, Falmouth, MA 02556

Below: Bob Dylan at Pilgrim Memorial State Park visiting the Mayflower II in October 1975

Left: The tour 'trail map' that details all the places and people involved in the Rolling Thunder Revue

Sandwich
Elvis Presley's gospel album cover

The cover of Elvis Presley's How Great Thou Art gospel album features a portrait of Elvis and a photo of the First Church of Christ, in Sandwich. Judging by his portrait on the 1967 LP he probably never visited the place.

Location 328: Sandwich is 60 miles south of Boston. The church is at 136 Main Street, near the junction with Water Street, Sandwich, MA 02563

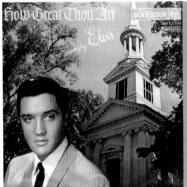

The First Church of Christ on the cover of Elvis's second full album of sacred songs

Watertown
Boston by Boston

When a Boston band were about to unleash what would turn out to be the biggest-selling debut album up to the end of the 20th century, they didn't have a name. Formerly Mother's Milk, Boston by Boston was how the band and its first release ended up being called, a suggestion from the album's producer John Boylan. However, the key figure in the writing and recording of the 1976 album, now nudging sales of 28 million worldwide, was the band's founder Tom Scholz. Despite Epic Records' insistence that he should not helm the project, as he wished to himself, Scholz, and Epic's hired producer Boylan, concocted a plan whereby Scholz got his way without the record company knowing too much about it. The album was mostly recorded in the basement at the then unknown Scholz's home. Foxglove Studios, Watertown, School Street, was where it all began for Boston.

Location 329: Watertown is seven miles west of Boston. Tom Scholz's home basement studio was on School Street, Watertown, MA 02472

Massachusetts

Worcester The Stones are 'The Cockroaches' at Sir Morgan's Cove

For the Tattoo You Tour in 1981 The Rolling Stones rehearsed at Long View Farm, North Brookfield, Massachusetts – see earlier Rock Atlas entry. The band's three-year absence from live performances meant a lengthy stay down on the farm to bond and mesh musically before they could confidently take to the stage once more. Their warm-up gig, 20 miles east of the farm at a club

in Worcester called Sir Morgan's Cove, was their way of thanking the locals for their hospitality. The cramped surroundings gave rock photographer Ron Pownall the opportunity to shoot the perfect picture of Mick, Keith, Ronnie, Bill and Charlie all pulling together as arguably the world's greatest live rock and roll band.

"I spent the afternoon of September 14th 1981 in a convertible, driving

around Worcester with Ian Stewart (the sixth Stone), taking photos of Stones fans. WAAF radio station urged their listeners to "show their love" and possibly win tickets to a special surprise concert by 'The Cockroaches' at Sir Morgan's Cove [now named The Lucky Dog Music Hall]. Fans plastered themselves with bumper stickers, posters, LPs, big lips, all in an effort to be selected by Ian and score free tickets. The

Ron Pownall captures the perfect Rolling Stones band picture: Ian Stewart, Ian McLagan, Ronnie Wood, Mick Jagger, Keith Richards, Bill Wyman, and an out-of-shot Charlie Watts rock Worcester

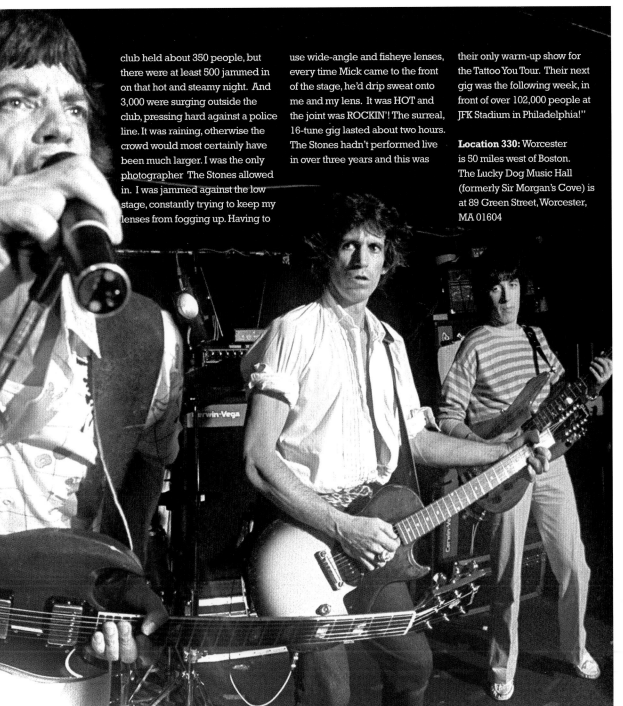

club held about 350 people, but there were at least 500 jammed in on that hot and steamy night. And 3,000 were surging outside the club, pressing hard against a police line. It was raining, otherwise the crowd would most certainly have been much larger. I was the only photographer The Stones allowed in. I was jammed against the low stage, constantly trying to keep my lenses from fogging up. Having to

use wide-angle and fisheye lenses, every time Mick came to the front of the stage, he'd drip sweat onto me and my lens. It was HOT and the joint was ROCKIN'! The surreal, 16-tune gig lasted about two hours. The Stones hadn't performed live in over three years and this was

their only warm-up show for the Tattoo You Tour. Their next gig was the following week, in front of over 102,000 people at JFK Stadium in Philadelphia!"

Location 330: Worcester is 50 miles west of Boston. The Lucky Dog Music Hall (formerly Sir Morgan's Cove) is at 89 Green Street, Worcester, MA 01604

Michigan

Ann Arbor
The MC5 'Kick out the Jams' on Hill Street

These days hailed as purveyors of punk's prototype, MC5 lived here on Hill Street in a counter culture commune in 1968 and 1969. Elektra Records scout Danny Fields was so impressed by what he saw of MC5 and their highly recommended "little brother band" The Stooges that he visited the Hill Street MC5 HQ to sign-up both bands in the mansion's kitchen in October 1968. Elektra then released the MC5's highly-rated debut album and locally-recorded live Kick out the Jams. The rented house MC5 occupied had once been owned by a former Ann Arbor mayor in the early 1900s. The band sound-proofed the garage and practiced endlessly while, upstairs, other members of the hippie commune designed the band's posters and flyers and created and mended their stage clothes, which included shirts made from Stars and Stripes flags. When the band decided to cut their ties with manager John Sinclair and his White Panther members, they used the windfall of an Atlantic Records advance to move out, 15 miles north to nearby Hamburg.

Location 331: about 40 miles west of Detroit, 1510 Hill Street, Ann Arbor, MI 48104

Photo by Leni Sinclair

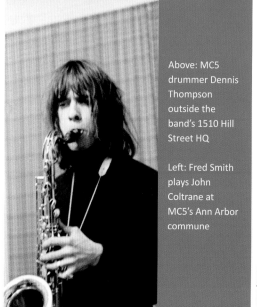

Photo by Leni Sinclair

❛We (that is me, my husband John Sinclair, and our baby daughter Sunny) had the room in the house right next to Fred Smith and his wife Sigrid Dobat. I fondly recall lying on my bed (which was a mattress on the floor, like everybody else's back then) and listening to Fred in the next room playing his tenor saxophone. He loved John Coltrane and would play John Coltrane solos almost note for note. No wonder he named his first band after the MC5 breakup Ascension, after one of John Coltrane's records ❜

Leni Sinclair, co-author of Detroit Rocks! A Pictorial History of Motor City Rock and Roll 1965-1975, by Gary Grimshaw and Leni Sinclair

Above: MC5 drummer Dennis Thompson outside the band's 1510 Hill Street HQ

Left: Fred Smith plays John Coltrane at MC5's Ann Arbor commune

Ann Arbor
The enduring Encore Records

Once the excellent Encore Recordings owned and run by Peter Dale, who first worked there in 1966, now slightly renamed as Encore Records and only slightly changed, this is THE place to buy or sell records in Ann Arbor. Part of the success appears to be the continuity of management from within the store. When owners or managers of this place retire, the staff step up to the plate and own it, as happened again recently. While going out of their way to help promote recordings by local bands (and hosting in-store performances by some), Encore's inventory is as expansive and international as any record store. This enduring little Ann Arbor institution, in various shapes and forms, has been a fixture on the local scene since 1939.

Location 332: Encore Records is in downtown Ann Arbor, 417 East Liberty Street, Ann Arbor, MI 48104

Photographer Joni Mitchell's feet, included in her artwork for the back cover of Miles of Aisles

Clarkston
Joni Mitchell's Miles of Aisles cover

The cover of Joni Mitchell's 1974 live album Miles of Aisles shows the empty concert venue seats and aisles at the Pine Knob Music Theatre ,where she performed on August 9th 1974 and announced from the stage that President Richard Nixon had just resigned. Earlier that day she had wandered the seating areas during a soundcheck for Tom Scott and The L.A. Express, taking photos of the venue. One of her pictures eventually surfaced on the front cover of Miles of Aisles and a second, including a shot of her feet, appears on the back.

Location 334: on the Detroit outskirts, the now renamed DTE Energy Music Theatre is at 7774 Sashabaw Road, MI 48348

Battle Creek
America's first rock star marker

Charles Weedon Westover (1934–1990) was born in Grand Rapids, grew up in Coopersville, and found fame when he changed his name to Del Shannon. Battle Creek, the town where he first used that name, lived, and first sang his six-million-selling 'Runaway,' has a waymark honouring the fact. The marker, on the site of the old LaSalle Hotel's groundfloor Hi-Lo Club, was America's first to a rock star. The base of the sign is formed by a reproduction 'Runaway' sculptured disc.

Location 333: Battle Creek is 120 miles west of Detroit. The historical marker and sculptured disc is on the east corner of Hamblin and Capital Avenues, Battle Creek, MI 49017

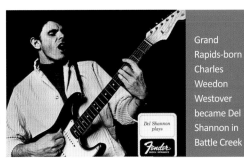

Grand Rapids-born Charles Weedon Westover became Del Shannon in Battle Creek

Michigan

Detroit
Hitsville U.S.A.

The blue and white house at 2648 West Grand Boulevard is world famous as the original home of Motown Records. Named Hitsville U.S.A. for good reason, this address is where Motown founder Berry Gordy bought the property in 1959 before setting up in business and kitting out a recording studio that would create Tamla Records and Motown Records, two labels that would dominate the U.S. and international music scene for decades to come. His $800 investment was inspired and astonishingly created not only a successful music business but one that also gave birth to a fantastic new music genre. In the early days Gordy both worked and lived (upstairs) at the house and the success of his enterprise necessitated the purchase of at least six more properties in the neighborhood to take care of all the business generated by his serial hit-making. By 1967 Gordy had accumulated enough wealth to move out and buy a large house in Detroit's Boston-Edison Historic District, a place dubbed Motown Mansion. Around the same time, the business moved to the Donovan building at 2457 Woodward Avenue (now demolished) before relocating out of Detroit almost completely to Hollywood in 1972. Today the historic Hitsville site has been brilliantly converted to serve as the Motown Museum. The organization that runs the place has preserved Berry Gordy's upstairs living quarters and the famous recording facility, Studio A, in a 1960s time warp. Add to that the memorabilia donated by the musicians who

Left: Smokey Robinson arrives for work at Hitsville

Centre: Marvin Gaye, The Supremes, Smokey Robinson, The Temptations and Stevie Wonder all worked here. Now the place is a visitor attraction complete with museum

Below: The Supremes and The Miracles at Detroit's music factory

Courtesy of Motown/Hitsville

were regular visitors to this creative hub and you have one of popular music's most remarkable tourist attractions.

Locations 335 and 336: the Hitsville U.S.A. building and Motown Museum is a mile or so north of downtown Detroit at 2648 West Grand Boulevard, Detroit, MI 48208. Motown Mansion, Berry Gordy's former home, is a mile north of Hitsville U.S.A. at 918 West Boston Boulevard, Detroit, MI 48202

Detroit
Eminem's house

Marshall Bruce Mathers III was born in St. Joseph, Missouri, in 1972 but grew up in Detroit, Michigan, where he transformed into Eminem. One of the most successful hip-hop albums of all-time, the autobiographical The Marshall Mathers LP features a picture of Eminem on a return visit to his childhood home in Detroit on the cover. The property is just south of the 8 Mile Road that gave the title to his 2002 movie 8 Mile – a symbolic dividing line between the neighborhoods of his eventful and difficult upbringing.

❝The guy who lives there now let me in and let me see the house. I had mixed feelings because I had a lot of good and bad memories in that house. But to go back to where I grew up and finally say "I've made it" is the greatest feeling in the world to me ❞

Eminem recalls an emotional return to his childhood home

Location 337: eight miles north of downtown Detroit at 19946 Dresden Street, Detroit, MI 48205

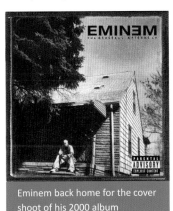

Eminem back home for the cover shoot of his 2000 album

Detroit
Jack White's Mexicantown and Indian Village homes

As the youngest in a family of ten children, Jack White grew up in the Mexicantown district of southwest Detroit in a neat white weather-boarded, detached house on Ferdinand Street. Ignoring the contemporary local cultures of hip hop and house, he gravitated from his early obsession, drums, to guitar, a less than cool instrument in 1980s Detroit. His chief influences came mostly from the unearthly blues music he came across on vinyl records, specifically Sun House. After forming The White Stripes in 1997 with wife Meg White, the duo's success with albums White Blood Cells (2001) and Elephant (2003) enabled them to purchase an imposing mansion on the eastern side of the city on Seminole Street, in 2003. This home studio was the location for the recordings of Get Behind Me Satan, the couple's fifth album.

❝The inspiration for what I do and the characters I write about come from this town. And I've become so obsessed with the pride of it and with living up to The Stooges and John Lee Hooker and joining that family, if I can so humbly ask to join the family. I'm obsessed with sounding "Detroit" ❞
Jack White (Guitar World)

Locations 338 and 339: Jack White's childhood home and location for early White Stripes recordings is at 1203 Ferdinand Street, Mexicantown, MI 48209. The house Jack and Meg moved to, a couple of miles east of downtown Detroit, is 1731 Seminole Street, Indian Village, MI 48214. Both properties are private residences.

Meg and Jack recorded Get Behind Me Satan at 1731 Seminole Street

Michigan

Rochester Hills
Madonna's childhood home

This is the place Madonna Ciccone spent something of a Cinderella existence as a child. As the eldest girl of seven sisters and brothers, she changed diapers, did kitchen chores, tended her father's vegetable garden and escaped to the basement where she danced alone to the radio. The house has had a checkered past since Madonna left it aged 18. It made the national news when a local family purchased the four-bedroomed house and then advertized it for sale on eBay, attracting huge, unsustainable bids from fans and hoaxers coinciding with the 9/11 disasters, which brought the 'sale' to an end. The house was then auctioned and became a family home again before more tragedy struck when the empty property became a burned-out shell following a likely arson attack. Four years later the place was purchased for $91,700.

Location 342: 25 miles north of Detroit at 2036 Oklahoma Avenue, Rochester Hills, MI 48309

The Ciccone family home where Madonna lived with her seven brothers and sisters, father Tony, and stepmother Joan

Detroit and Warren
Florence Ballard's grave

Detroit girl Florence Ballard died in 1976 aged just 32. The Supremes founder member's funeral was attended by 5,000 fans at New Bethel Baptist Church, who congregated outside. Her light blue coffin was then transported to her final resting place at Detroit Memorial Park. The grave site memorial for the singer nicknamed "Blondie" spells out her married name, "Florence Glenda Chapman." The New Bethel Baptist Church has a second claim to fame. It was the recording location for Aretha Franklin's 1987 gospel album, One Lord, One Faith, One Baptism, at the church founded by her Baptist minister father, who was fatally wounded in a robbery in 1979.

Locations 340 and 341: the church is at 8430 C. L. Franklin Boulevard. The cemetery is 10 miles north of Detroit at 4280 East Thirteen Mile Road in Warren, MI 48092

Rothbury's Electric Forest Festival is a visual treat if the festival website is anything to go by

Tobin Voggesser

Rothbury
The Electric Forest Festival

This annual late June festival provides an outdoor experience with sound relegated to just one of the senses you will be working overtime here. The visually stunning area at the heart of the festival is Sherwood Forest, "with no exaggeration at all, the most well produced and artistically inspired area ever seen at a music festival" according to Magnetic magazine. The artfully created light displays, marrying high technology and the location's beautiful wooded area, draw around 30,000 music fans a year to this extraordinary festival. The delightfully-named The String Cheese Incident from Colorado, have headlined all three years of the event. They are a perfect fit. The band's integration of art, music, and their fan participatory vibe is exactly what this festival stands for.

Location 343: Rothbury is 65 miles northwest of Grand Rapids. The Electric Forest Festival is held at the Double JJ Resort at 5900 Water Road, Rothbury, MI 49452

Minnesota

Bloomington
Eagles beat Beatles

The Metropolitan Stadium might have had an illustrious sporting history but the Met's record attendance was for a rain-soaked rock concert when the Eagles, supported by the Steve Miller Band and Pablo Cruise, drew a 65,000 crowd on August 1st 1978. Despite the fact that it was The Beatles' one and only visit to Minnesota, their August 21st 1965 appearance in Bloomington failed to sellout at the box office. Of the 45,919 available tickets, only a reported 25,000 fans turned up for an appearance that also lacked the 'Fab Four''s usual rip-roaring opening. With John Lennon having throat problems, their first number, the raucous 'Twist and Shout' was dropped from the set list. The Metropolitan Stadium where they played (home to the Minnesota Twins baseball team and the Minnesota Vikings football team at that time) was demolished before the Mall of America was built on the site in 1992.

Location 344: Bloomington is 15 miles south of Minneapolis. A Metropolitan Stadium Home Plate plaque embedded in the floor of Nickelodeon Universe is a reminder of this sporting structure's existence at the Mall of America, 8100 24th Avenue South, Bloomington, MN 55425

Fit for a Prince: the fabulous Paisley Park Studios

Chanhassen
Prince's Paisley Park Studios

In a prosperous town in a suburb of the twin cities sits this extravagant structure owned by Prince. A few years after creating his own record label – the relatively short-lived Paisley Park Records - Prince opened Paisley Park Studios here in Chanhassen in 1987. The striking $10 million complex includes a hangar-size sound stage and state-of-the-art studios, accompanied by a trophy room of gleaming awards, a jukebox, arcade games, opulent carpeting, and a bird cage high up above the atrium which is home to a pair of doves - naturally. The place attracted TV and movie-makers in its heyday, although as a going concern reports suggest Paisley Park is not exactly a hotbed of activity these days. Back in the day though, aside from recording his own albums including Lovesexy, the Batman soundtrack, Graffiti Bridge, and Diamonds and Pearls, the studios have been used as a recording and mixing facility by George Clinton, Madonna, Paula Abdul, Fine Young Cannibals, Steve Miller, R.E.M.,and Sheila E.

Location 345: Paisley Park Studios lie approximately 20 miles west of Minneapolis in Chanhassen, at 7801 Audubon Road, MN 55317

Minnesota

Richard Sheehan

Duluth
Bob Dylan's early childhood home

Robert Allen Zimmerman (Bob Dylan) was born on May 24th 1941 at Duluth's St. Mary's Hospital, a block away from the top floor apartment in the house where he spent his early childhood. Here he spent the first six years of his life, in the city on the edge of Lake Superior, returning many times in his teens;

significantly, on one occasion, to witness performances by Buddy Holly, The Big Bopper, and Ritchie Valens on the ill-fated 1959 Winter Dance Party tour. The 18-year-old Dylan was present at the Duluth Armory three days before all three perished in an air crash on what was later dubbed "The day the music died."

Locations 347 and 348: Duluth is 150 miles north of Minneapolis. The Zimmerman family home is close to downtown Duluth at 519 North 3rd Avenue East, Duluth, MN 55805. The Duluth National Guard Armory overlooks Lake Superior north of downtown Duluth at 1307 London Road, Duluth, MN 55805

Bob Dylan's Duluth home from 1941 to 1947

Detroit Lakes
WE Fest at Soo Pass Ranch

Head for the Soo Pass Dude Ranch if you want a great country music festival, Minnesota style. WE Fest has been an annual event since 1983. The big difference here is the permanent nature of the location. The festival area at Soo Pass Ranch has a permanent concert bowl and established sanitation, rest rooms, and piped-in water.

That doesn't mean that the natural side of things is diminished. The extra comfort as a festivalgoer is enhanced by the woods and meadows on the shore of Lake Sallie. This August festival has attracted the biggest names in country down the years. Tim McGraw, Jerry Lee Lewis, Taylor Swift, Keith Urban, and Vince Gill have all entertained a

fanbase that hit 83,000 in a WE Fest record-breaking weekend attendance in 2007.

Location 346: Detroit Lakes is 50 miles east of Fargo, North Dakota, and 200 miles west of Duluth, Minnesota. The Soo Pass Ranch is four miles south of Detroit Lakes, 25526 County Highway 22, MN 56501

Hibbing
Bob Dylan's teenage home

Although Bob Dylan was born and spent his early childhood in Duluth, 70 miles away, he was raised from the age of six in the iron-mining city of Hibbing. The house where Dylan grew up is easy to spot. Just look out for the huge garage door image of Dylan's Blood on the Tracks album cover which the current owners have created. The property comprises two bathrooms, three bedrooms, a living room, dining room, and basement room. Dylan's father, Abe Zimmerman, worked at the family business, an electrical appliance store on Fifth Avenue. Zimmerman Furniture and Electric also gave the teenage Bob Dylan the opportunity to earn some pocket money, helping with the store's deliveries. A short walk from the Zimmerman family home brings you to Hibbing High School, where Dylan was a student and made some of his first public appearances as a musician. On East Howard Street is one of the few locations where Dylan is actively remembered, even though the building itself has no Dylan history. Zimmy's is the unofficial restaurant and museum commemorating Bob's place in Hibbing history. The establishment is co-owned by Linda Stroback-Hocking, who, despite never having met the man, has enthusiastically promoted the spirit of Dylan in Hibbing. An event that began informally at Zimmy's back in 1991 has transformed into the

Richard Sheehan

Bob Dylan's teenage home in Hibbing, on the street renamed after him

Dylan Days festival, which each May celebrates Bob's birthday with music performances, an art competition, and even a Bobby Zimmerman bus tour to 15 Hibbing Dylan locations. If you want to take that kind of trip any other time then head to the Hibbing Library or go online to get the library's tailor-made map of the places listed here and plenty more with connections to the great man. Bob himself has returned to Hibbing on a few occasions. With his propensity for such things, maybe he's even taken his own tour. In 1969 he attended a school reunion at Hibbing High, and on the occasion of a 1984 nostalgic visit to the Zimmerman family home he reportedly expressed the common reaction that his childhood bedroom looked much smaller than he remembered it.

Locations 349, 350, 351, 352, and 353: Hibbing is 70 miles northwest of Duluth. The privately-owned former Zimmerman family home (not open to the public at any time) is at 2425 Seventh Avenue East, Hibbing, MN 55746. Hibbing High School is at 800 East 21st Street, a short walk up Seventh Avenue from the Zimmerman home. Seventh Avenue East has been renamed Bob Dylan Drive for the stretch between Howard Street and 25th Street. Zimmerman Furniture & Electric (now Excel Business Systems) was at 1925 Fifth Avenue East, Hibbing, MN 55746, next to the Hibbing Bowling Center where Dylan bowled as a kid. Zimmy's is at 531 East Howard Street, Hibbing, MN 55746.

Minnesota

Minneapolis
The Electric Fetus record stores

Here's a place to "get turned on to something a little out of the ordinary," as the Electric Fetus website puts it. With an inspired name and an excellent record store philosophy, Electric Fetus has served the record-buyers of Minnesota well since 1968. The Minneapolis store is one of three: the others are in Duluth and St. Cloud. These well-arranged stores – you can check them out on the website's virtual tours, soundtracked by some of Minnesota's finest funk and soul - have broadened their service to include just about any music-related product you might want to hear, plus gig ticket sales and live in-store performances. You can get underwear, hats, and soap here too! Aren't record stores the best way to make new friends and develop new listening habits? Electric Fetus encourages all that. They've come a long way since one of the owners was given a citation for refusing to take down a drawn, caricature poster of John and Yoko's Two Virgins with Richard and Pat Nixon's faces on the bodies. Or the time another of the owners was arrested for having a "peace flag" in the store window.

Locations 354, 355, and 356: visit an Electric Fetus at 2000 4th Avenue South, Minneapolis, MN 55404, 12 East Superior Street, Duluth, MN 55802, and 28 5th Avenue South, St. Cloud, Minnesota, MN 58301

New Ulm's traditional museum reflecting mostly traditional music

New Ulm
The Minnesota Music Hall of Fame Museum

The inductees in this Music Hall of Fame museum range from the Minneapolis Police Band to Bob Dylan. For just $5 you can visit the museum which honors and exhibits the achievements of all Minnesota musicians.

Location 359: New Ulm is 95 miles southwest of Minneapolis. The museum is situated next to the public library at the junction of First North Street and Broadway, 27 North Broadway, New Ulm, MN 56073

Minneapolis
Purple Rain at the First Avenue nightclub

Covered in more than 500 silver stars on the outside which commemorate past performers at the venue, the First Avenue nightclub in Minneapolis became a star itself when it appeared in Purple Rain, the 1984 Prince movie. First Avenue and the smaller venue, 7th St. Entry, are located in a former Greyhound bus station, a venue where Prince and local bands: The Jayhawks, The Replacements, Hüsker Dü and Soul Asylum have all appeared on their rocky upward road to success. The Hard Rock Cafe across the street from First Avenue which once housed an exhibition of the diminutive one's white Cloud guitar, stage gear and original hand written lyrics has sadly closed.

Location 357: located in downtown Minneapolis, The First Avenue and 7th Street address is 701 North First Avenue Minneapolis, MN 55403

Minneapolis
Tom Waits' Dangerous Donut Shop

Tom Waits plucked an incident in a Minneapolis Donut shop from his memory banks when creating '9th & Hennepin,' a track from his 1985 album, Rain Dogs. Tom Waits explains:

❛It's just that I was on 9th and Hennepin years ago in the middle of a pimp war, and 9th and Hennepin always stuck in my mind. "There's trouble at 9th and Hennepin." To this day I'm sure there continues to be trouble at 9th and Hennepin. At this donut shop, they were playing 'Our Day Will Come' by Dinah Washington when these three 12-year-old pimps came in in chinchilla coats armed with knives and, uh, forks and spoons and ladles and they started throwing them out in the streets. Which was answered by live ammunition over their heads into our booth. And I knew "Our Day Was Here"❜

Location 358: downtown Minneapolis, 9th Street and Hennepin Avenue, Minneapolis, MN 55403

Walker
Moondance Jam: 'where people come to play'

If you're a classic rock camper then the annual Moondance Jam will tick just about any box on your list. Aside from attracting the biggest names in the genre – Def Leppard, Crosby, Stills & Nash, Journey, KISS, and Heart have all played this summer event in the last five years – the location couldn't be more beautiful. Set in 300 acres of fields and woodland in the Chippewa National Forest, the Moondance Jam is a few miles from the small city of Walker, whose nickname reads, aptly enough, "Where People Come to Play." The owner of Moondance is Kathy Bieloh, who, together with her late husband Bill Bieloh, started the whole thing as a family BBQ for a few hundred back in 1992. Described by a colleague as "a truly amazing woman with an unreal work ethic," Kathy now runs Minnesota's largest rock festival and the country's premier classic rock event along with the Moondance Jammin Country Fest in June. It's a true family affair, with Kathy's son Jon managing the grounds and daughter Bri working with sponsorship and promotion.

❛Moondance started because Bill and I just loved to party and have fun with our family and friends. What better way of doing it than throwing a little music festival? ❜

Moondance owner, Kathy Bieloh

Location 360: three miles east of the Highway 371/Highway 200 intersection, the Moondance Jam is 6.5 miles east of Walker, 7050 39th Avenue Northwest, MN 56484

The Moondance Jam crowd turn out in record numbers for Kid Rock in 2012. An attendance of 23,000 on the day and 60,000 for the event were the festival's best ever

Shannon Northbird

KISS wow classic rock fans at Moondance Jam in 2011

Dean Morrill

Right: Sheryl Crow wraps up as the temperature drops at Moondance 2009

Far right: owner and founder of the Moondance Jam, Kathy Bieloh (left), with her trusty right-hand woman, Renee McAllister

Left: Matt Becker Right: Beau Seeger

Mississippi

Clarksdale
The land "where the blues began"

Clarksdale, Mississippi, is the place of myth and legend where bluesman Robert Johnson infamously sold his soul to the devil at the town's crossroads – the crossroads immortalized in guitar-based blues songs by everyone from Johnson to Eric Clapton since Johnson first recorded 'Cross Road Blues' in 1936. As Clarksdale and its surrounding area is recognized as "the land where the blues began" it's no surprise that this is the home of the Delta Blues Museum. Since 1999, the museum has been housed in the historic Clarksdale freight depot, built in 1918 for the Yazoo and Mississippi Valley Railroad. The building, which was designated a Mississippi Landmark in 1996, has about five-thousand square feet devoted to permanent and traveling exhibits. There's a stage adjacent to the museum classroom which hosts a year-round music education program as well as lectures and symposia. The Delta Blues Museum stage serves as the main venue for local festivals such as the Sunflower River Blues & Gospel Festival (August) and the Juke Joint Festival (April). But Clarksdale boasts a second museum. The Rock & Blues Museum exhibits memorabilia covering the period from the 1920s to the 1970s. Reinforcing the evolution of blues music down

the decades, they added a special exhibition centered on the British rock titans Led Zeppelin, who channeled the blues in their own respectful way. Zeppelin's vocalist Robert Plant (who along with Jimmy Page autographed one of the museum guitars) headlined Clarksdale's Sunflower River Blues & Gospel Festival in 2012. When walking round Clarksdale, look out for the Clarksdale Walk of Fame markers dotted around the place. These honor a dozen or more worthies who have made significant contributions to the area or who are from the region.

Locations 361, 362, 363, 364, and 365: Clarksdale is 80 miles south of Memphis, Tennessee, and 155 miles north of Jackson, Mississippi. The Clarksdale crossroads are marked by a giant triple guitar signpost at the junction of old US Routes 61 and 49, State Street, and Desoto Avenue, Clarksdale, MS 38614. The Delta Blues Museum is at 1 Blues Alley, Clarksdale, MS 38614. The Rock & Blues Museum is at 113 East 2nd Street, Clarksdale, MS 38614. The Clarksdale Walk of Fame sidewalk plaques are scattered around the town. Son House is one of the sidewalk-honored at Cat Head Delta Blues & Folk Art, 252 Delta Avenue, Clarksdale, MS 38614, and the ZZ Top band plaque is on the sidewalk leading up to the old entrance of the Carnegie Public Library at 114 Delta Avenue, MS 38614

Three blues guitars mark the famous crossroads, in Clarksdale

❛When Robert Johnson got through playing, all our mouths was open. He sold his soul to the devil to get to play like that ❜

Son House

❛Clarksdale is a very sleepy town now, but it carries a history which had an amazing effect on both of us [Page and Plant]. Up a bit further you get to Helena, Arkansas, where the King Biscuit Flower Hour was recorded with Sonny Boy [Williamson] and Robert Junior Lockwood, and then a little further up is Robinsonville where Robert Johnson was raised, and then on up to Memphis. There's a little trail now ❜

Robert Plant points the way in a 1998 Mojo interview

Clarksdale
Muddy Waters' cabin

One-hundred miles north of his birthplace in Rolling Fork, Mississippi, is the site of Muddy Waters' cabin. There's a Blues Trail marker and a granite-engraved stone to show where his very basic, rural home once stood before the dilapidated parts of it were preserved in the nearby Delta Blues Museum in Clarksdale. Some sections of the cabin even went on a world tour! A few miles north of Clarksdale was the family base at Stovall Plantation, where Muddy Waters drove a tractor and worked the cotton fields. He began his career in music when, on the property's front porch, he was recorded by Alan Lomax on a field recording expedition sponsored by the Library of Congress and Fisk University, in 1941. By the 1980s the cabin had started to become a shrine to fans of Waters, but the structure of the property was virtually beyond repair. Aside from the preserved portion exhibited by the Delta Blues Museum, some planks were retrieved for an imaginative recycling project by guitarist Billy Gibbons in 1987. The ZZ Top band member crafted special "Muddywood" guitars from the cabin planks and used his idea to raise funds for the Delta Blues Museum.

Location 366: the Blues Marker and granite stone at the site of Muddy Waters' former home can be found by taking the Stovall Road north out of Clarksdale until you hit Burnt Cane Road, where a little raised grassy bank indicates the place on the left-hand side of Stovall Road, Clarksdale, MS 38614

Elmore James, depicted in familiar slide guitar action on his Mississippi gravestone

T.O. File

Ebenezer
Elmore James' slide guitar headstone

As it says on his striking gravestone, Elmore James was "King of the Slide Guitar," a modern electric Chicago bluesman whose signature songs, 'Dust My Broom' and 'Shake Your Money Maker' both feature in the Rock and Roll Hall of Fame's rundown of the '500 Songs that Shaped Rock and Roll.' The headstone was paid for by Phil Walden of Capricorn Records in 1991. He hit upon the headstones design while under the effects of anesthesia administered by his dentist, an amateur sculptor who dreamt up the bronze figure of James playing a guitar that tops the headstone. About 20 feet from James' grave is the pictorial headstone of another Delta bluesman, instrument maker Lonnie Pitchford. A feature of Pitchford's headstone is the single guitar string attached to the side of the stone. The one-string diddley bow was his trademark.

Locations 367 and 368: about 10 miles south of Lexington at the Newport Missionary Baptist Church cemetery, 2028 Newport Road, near Ebenezer, MS 39095

Friars Point
Robert Johnson's 'Traveling Riverside Blues'

Aside from being famous as the birthplace of chart-topping singer Conway Twitty, Friars Point is where blues guitarist and inveterate traveler Robert Nighthawk (Robert McCollum) made his occasional home, now marked by a Mississippi Blues Commission waymark on the site of Hirsberg's drugstore. Outside the store, along with the local juke joints, was where the legendary Robert Johnson would play – a fact endorsed by none other than Muddy Waters, a young, rather intimidated eyewitness, by all accounts. Friars Point gets a namecheck in the lyrics of at least one Robert Nighthawk lyric line "Going back to Friars Point, down in sweet old Dixie Land" – and Robert Johnson's 'Traveling Riverside Blues' also gives the town a mention.

❝On tour in Memphis, I rented a car and drove down to Mississippi, to Friars Point, as in the song. Very strange place, very African, very other-worldly. Sleepy, woodsmoke fires, big trees all around, burnt-out motels, deserted gas stations ...❞

Led Zeppelin's Robert Plant describes Friars Point in a 1990 Q magazine interview

Location 369: Hirsberg's store is close to the junction with 2nd Street and Webb Street, marked by the Mississippi Blues Commission waymark at Friars Point, MS 38631

Mississippi

B.B. King Museum

Indianola
The B.B. King Museum and Delta Interpretative Center

Indianola's B.B. King Museum and Delta Interpretive Center is a beautifully created homage to the great bluesman, who was born 20 miles west of here near Berclair, Mississippi. This multi-media, multi-million dollar museum in his hometown is designed to enable visitors to experience several different chronological periods in B.B. King's life, from sharecropper to music legend. The museum features the now restored brick cotton gin building where the great man (Riley B. King then, Beale Street Boy, and finally "B.B.") worked in the 1940s.

Location 372: Indianola is 90 miles north of Jackson and 130 miles south of Memphis, Tennessee. The B.B. King Museum is at 400 Second Street, in downtown Indianola, MS 38751

Above: the B.B. King Museum interior tells his story but also that of many other Delta musicians Opposite: the man himself performs at the B.B. King Museum

Clarksdale
Sam Cooke's childhood home and plaque

Soul and R&B singer Sam Cooke was born on January 22nd 1931. His family moved from their 7th Street, Clarksdale, home to Chicago when Sam was three. Just over a mile west of his former home is the New Roxy Theatre where a Blues Trail blue plaque commemorates his time in the town. In addition, look out for his Clarksdale Walk of Fame sidewalk plaque. Cooke had the distinction of being the first recipient of this honor. Although this singing legend only lived a short time in Clarksdale, he returned to his home town on a number of occasions and sang at Higgins High School, Geo Oliver School, and the 1st Baptist Church.

Locations 370 and 371: Sam Cook's childhood home (his birthname was Cook without an 'e') is on the edge of town at 2303 7th Street on the corner with Illinois Avenue, Clarksdale, MS 38614. The blues trail and sidewalk plaques are outside the old New Roxy building at 357 Issaquena Avenue, Clarksdale, MS 38614

❝[The museum] honors my name but we want it to be educational to people about the origins of blues music ... to let people of the world know that we are proud of it ❞

B.B. King

B.B. King Museum

Mississippi

Greenwood
Robert Johnson's probable gravesite

Blues icon Robert Johnson died penniless and in poor physical condition aged 27 in 1938. He'd been poisoned by the owner of Greenwood's Three Forks juke joint, who had taken exception to the close attention Johnson had been paying his wife. There are three potential gravesites for Johnson. The only certain fact is that he was buried in an unmarked grave. All three claims have worthy stories as the correct spot, but if you only have time to visit one make for the Little Zion Missionary Baptist Church near Greenwood, where a Mississippi Blues Commission waymark indicates you are in the right place. The exact location of Johnson's grave is marked by a memorial stone "at the base of this old pecan tree" (as it says on the stone) – a position recalled by local woman Rosie Eskridge, husband of Tom "Peter Rabbit" Eskridge who dug the grave. Tom and Rosie (who died as recently as 2006) are both also buried here.

Location 373: two miles north of Greenwood outside the Little Zion Missionary Baptist Church on County Road 518, Money Road, Greenwood, MS 38390

Morgan City and Holly Ridge
John Fogerty's blues pilgrimages

In the early 1990s, Creedence Clearwater Revival founder member John Fogerty made more than one pilgrimage to the South to discover the roots of the blues he fused into his own music. His expeditions south of Memphis through Robinsonville and Lula down Highway 61 resulted in dual epiphanies for the Californian musician when, in 1992, he went searching for the grave of legendary bluesman Robert Johnson at Mount Zion Missionary Baptist Church graveyard. A chance meeting there with fellow blues pilgrim Skip Henderson at the overgrown graveyard led to Fogerty's sponsorship of guitar salesman Henderson's project to erect some kind of monument to Johnson. With the financial support of Columbia Records, who had released a lucrative Robert Johnson boxed set in 1990, a monument was erected and the church's mortgage paid off. Not done yet, Fogerty suggested that Henderson make similar plans for another monument to Robert Johnson's mentor Charley Patton. At the dedication ceremony at nearby New Jerusalem Missionary Baptist Church in Holly Ridge, Fogerty stood side-by-side with Pop Staples, who also attended what turned out to be a significant turning point in Fogerty's life. Fogerty's well-documented epiphanies had him imagining his own gravestone and the lost legacy of his own Creedence Clearwater Revival songs he hadn't sung in years, and how he should utilize the songs before it was too late. Poor Charley Patton and Robert Johnson: if they'd had a dollar in life for every blues pilgrim who visited their stone memorials in the decades after their deaths they would have been, materially, very rich men.

> ❝Lula and Robinsonville are just a little south of Memphis. They're the first true Delta towns and it's strong with Robert Johnson and Charley Patton, their presence and history and lore. It's like learning about Canaan or learning about Galilee. Just the names, you go, 'yeah, and then he went down to Lula' ❞
>
> *John Fogerty*

Locations 377 and 378: the Robert Johnson memorial marker inscribed with all his song titles is at Mount Zion Missionary Baptist Church, three miles northeast of Morgan City, MS 38946. This is the spot where Johnson's death certificate states he was buried, but check out two more claims elsewhere in Rock Atlas for this iconic gravesite. The New Jerusalem Missionary Baptist Church where Charley Patton's monument can be found is in Holly Ridge, MS 38751

Jackson
The Mississippi Musicians Hall of Fame Museum

Located at the Jackson-Medgar Wiley Evers International Airport, the museum is part exhibition, part restaurant and has a busy footfall due to the two million or so passengers that use the airport annually. The Hall of Fame slogan describes why Mississippi music history needs a showcase: "Mississippi, birthplace of America's music. The blues was born in the Delta; country music with the father of country music, Jimmie Rodgers; and rock-n-roll with Ike Turner, Jackie Brenston and Blind Roosevelt Graves. All forms of American music came from one of these roots."

Location 374: the museum is inside the airport (east of the city center), accessed at International Drive, Jackson, MS 39208

Money
Bobbie Gentry's Tallahatchie Bridge story

A sawmill at Choctaw Ridge and the nearby Carroll County picture show both get a passing mention but it's the Tallahatchie Bridge that's the most famous landmark in Bobbie Gentry's 1967 chart-topping hit 'Ode to Billie Joe.' The haunting country song story has Billie Joe McAllister jumping off the bridge over the Tallahatchie River in an apparently successful suicide bid. The genius of Gentry's songwriting has left an unsolved mystery. As time goes by, more and more theories have been added to the list as to what the song is actually all about. Sensibly, to prolong the debates, Bobbie Gentry is rather vague when it comes to revealing any answers as to what happened on that "sleepy, dusty, Delta day." Which bridge? Her coy description is that it was the one "right outside Greenwood."

Location 376: the bridge might be on County Road 559, just west of Money Road, Money, MS 38930, 10 miles north of Greenwood. Some locals claim the bridge nearer to Greenwood at the end of Grand Boulevard is the bridge Bobbie Gentry wrote about.

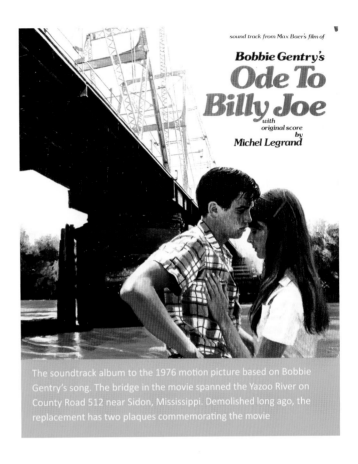

The soundtrack album to the 1976 motion picture based on Bobbie Gentry's song. The bridge in the movie spanned the Yazoo River on County Road 512 near Sidon, Mississippi. Demolished long ago, the replacement has two plaques commemorating the movie

Jackson
Johnny Vincent's Ace Records HQ

Founded in 1955 by Johnny Vincent, Ace Records was, as today's waymark locating the place says, "the most successful Mississippi-based record label of the 1950s and 1960s." From the now disused building, Ace released blues, soul, R&B, pop, and rock records by a variety of artists ranging from Arthur "Big Boy" Crudup to Lee Dorsey. The label played a significant part in the early career of Dr. John, when as 16-year-old Mac Rebennack he furthered his musical education when hired as a producer by Johnny Vincent, working with the likes of James Booker and Earl King.

Location 375: Ace Records' former HQ is revealed by a waymark almost on the corner of West Capitol Street and South Roach Street, Jackson, MS 39201

Quito
Robert Johnson's Tombstones tribute

There are three potential burial sites for blues legend Robert Johnson. This is the least likely, but still has an interesting fact or two attached. An elderly local woman called Queen Elizabeth claimed that she was a former girlfriend of Johnson and that he had been buried at the Payne Chapel Missionary Baptist Church in Quito. Following the publication of this account in 1991, Atlanta swamp rockabilly band The Tombstones were sufficiently convinced in the story to have a simple stone marker placed on the lawn outside the church. There are at least two other Mississippi locations where Robert Johnson is said to be buried. Check out these claims elsewhere in Rock Atlas for this iconic gravesite at the entries listed for Greenwood and Morgan City.

Location 379: the stone marker is at Payne Chapel Missionary Church, seven miles south west of Greenwood at 32380 County Road Highway 167, MS 38941

Mississippi

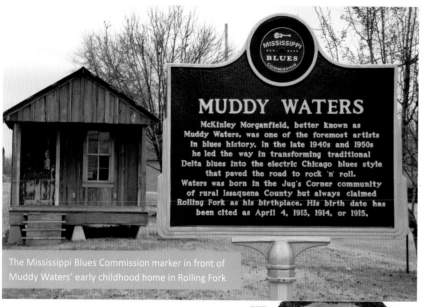

The Mississippi Blues Commission marker in front of Muddy Waters' early childhood home in Rolling Fork

Rolling Fork
Birthplace of Muddy Waters

McKinley Morganfield, the small child who was forever playing in the Mississippi mud, was born in Rolling Fork, Mississippi. His grandmother called her grandson "Muddy" - a name extended by friends that would serve as the name of world-famous blues legend Muddy Waters. A Mississippi Blues Commission marker stands on the spot near the corner of Chestnut Street and Walnut Street where he claims to have been born sometime between 1913 and 1915.

Location 380: Rolling Fork is approximately 80 miles northwest of Jackson. The Blues Commission marker is at 130 Walnut Street, Rolling Fork, MS 39159

Six decades on from his "Muddy" 'christening' in Rolling Fork: The Grammy award-winning album Muddy Waters cut in 1977

West Point
The Howlin' Wolf museum, statue, and marker

Opened as recently as 2005, the Howlin' Wolf Blues Museum celebrates the life of Chester Arthur Burnett, aka Howlin' Wolf. The man famous for powerhouse blues numbers such as 'Smoke Stack Lightning' was born a little way north of West Point at White Station, where by the age of 13 he was playing at Roxy's juke joint. In addition to the museum, the town proudly remembers Howlin' Wolf each late August/early September with a dedicated festival, and there's a statue in the town center.

Locations 385, 386, and 387: West Point is 50 miles south of Tupelo. The museum is iat 307 West Westbrook Street, West Point, MS 39773. The statue is in "Kitty" Bryan Dill Memorial Parkway, West Point, MS 39773. The Blues Trail marker is at 510 East Broad Street, West Point, MS 39773

Tupelo
Birthplace of Elvis Presley

For the first 13 years of his life, Elvis Presley lived here in Tupelo, a city called after the gum tree of that name. His birthplace, a two-room house, draws tens of thousands of visitors a year to a site now expanded to include a museum and chapel dedicated to the 'King of Rock and Roll.' Within the grounds you can read memories of the young Elvis written by locals on a story wall, tread the Walk of Life, a kind of annotated timeline, visit the Fountain of Life water feature, and have your photo taken next to a bronze statue of the 13-year-old Elvis. There's even a replica 1939 green Plymouth sedan car which symbolizes the journey the Presley family made to Memphis from Tupelo in 1948 in just such a vehicle. Nearby is the First Assembly of God Church which the Presleys attended regularly, now carefully restored to its original 1930s décor. In the city itself you can visit Elvis' schools (Lawton Elementary and Milam Junior High), his favorite burger and soda hang-out at Johnnie's Drive-In, Tupelo Hardware Co. where he bought his first guitar, and Lee County Courthouse where he performed his first live radio show for station WELO. Elvis' Tupelo connections don't finish there. In August 2012, a larger-than-life (grown-up) statue of Elvis, by Mississippi sculptor William Beckwith, was unveiled at the former Tupelo fairgrounds where he performed a famous homecoming concert 35 years earlier.

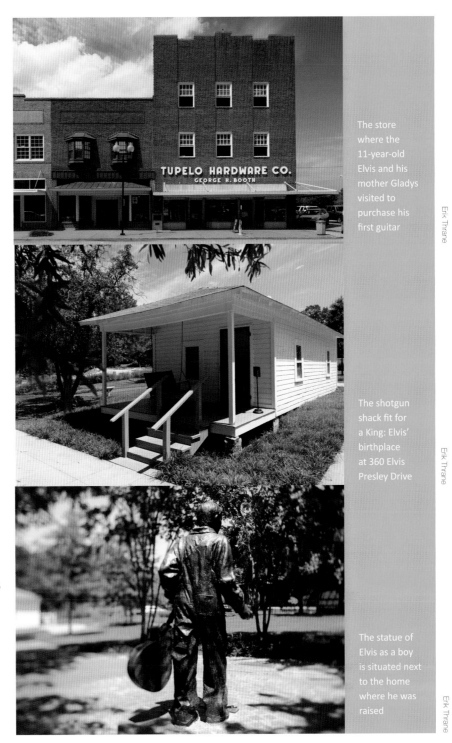

❝I can well remember the afternoon when Elvis Presley and his mother came into Tupelo Hardware, where I worked for 20 years. He wanted a 22 cal. rifle and his mother wanted him to buy a guitar. I showed him the rifle first and then I got the guitar for him to look at. I put a wood box behind the showcase and let him play with the guitar for some time. Then he said that he did not have that much money, which was only $7.75 plus 2% sales tax. His mother told him that if he would buy the guitar instead of the rifle, she would pay the difference for him❞

The words of Tupelo Hardware shop assistant Forrest L. Bobo, quoted aged 78, in 1979

Locations 381, 382, 383, and 384: the house where Elvis was born and raised is part of Elvis Presley Park, which is a short distance due east of downtown Tupelo at 360 Elvis Presley Drive, MS 38804. You'll also find the statue of the young Elvis here. Johnnie's is at 908 E Main Street, Tupelo, MS 38804. The Tupelo hardware store is at 114 W. Main Street at the junction with Front Street, Tupelo, MS 38802. The Lee County Courthouse is at the intersection of Court and Spring Streets, Tupelo, MS 38804

The store where the 11-year-old Elvis and his mother Gladys visited to purchase his first guitar

Erik Thrane

The shotgun shack fit for a King: Elvis' birthplace at 360 Elvis Presley Drive

Erik Thrane

The statue of Elvis as a boy is situated next to the home where he was raised

Erik Thrane

Missouri

Kansas City
No night off for The Beatles

When The Beatles played Kansas City on their first US tour in 1964, it was a unique appearance. When the tour began in San Francisco on August 19th Kansas City wasn't even on the list of cities to host a Beatles concert. But the owner of the local baseball team and stadium was determined that his home city wouldn't miss out. Charles O. Finley met with Beatles manager Brian Epstein and eventually persuaded him and the group to cancel a September 17th day-off, sight-seeing around New Orleans, with a check for $150,000. So, a Kansas City, Municipal Stadium gig was squeezed into the hectic schedule and became the only appearance of the tour not to sell out. Of the 35,561 tickets that went on sale, only 20,124 were sold, due partly to a reluctance on the part of the local media to promote the historic event as Finley was an unpopular figure with the local newspapers and radio stations. Final negotiations rumbled on after the group's arrival at the Muehlebach hotel, where The Beatles booked into the 18th floor Terrace Penthouse. Finley still had one more request. He wanted the 'Fab Four' to extend their usual 30-minute set and tried to top his already excessive offer to get what he wanted. John Lennon was having none of it and countered by replying that The Beatles were not for sale. When they did finally get on stage they made one concession, adding band favorite 'Kansas City' to the set list as a treat for the Kansas City fans who turned out on The Beatles' 'night off.'

❝Today's Beatles Fans Are Tomorrow's Baseball Fans❞

Charles Finley's typically gimmicky slogan

Location 388: all that remains of the now demolished stadium is a plaque at 22nd Street and Brooklyn Avenue. Now part of the Kansas City Marriott Downtown, the Muehlebach hotel has been restored, complete with original lobby, at 12th and Baltimore Avenue, MO 64105

Photo: Hope Edwards

"One night in 1996 when reminiscing about the early days of his career, Chuck mentioned to me that he'd like to play a place the size of the clubs he played when he first started out. We looked at each other for about a second and I said, 'Let's do it at Blueberry Hill.'" Joe Edwards describes the beginning of the legendary concert series at his Blueberry Hill venue

St. Louis
The Chuck Berry statue and Blueberry Hill

Mostly legends are accorded the honor of statues after their death. Not Chuck Berry. The St. Louis-born rock and roller who so inspired The Beatles, The Rolling Stones, Bob Dylan, and everyone who followed even went to the dedication of his own eight-foot-high bronze likeness. The statue stands in a plaza with colored lights that make musical notes, across the street from the restaurant, venue, and memorabilia museum of pop culture, Blueberry Hill. Chuck Berry was the first Rock and Roll Hall of Fame inductee, which says a lot about his place in the popular music firmament of genuine stars. What makes this location doubly special is that you can have your photo taken next to the great man's statue and, if your visit is timed right, head across the street to Blueberry Hill's Duck Room to see him play his monthly live show. Blueberry Hill is the creative vision of Joe Edwards, who in 1972 set out to open a place "where I could program a jukebox with my personal record collection and display the pop-culture and music memorabilia I'd been collecting since childhood," as he puts it. "I

Sculptor Harry Weber's statue of Chuck Berry stands on Delmar Boulevard, across the street from where the "real" Chuck plays at Blueberry Hill

Photo: Hope Edwards

wanted visitors to feel comfortable and enjoy the atmosphere as much as the food and drink." Aside from the statue and delights of Blueberry Hill, the sidewalk outside along Delmar Boulevard has the St. Louis Walk of Fame. Chuck is honored in this way at address: #6504 Delmar Boulevard. Others honored in this fashion are Fontella Bass (#6691), Miles Davis (#6314), Johnnie Johnson (#6628), Albert King (#6370), David Sanborn (#6306) Ilke Turner (#6659), and Tina Turner (#6378).

Location 389: eight miles west of downtown St. Louis, Blueberry Hill is at 6504 Delmar in The Loop, on Delmar Boulevard across the street from the Chuck Berry statue, University City, St. Louis, MO 63130

❛The challenge I had was to make the statue have the same kind of life and joy that Chuck displays when he performs. We wanted it at street level so that people could come up and have their pictures taken with him. He wanted to be shown in the era when rock and roll singers still wore tuxedos and he still had a lot of hair! ❜

Sculptor Harry Weber

Missouri

Dan Torchia

Tipton
Gene Clark's gravestone

A founding member of The Byrds, singer songwriter Gene Clark was born (1944) and buried (1991) in Tipton. His gravestone, clearly marked "Harold Eugene Clark" and "No Other" – the title of his 1974 solo album - is set among the grassy slopes of St. Andrews Cemetery. Although No Other failed to sell following its release it has come to be regarded as one of those lost and found masterpieces that some singer-songwriters create but never see the benefit from in life. Some music commentators think it on a par with anything as poetic and affecting as recordings made by Bob Dylan or Gram Parsons at their best.

Location 391: the tiny city of Tipton is approximately 100 miles east of Kansas City, where Gene Clark later grew up. To find St. Andrews Cemetery, turn right down a narrow lane off Route 50, approaching Tipton from the west, MO 65081. The gravestone is to the left of the angel stood in the middle of the cemetery

Gene Clark was 46 years old when he died at his home in Sherman Oaks, California

Tipton is where Gene Clark was born and buried

St. Louis
The Beatles play two states in one day

On August 21st 1966, The Beatles played two concerts in two major cities, in the same day. They rescheduled a rain-wrecked show in Cincinnati, Ohio, on the evening of August 20th and played that gig the following afternoon. Immediately afterwards, the entire entourage drove across the Ohio state border to Boone County Airport in Kentucky, from where they flew the 300-plus miles to St. Louis to keep their scheduled evening performance at the Busch Memorial Stadium. Many of the largest rock tours have played the place since, including The Rolling Stones' Steel Wheels Tour (1989), The Who's Tommy Tour (1989), U2's Zoo TV Tour (1992), and Paul McCartney's The New World Tour (1993).

Location 390: the current Busch Stadium was built on the site of the Busch Memorial Stadium, which was demolished in 2005. The address is 250 Stadium Plaza, St. Louis, MO 63102

Montana

Billings
ZZ Top and Elton John play key concerts at MetraPark

Elton came to Billings for the first concert after tornado damage had closed the METRA. Below: "Takin' Texas to the people": the London Records radio sampler for possibly the most ambitious tour in rock history, which drew 10,086 fans to the METRA

For a big cattle-ranching state like Montana it was only right that in 1976 ZZ Top's famous Worldwide Texas Tour, featuring on-stage livestock, should make a stop at Billings. That year, on September 18th, between dates at Bismarck, North Dakota, and Boise, Idaho, the 38th show of one of the most remarkable and ambitious rock concert tours hadn't even reached its halfway point. Aside from performing on a huge, gently sloping stage shaped like the state of Texas, backed by a 3D prairie and mountain panorama, ZZ Top were joined on stage by support band REO Speedwagon, a long-horned steer, a black buffalo, two black vultures,

and two diamond back rattlesnakes. A reported $140,000 budget was set aside for the comfort of the animals. The ZZ Top menagerie lived the rock star lifestyle, transported from city to city in a specially ventilated goose-neck trailer with private quarters for each animal, accompanied by their very own animal expert/roadie. The METRA (Montana Entertainment Trade and Recreation Arena), which hosted the Billings concert, was only a year old but for sheer spectacle and drama it's hard to imagine anything topping the Worldwide Texas Tour, except perhaps the 2010 tornado which severely damaged the building. The venue survived but only

after major renovation that saw Elton John perform a year later on April 10th in the very first concert at, what was by then, the renamed Rimrock Auto Arena .

Location 392: Billings is 550 miles north of Denver, Colorado. The Rimrock Auto Arena at MetraPark is a mile northeast of downtown Billings at 308 6th Avenue North, Billings, MT 59101

Nebraska

Alliance
Steely Dan's Carhenge cover

The automobile version of Britain's ancient stone circle, Stonehenge, is featured on the cover of The Best of Steely Dan: Then and Now, released in 1993. Carhenge is a western Nebraska visitor attraction with free admission. The giant 36-vehicle sculpture is the work of artist Jim Reinders.

Location 393: Alliance is 250 miles northeast of Denver, Colorado. Carhenge is about three miles north of Alliance, 2141 County Road, 59 Alliance, NE 69301

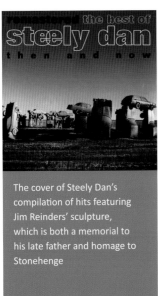

The cover of Steely Dan's compilation of hits featuring Jim Reinders' sculpture, which is both a memorial to his late father and homage to Stonehenge

Despite being a low-key collection of demos, Springsteen's Nebraska still hit No.3 on Billboard's albums chart

Lincoln
Bruce Springsteen's 'Nebraska'

Lincoln is the starting point for Bruce Springsteen's haunting title track to his 1982 album Nebraska. It's the first stop on a tragic journey in the lyrics of the ballad Springsteen penned about Lincoln-born teenager Charles Starkweather, who murdered 11 people on a bloody road trip in the winter of 1957/58.

Locations 394 and 395: Springsteen's song takes the listener from Starkweather's first murder at the Crest gas station on Cornhusker Highway, Lincoln, NE 68521, "through to the Badlands of Wyoming," where the serial killer was eventually captured, in Douglas, WY 82633

Omaha
Birthplace of 311

The funk-rock outfit from Omaha took their name from the Omaha police department's code 311 for indecent exposure, a crime number used during the arrest of the band's original guitarist for streaking. The city may have created the band but it also almost destroyed them. A year before their major breakthrough with the album Grassroots, the band members were traveling into the city to play a gig when the their RV caught fire descending a hill. The fire forced them to jump out of the burning vehicle, an incident that saw them lose all their equipment in the bus towed behind. Escaping the blaze, 311 later released 'Omaha Stylee,' a track on Grassroots with lyrics describing their "leaping through fire surviving." If you want a music bar where 311 is played proudly and regularly on the jukebox, check out Omaha's Hive Lounge.

When people ask us how we've been able to maintain a certain fan base, we tell them it's because of our upbringing in Omaha. Omaha is a part of us. We wear it proudly

311's Nick Hexum talking to Lazy-i.com

Location 396: The Hive Lounge is downtown at 1951 St. Marys Avenue, Omaha, NE 68102

Nevada

Rick Elmore

The Las Vegas Elvis statue commemorates 'The King''s eight-year run of concert appearances at the Hilton hotel, starting on July 31st 1969

Las Vegas
The Elvis Presley statue

"To Elvis" reads the Las Vegas Hotel plaque, "who will be remembered by the many great artists in the Hilton Showroom and by the millions who enjoyed his great performances on our stage." The accompanying statue is outside the main entrance of the LVH (Las Vegas Hotel), a location where Elvis Presley appeared 837 consecutive times at the Showroom, which is toward the back of the hotel's casino, in the southwest corner. Sculptor Carl Romanelli's 7-foot-high creation was dedicated in 1978 by Presley's father, Vernon, and former wife, Priscilla.

Location 397: the Las Vegas Hotel (Las Vegas Hilton back in Elvis' day) is at 3000 Paradise Road, Las Vegas, NV 89109

Las Vegas
The Beatles upsize in Vegas

In 1964 The Beatles stayed at the Sahara hotel in Las Vegas and played two shows (4 p.m. and 9 p.m. with 8,408 attending each) at the nearby Las Vegas Convention Center. Arriving at 1 a.m. at the Old McCarran Field International Airport, the tired 'Fab Four' were greeted by 2,000 Las Vegas city curfew-busting fans, who watched as the objects of their desire sped away to spend the rest of that night and the next morning asleep in room 2344 on the 23rd floor of the Sahara. The hotel where Elvis Presley played the slot machines as he filmed his movie Viva Las Vegas closed its doors for the last time in 2011. The Convention Center, where The Beatles switched their shows from the Sahara hotel's Congo Room when a rush on tickets demanded a bigger venue, still remains.

Locations 398 and 399: the Sahara hotel was at 2535 Las Vegas Boulevard South, Las Vegas, NV 89109. The Las Vegas Convention Center is at Paradise Road, Las Vegas, NV 89109

When hosting The Beatles in 1964, the Convention Center stretched its capacity to accommodate 8,408 excited fans

Las Vegas
The Hard Rocks

Founded in 1971 in London, England, there are now more than 150 Hard Rock Cafés and Hotels worldwide. The hotels offer the expected rock star luxury and this one in Vegas can boast a casino (naturally) and a concert venue. Out front a giant Fender Stratocaster guitar greets guests, and inside the rock memorabilia on display features some of the most high-profile exhibits in the Hard Rock collection. Sadly, this Hard Rock has the unhappy distinction of being the hotel where John Entwistle died. The Who's bass player is reported to have spent his last night in room 658 at the Hard Rock on June 27th 2002, a day before The Who's US tour was due to begin at The Joint, the hotel's rock venue.

Location 400: the hotel and casino are at 4455 Paradise Road, Las Vegas, NV 89169, with a Hard Rock Café at 4475 Paradise Road, NV 89169. If that wasn't enough there's a more centrally placed Hard Rock Café at 3771 South Las Vegas Boulevard, NV 89109

David Roberts

Above: a giant Fender Stratocaster at the entrance to the Hard Rock Hotel, Las Vegas. Below: memorabilia inside the hotel and casino includes the baseball outfit worn by Elton John at his 1975 Dodger Stadium gig and hundreds of other exhibits like these Rolling Stones goodies

David Roberts

New Hampshire

Sunapee
Aerosmith beginnings at the Anchorage

Aerosmith is a band made in Boston, but the origins go back way further to the tiny tourist town of Sunapee where their singer, Steven Tyler, still has a home. It was the resort's Anchorage ice cream parlor where Aerosmith's 'Toxic Twins', Steven Tyler and Joe Perry, met up during childhood summers around Lake Sunapee. Perry had a job at the Anchorage while Tyler mowed lawns and dug ponds on the family's land, bought by his grandfather. Tom Hamilton, who would become the band's bass guitarist, lived year-round in the town. In 1964 Tyler formed The Strangeurs and in 1966 Chain Reaction and when Chain Reaction, and Perry and Hamilton's Jam Band played at the same local gig (at The Barn in Sunapee) in 1970, it prompted an enthusiastic joining of forces to create Aerosmith. There are still a couple of reminders that Sunapee was the important birthplace of the band. A red brick walkway down to the harbor has one stone engraved simply with the word "Aerosmith" and the Anchorage still serves ice-cream, and still has

Steven Tyler as a customer. The singer has a home here on the shore of Lake Sunapee and is often seen joining in community events and activities.

❝He came over here and was looking in a paper in New York and saw Sunapee, which was worth three grand in those days. He got a bit of money together and bought this piece. We've still got 212 acres left. That whole mountain there is mine. Sunapee is only a teeny resort, but it's decent ❞

Steven Tyler, talking about his grandfather's property purchase

Locations 401 and 402: Sunapee is 100 miles northwest of Boston. The Anchorage at Sunapee Harbor has grown into a restaurant and lounge. It's on the lakeside at 71 Main Street, Sunapee, NH 03782. Steven Tyler's private residence is east of the harbor on Lake Avenue,

❝Steven Tyler is my neighbor in Sunapee! He participated in the 4th of July parade by riding in the police car. The car stopped and he asked me for a kiss. I should have asked him if Aerosmith could play at our class reunion ❞

Sunapee resident Martha Keenan

Above left: Steven Tyler's wooded, lakeside paradise - his private home on Lake Sunapee

New Jersey

Courtesy of Cicada Mania at Panoramio

Asbury Park
The Jersey shore sound at The Stone Pony

Apart from being an historic, world famous venue, The Stone Pony has one distinct location advantage: it's right on the beach. Still attracting teenagers and seasoned Asbury rockers – Limp Bizkit were scheduled to appear at the time of writing – this black cavern of a venue has a Tardis-like capacity to surprise and is packed with music memorabilia and autographed guitars to help you while away a drink or two before the entertainment kicks into action. The Stone Pony first opened in 1974, and despite suffering more than one closure it finally got a significant makeover in 2000 which exploited the history of the place, a history which has seen locals Bruce Springsteen, Jon Bon Jovi, and Southside Johnny and The Asbury Jukes all acknowledge its part in their career development. Springsteen owes the venue in more ways than one. It was here he first met Patti Scialfa, his future wife, when she was guesting on vocals at a gig by Bobby Bandiera in 1982.

Location 403: on the beachfront at 913 Ocean Avenue, Asbury Park, NJ 07712

The small on the outside and large on the inside, Tardis-like Stone Pony

New Jersey

Asbury Park
Bruce Springsteen's Asbury Park connections

Bruce Springsteen announced himself to the world and left nobody in any doubt where he belonged when releasing his debut album Greetings from Asbury Park N.J. in 1973. Few artists are so firmly connected to a sense of place as Springsteen. The sights and sounds of New Jersey and the Jersey Shore permeate much of his lyric writing. The cover of Greetings from Asbury Park is a postcard advertising the entertainment to be had on the shore 60 miles south of New York. Springsteen is said to have seen the postcard for sale on the Asbury Park boardwalk. He bought it, took it to Columbia, and told the record company that the message on the postcard was what he wished his first album to be called. The story goes that Joey Ramone once had an Asbury Park meeting

with Springsteen and asked the future 'Boss' to write a song for The Ramones. Later that same day Springsteen created 'Hungry Heart,' reportedly written in a matter of half-an-hour, but ended up keeping the song and including it on his 1980 album, The River. Released as a single, the cover of 'Hungry Heart' shows Springsteen in familiar territory, on the boardwalk at Asbury Park.

Location 404: Springsteen's cover shoot on the boardwalk can be pinpointed by the Empress hotel in the background, which is at 101 Asbury Avenue, Asbury Park, NJ 07712

Above: Bruce on familiar territory: on the Boardwalk, Asbury Park Left: the emerging Bruce sends his postcard to the world

Atlantic City
Bruce's ballad of 'Atlantic City'

Bruce Springsteen's 'Atlantic City' single, taken from his 1982 album Nebraska, paints a not altogether flattering picture of the boardwalk and streets of this city on the Jersey Shore. It's one of Springsteen's darker, more desperate songs about escaping – in this case the organized crime and poverty prevalent at that time.

Location 405: Atlantic City is 60 miles southeast of Philadelphia, NJ 08401

Long Branch
Bruce Springsteen's 'Born to Run' home

Long Branch is where Bruce Springsteen wrote his Born to Run album, released in the summer of 1975. The very definition of a breakthrough album, Born to Run sheds much of Springsteen's previous tendency to write songs based around places in New Jersey and makes a bigger, bolder, and more involving statement. Those songs were created at a small two-bedroom bungalow he rented close to the beach. Mostly created at the piano, the title track was an exception, written while playing guitar sitting on the end of his bed one day, when according to Bruce "the words 'born to run' just came to me." The Ink Well Coffee House where the E Street Band's earlier incarnation Steel Mill were formed is around the corner from the property. Rock pilgrims seeking out the place beware. Famous for visiting the homes of his peers Neil Young, John Lennon, and Jim Morrison, Bob Dylan was detained by police one rainy day in 2009 trying to track down Bruce's place. Apparently he went to the wrong address, got lost, and was not recognized by the young officer detaining him after a report of "an eccentric-looking man" was phoned in by a concerned homeowner who saw a soaked, disheveled Dylan in their yard.

Locations 408 and 409: Long Branch is a beach resort a few miles up the shore from Asbury Park. A block from the beach, the bungalow where Springsteen wrote songs for Born to Run is at 7 ½ West End Court, Long Branch, NJ 07724 . The Ink Well is at 665 2nd Avenue, Long Branch, NJ 07724

Belmar
Bruce Springsteen's giant E Street Fender

A replica of Bruce Springsteen's Fender guitar stands on the corner of E Street in Belmar. Authentically distressed and battered, the Fender Esquire is eight feet tall and stands on the street that gave its name to The E Street Band, a street where original band member and keyboard player David Sancious had his home back in the 1970s at No.1105. The guitar is the work of artist Bob Mataranglo, who had already impressed the local Belmar Tourism Commission with his Springsteen-themed wall mural across town.

Locations 406 and 407: the guitar stands on the front lawn of the library building on the corner of 10th Avenue and E Street, Belmar, NJ 07719. The giant wall mural can only be seen traveling north on Main Street. It's on the outside wall of the Yarnold building, on the corner of Main Street and 10th Avenue, Belmar, NJ 07719

E Street tributes: Bob Mataranglo and his eight-foot Fender and the mural he created a block away

New Jersey

Freehold
Springsteen's childhood homes

From his birth in Long Branch Hospital to his late teenage years Bruce Springsteen was raised and began his extraordinary life in music in Freehold. Two of the three houses he grew up in are still around today, and if you want a guided tour around haunts he hung out at listen to or search out the lyrics to 'In Freehold,' his unreleased mid-90s live ballad. The convent, church, school, and YMCA canteen all get a mention as does Randolph Street, his first home. Here he spent the period from birth to the adolescent years when his parents bought him his first guitar after being inspired by watching Elvis Presley on The Ed Sullivan Show. Although this house was eventually demolished, there is "that big red maple tree" Springsteen refers to in 'In Freehold' that still survives today. There's much more to see at the home a short distance away where the family moved to when Bruce was still at grammar school. Here on Institute Street, Springsteen is pictured next to the sycamore tree near the property inside his 1985 album Born in the USA and on the cover of the single 'My Hometown.' The last family home was on South Street, where his mother and father stayed until heading west to California. Bruce remained in New Jersey when they left in 1969.

Locations 410, 411, and 412: Freehold is 20 miles inland east of Asbury Park. Springsteen's first childhood home was at 87 Randolph Street where the maple tree he wrote about still stands, Freehold, NJ 07728. A quarter of a mile away is the second home, at 39½ Institute Street on the corner with Parker Street, Freehold, NJ 07728. 68 South Street was home in the mid-sixties, where Springsteen stayed when the family moved west to California in 1969. The Springsteens lived in the right-hand side of the property, Freehold, NJ 07728

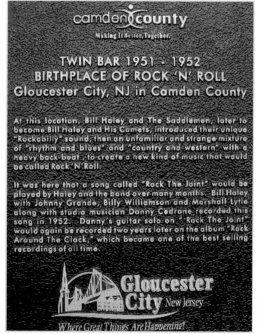

Scott Clark

Gloucester City
Birthplace of rock and roll?

Gloucester City and Wildwood (85 miles farther south) both have strong claims to be the birthplace of rock and roll, where Bill Haley strutted his stuff in the early 1950s. A bronze plaque marking the exact spot the genre is said to have kicked off has pride of place at what is now Jack's Twin Bar.

Location 413: Gloucester City is just south of Philadelphia. The Twin Bar (Jack's Twin Bar) is at the intersection of Broadway and Market Street at 200 South Broadway, Gloucester City, NJ 08030

Paramus
R&B memorials

The eldest member of The Isley Brothers, vocalist O'Kelly (Kelly for short) Isley Jr. and youngest member, bass guitarist Marvin Isley, are both buried at The George Washington Memorial Park. Luther Vandross and Drifters founder Clyde McPhatter are also buried here.

Location 416: The George Washington Memorial Park is at 234 Paramus Road, Paramus, NJ 07653

Bruce Springsteen exits the back yard of his childhood home on the corner of Institute and Parker Streets

West Long Branch
Springsteen's Special Collection

If you have a serious interest in Bruce Springsteen's life and career, the Monmouth University campus is where you need to go. More a library than a museum, fans, scholars and anyone researching the rock legend's activity can indulge themselves at the Bruce Spingsteen Special Collection housed here. The initiative of Springsteen Backstreets magazine in 2001, the archives consist of documents, music releases, memorabilia, posters, and seemingly just about every word written about the great man.

❛The Collection has almost 1,000 books and magazines on myself and the band – more stuff than every place except my mother's basement! ❜

Bruce Springsteen

Location 419: open to visitors only by appointment, at the Monmouth University campus at Cedar Avenue near the intersection of Norwood Avenue, 400 Cedar Avenue, West Long Branch, NJ 07764

Totowa
'Soul Man' grave

Dave Prater was half of the soul duo Sam & Dave. A resident of nearby Paterson, he died in a Georgia automobile accident in 1988 and his Totowa gravestone reads simply "Soul Man," the duo's 1967 hit.

Location 418: the Holy Sepulchre Cemetery is at 52 Totowa Road, Totowa, NJ 07512

Elizabeth Colrick

Lyndhurst
Joey Ramone's gravestone

The Ramones' lead vocalist is buried at the Hillside Cemetery in Lyndhurst. The spot is much visited by Ramones fans, who leave a variety of objects (even a Joey-type leather jacket in the case of one tuned-in fan) at the site. The large, simple headstone has an inscription which reads "Jeff Hyman," Joey Ramone's real name and describes him as a "Rock and Roll Hall of Famer."

Location 414: Hillside Cemetery is a couple of miles north of the New Jersey Turnpike Toll Road at 742 Rutherford Avenue, NJ 07070

Manasquan
The Bruce Springsteen sculpture

Artist Stephen Zorochin's sculpture "Bruce Springsteen, Soulful Humanitarian" can be found a few miles down the coast from Asbury Park at Manasquan. The hand-painted bronze on cement bust was completed by Zorochin in 2011. Recently relocated, it's in the borough of Manasquan at the southern end of Monmouth County, a spot the real 'Boss' is said to frequent regularly.

Location 415: the Springsteen bust is at 475 Euclid Avenue, Manasquan, NJ 08736

The bronze 'Boss' looking thoughtful on Euclid Avenue

Sayreville
Jon Bon Jovi's boyhood home

In 1989, MTV ran a Bon Jovi Home Contest when, amazingly, the prize was Jon Bon Jovi's boyhood home. The winners were Jay and Judy Frappier, who were handed the deeds to the place and given a guided tour by the rock star while hundreds of Bon Jovi fans screamed themselves hoarse outside. Showing the couple round the colonial-style property, complete with pool and motorcycle, Jon drew their attention to the basement window where he sneaked girls into the house, and the stove burner where his father would make special spaghetti sauce on Sundays.

❛It's my boyhood home, man. This is the place where I learned about the finer things in life. Like rock 'n' roll ... and women ❜

Jon Bon Jovi does the real estate soft sell

Location 417: a short distance west of the Garden State Parkway, at 16 Robinhood Drive, Sayreville, NJ 08859

New Jersey

Wildwood

Birthplace of 'The Twist' (and rock and roll?)

There's a question mark hanging at the end of Wildwood's headline as some music fans in nearby Gloucester City (85 miles northwest) claim it to be the location where Bill Haley first performed his earth-shatteringly epic 'Rock Around the Clock' for the first time. There's better evidence that the first time he played the song as Billy Haley and His Comets was at Wildwood's HofBrau Hotel. The song had already been recorded by the band in April 1954 when, on Memorial Day weekend, 500 fans packed into the hotel and Haley and co let rip with the opening line "One, two, three o'clock, four o'clock rock…" There's a plaque to mark the event where the HofBrau Hotel used to be and Wildwood stakes another, more certain, rock and roll claim to fame and a second plaque at what was once the Rainbow Club but is now Irish restaurant Cattle 'n Clover. Here is where Chubby Checker is first thought to have performed his equally world famous song and dance 'The Twist' back in the summer of 1960. And Wildwood isn't done yet. Scott Clark, who hails from Albany, NY, via Montreal, Canada, and has "rock and roll and South Jersey in my blood!" remembers a great story radio and TV host Dick Clark would tell about how Wildwood was responsible for Buddy Holly's 'That'll be the Day' getting so popular so fast. Shortly after Dick took over American Bandstand in Philadelphia, he would host a weekly "Record Hop" at the Starlight Ballroom on

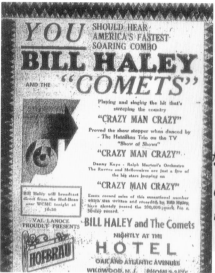

Chubby Checker

Wildwood's boardwalk. One night he tested the Holly record and the kids went crazy, asking him to play it again and again. He must have played it six times that night! Buddy, Bill, and Chubby owe a big rock and roll debt of gratitude to Wildwood. As do KISS, as some of their first Top 10 album, Alive!, was recorded at the Wildwood Convention Center in 1975. And we're still not finished with Wildwood … Bobby Rydell immortalized the place in his Top 20 1963 hit 'Wildwood Days,' while others putting it into song include The Treniers (with fifties release 'Everything's Wild in

Wildwood') and 1960s rock band Nazz's 'Wildwood Blues.'

> ❝Rock and roll had a sound, a beat, but it didn't have a dance, not until Wildwood and 'The Twist' ❞
>
> Chubby Checker

Locations 420, 421, and 422: the resort town of Wildwood is 45 miles south of Atlantic City. The 'Rock Around the Clock'

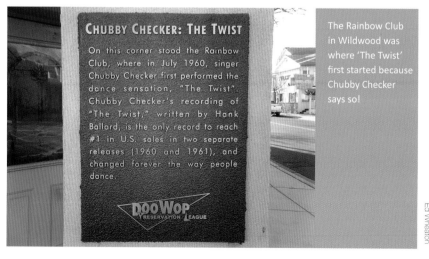

CHUBBY CHECKER: THE TWIST

On this corner stood the Rainbow Club, where in July 1960, singer Chubby Checker first performed the dance sensation, "The Twist". Chubby Checker's recording of "The Twist," written by Hank Ballard, is the only record to reach #1 in U.S. sales in two separate releases (1960 and 1961), and changed forever the way people dance.

DOO WOP RESERVATION LEAGUE

The Rainbow Club in Wildwood was where 'The Twist' first started because Chubby Checker says so!

Above: the HofBrau Hotel (and advert opposite page for his broadcast in 1953), where Bill Haley performed

Left: the Rainbow Club back in the day, now restaurant Cattle 'n Clover, and (opposite) its present-day Twist plaque

plaque is on an outside pillar of the Motor Inn Beach Terrace at the site of the former HofBrau Hotel at 3400 Atlantic Avenue, Wildwood, NJ 08260. The Chubby Checker plaque is at Cattle 'n Clover (known as the Rainbow Club in 1960) at 3817 Pacific Avenue and Spicer Avenue, Wildwood, NJ 08260. At some point, a block from here, where Pacific Avenue joins Garfield Avenue, there was once a sign that read "Chubby Checker Way" but sadly that appears to have vanished, although a sign reading "Chubby Checker Ave" now sits at the intersection of Spicer Avenue and Atlantic Avenue. The Starlight Ballroom was on the boardwalk at Oak Avenue, Wildwood, NJ but was destroyed by the devastating boardwalk fires of 1981.

RockAtlasUSA

New Mexico

Clovis
The Norman & Vi Petty Rock & Roll Museum

There are two good reasons for the rock and roll tourist to visit Clovis. This is the town where Buddy Holly, The Fireballs, Buddy Knox, Waylon Jennings, Bobby Vee, LeAnn Rimes, and Roy Orbison recorded at Petty's studio and created the "Clovis Sound." Norman Petty was the Clovis-born producer and musician who also helped write some of Buddy Holly's biggest hits. You can visit the studio and get a real feel for what it must have been like back in the fifties when this kind of music broke through and swept across the nation. The studios are the reason for the second good location worth making for in Clovis. The significance of the studios has led to the creation of a great little rock and roll museum nearby. The Norman & Vi Petty Rock & Roll Museum (wife Vi was also a member of The Norman Petty Trio) has two re-created studios, the original fifties mixing board, a fifties style diner, and plenty of artefacts and neon to help transport you back to the time when Clovis contributed hugely to the history of rock.

Locations 424 and 425: Clovis is close to New Mexico's eastern border with Texas. The Norman Petty Recording Studios are open

for tours by appointment only at 1313 West 7th Street, Clovis, NM 88101. Just over a mile east of the studios is the Norman & Vi Petty Rock & Roll Museum at 105 East Grand Avenue, Clovis, NM 88101

Right: One of the many Buddy Holly record releases to carry the Norman Petty and 'Clovis' stamp of quality

Above and opposite: transport yourself back in time through the memorabilia on display at the Norman & Vi Petty Rock & Roll Museum

Bethel
The Woodstock Festival

Along with the moon landing, the 1969 Woodstock Festival has become not only an iconic event in American cultural history for that year but for all time. As everyone probably knows by now, the Woodstock Music & Art Fair, to give it its proper name, didn't take place in Woodstock at all: plenty of other interesting stuff did, so check out the real "Woodstock" entry at the end of this section. Wallkill, 40 miles south of Woodstock, was selected as the preferred festival site and a bridge was constructed before, as organizers put it, they were run out of town. The site then switched to dairy farmer Max Yasgur's property up at White Lake, Bethel, 45 miles west of Wallkill. With an ambitious bill planned for August 15th, 16th, and, 17th featuring "3 Days of Peace & Music," as the posters advertised, everything was set, awaiting the expected 100,000 ticket holders. The astonishing line-up of acts - Jimi Hendrix, The Who, Crosby, Stills, Nash & Young, Santana, Joan Baez, and Sly & The Family Stone were highlights – was eclipsed by the half-a-million strong crowd (turning it into a free festival) which made this an event so newsworthy that it headlined front pages around the world. Just as well Max Yasgur's land, sloping

Picture courtesy Warner Bros.

It was made in heaven. It was a bowl with a rise for a stage. What more could you want?

Woodstock co-producer Michael Lang finds the perfect site at Yasgur's 600-acre farm

fields, and large lake (Filippini Pond), which was a magnate for nude skinny-dippers, was able to cope. Largely trouble free, Woodstock, despite the rain and mud, made headlines for all the right reasons. The behavior of the hippie hoards turned first local, then national opinion around. Here were 500,000 young people helping one another in what some compared to a disaster area or war zone – a feature of the festival amplified in director Michael Wadleigh's Oscar-winning movie, Woodstock, a year later. The

Woodstock Festival name was resurrected most notably in 1994 for Woodstock II at Winston Farm in Saugarties with a bill featuring Bob Dylan, Green Day, Red Hot Chili Peppers, and Sheryl Crow, and again in 1999 when James Brown, Metallica, Dave Matthews Band, and Alanis Morissette played Griffiss Air Force Base outside of Rome, New York. Befitting one of popular music's milestones, the whole Woodstock experience is celebrated and remembered by a beautifully designed museum on the site of the original 1969 festival. Part of the Bethel Woods Center for the Arts, which includes performance venues, the museum sets out to tell the Woodstock story using interactive displays and artefacts in a 6,728-square-foot exhibit gallery. When Richie Havens, the

Above: in a movie still from Woodstock, dairy farmer Max Yasgur begins to comprehend the enormity of what he's signed up to

Right: Bethel Woods Center for the Arts transports visitors back to 1969

performer who famously went on stage first at Woodstock, died in 2013 it was announced on his website that his ashes would be scattered at the site.

Locations 426, 427, 428, and 429: the Woodstock monument (on the corner of Hurd Road and West Shore Road) can be accessed from the public routes in Bethel, NY 12720. The actual position of the festival's stage can be found by taking West Shore Road, heading southeast, and looking right just before the right-hand turn into North Access Road, Bethel, NY 12720. The museum entrance is addressed as 200 Hurd Road, Bethel, NY 12720. Note that the museum is closed for the winter season and re-opens every April. Max Yasgur's farm is marked by landmark signs in memory of Max and wife Miriam Yasgur at Yasgur Road (a small track road north off State Route 17B, about two miles west of the museum site), Bethel, NY 12726

California

Buffalo
Rick James' Street Songs monument

Motown funk and soul legend Rick James is remembered in his birth city, Buffalo, by an illustrated black granite gravestone.

Location 430: the Forest Lawn Cemetery is in the city center at 1411 Delaware Avenue, Buffalo, NY 14216. The grave is in a section of the cemetery near the Delaware Avenue S-curve, and it's close to Scajaquada Creek.

Rick James' brother Carmen Sims and family friend Ron Fleming visit the gravestone. The image comes from a photo on James' 1981 album Street Songs

Buffalo News

Cold Spring
The Don McLean album cover shoot

Cold Spring is the village where Don McLean wrote a good deal of his epic song 'American Pie.' He lived here for a time in a house he once described as leaking like a sieve. His self-titled 1972 album has a cover that pictures the singer-songwriter in the chilly Cold Spring landscape on a hill up above the village.

Location 431: Cold Spring is north of New York City, a little over 20 miles south of Poughkeepsie. The album cover was shot in a spot overlooking the village, NY 10516

❝This is taken by a man named John Olsen for a feature on me in Life magazine in 1972. It was taken on a bluff overlooking the Hudson River in Cold Spring, which was near the little gatehouse where I used to live at that time ❞

Don McLean describes the location of his self-titled album cover photo

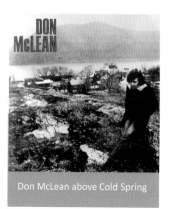

Don McLean above Cold Spring

Montauk
The Stones use 'Memory Motel'

'Memory Motel' is a track on The Rolling Stones' 1976 album Black and Blue and here in Montauk is the motel and bar that sparked the lyric-writing of one of the Stones' longest tracks. Although the band never stayed here, the place caught the attention of songwriters Mick Jagger and Keith Richards when they relaxed and rehearsed for a tour in the Montauk area at Andy Warhol's house in 1975.

Location 433: at the eastern end of Long Island at 692 Montauk Highway, Montauk, NY 11954

Montauk
The Rufus Wainwright song

Montauk is home to Rufus Wainwright and the place where he got married to Jörn Weisbrodt in 2012. The seaside town features in the song simply titled 'Montauk' that he recorded for his album Out of the Game. The track describes the love between Wainwright, Weisbrodt, and their baby daughter Viva.

Location 434: Montauk, NY 11954

Hunter
The Mountain Jam

Good music and a good degree of comfort are what you can guarantee at the Mountain Jam in this ski resort in the Catskill Mountains. This comparatively young annual event, held each weekend after Memorial Day, uses the winter ski chalets and on-site facilities, although the rolling mountain slopes make for an attractive camping spot. The regular fans must love Gov't Mule. The Southern rock outfit made their 9th consecutive appearance when they headlined in 2013. The kind of music you are likely to get is illustrated by the bands who have attended the Mountain Jam since it began in 2005. My Morning Jacket, The Felice Brothers, Steve Winwood, Toots and The Maytals, and Ray LaMontagne have all played their part in bagging Mountain

Fans eye view: the ski resort facilities and breathtaking views at the Mountain Jam

Courtesy of Mountain Jam

Jam a Pollstar nomination for Music Festival of the Year and a high ranking in Rolling Stone magazine's run down of the best festivals.

Location 432: Hunter Mountain is just over 2 hours north of New York City. Mountain Jam is at the Hunter Mountain ski resort, 64 Klein Avenue, Hunter NY 12442

New York City/Brooklyn
Woody Guthrie's favorite place

From 1943 until 1950, Mermaid Avenue, Coney Island was where folk legend Woody Guthrie lived during the most settled period of his life. The creator of 'This Land is Your Land,' released in 1940, Guthrie immersed himself in his writing and family life in a first-floor apartment a couple of blocks from the beach. A favorite destination at meal times for Guthrie and family was the Nathan's Famous restaurant, still serving hot dogs today on Surf Avenue. Favorite of all the Coney Island places he loved, though, is the beach area down by the jetty at the end of the boardwalk.

Here's where Guthrie's ashes were scattered following his death in 1967 in a family ceremony ended by a visit to Nathan's Famous, for hot dogs and fries.

Locations 435, 436, and 437: now a senior citizens home, 3520 Mermaid Avenue, Coney Island, NY 11224, was where Woody Guthrie's apartment stood. Nathan's Famous hot dog restaurant is still at 1310 Surf Avenue, NY 11224. The spot where his ashes were scattered is off the rocks by the boardwalk jetty at 1208 Surf Avenue, NY 11224

Woody and his children on the beach he loved so much. This LP was a collection of tracks featuring previously unheard lyrics of Guthrie

❝We climbed out on the rocks and it was really windy and we were slipping on the rocks. We threw the whole can in, and it bobbed along and came back on shore. It kept happening. Finally, we held the can down in the water, filled it with a little water, and chucked it in. The can is probably still out there❞

Nora Guthrie recalls the "comedy of errors" as she describes the scattering of her father's can of ashes to Rolling Stone magazine

New York

New York City/Brooklyn
Swing Out Sister on the boardwalk

British pop duo Swing Out Sister are pictured at an amusement park on the Coney Island boardwalk for the cover of their fifth studio album, Shapes and Patterns, which got its US release in 1998.

Location 441: the Astroland park closed in 2008, 1000 Surf Avenue (corner of West 10th Street), Coney Island, Brooklyn, NY 11224

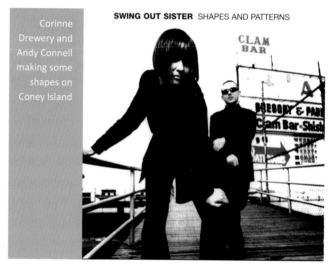

Corinne Drewery and Andy Connell making some shapes on Coney Island

SWING OUT SISTER SHAPES AND PATTERNS

New York City/Brooklyn
Phish Live in Brooklyn

KeySpan Park is the almost sci-fi landscape location pictured on the cover of the Phish Live in Brooklyn album the band released in 2006. The June 17th 2004 gig, at the South Brooklyn peninsula on Coney Island, was the opening night of their final tour and was broadcast live to theaters and captured on a DVD.

Location 439: the cover pictures their gig at the baseball field at Keyspan Park, Coney Island, NY 11224

New York City/Brooklyn
The Manic Street Preachers' bridge cover

The 2007 album Send Away the Tigers by Welsh band the Manic Street Preachers has a cover featuring two girls walking along Shore Road, with the Verrazano-Narrows Bridge leading to Staten Island in the background.

Location 440: Shore Road, Brooklyn, NY 11209

The band used a picture by New York-born fashion photographer Valerie Phillips for the cover of what was their eighth studio album

MANIC STREET PREACHERS
SEND AWAY THE TIGERS

Newburgh
The Folk Music Hall of Fame

At the time of writing there is no bricks and mortar Folk Music Hall of Fame Music Center but the building could be a reality by the time you're reading this. The set-up is a non-profit educational, literary, cultural corporation dedicated to the promotion and preservation of traditional, contemporary, and international folk music.

Location 438: Newburgh is 60 miles north of New York City. The FMHF will be housed at 63 Liberty Street, Newburgh, NY 10550

New York City/ Manhattan
Neil Young's After the Gold Rush cover

The memorable solarized cover photo on Neil Young's After the Gold Rush album was shot by Joel Bernstein and art directed by Gary Burden in 1970. As they went about their photo shoot, first in nearby Washington Square Park, Bernstein spotted his photo opportunity. Just as Young was walking down Sullivan Street the 18-year-old photographer caught sight of a tiny old lady headed in the opposite direction and waited until both figures passed each other, capturing one of rock's enduring images. Interestingly, the uncropped photo shot by Bernstein shows fellow musician and enthusiastic photographer Graham Nash in the foreground, looking on.

Location 442: thanks to detailed detective work by Bob Egan of the PopSpots website it is clear that this Neil Young cover was photographed against the bricks and railings on Sullivan Street, where it meets West 3rd Street in Greenwich Village, NY 10012

The cover solarization was added by photographer Joel Bernstein to disguise the slight lack of sharpness in capturing the moment Neil Young and the little old lady passed each other

New York City/Manhattan
Joe Strummer's mural

A colorful memorial to the late great Joe Strummer appears as a mural on the wall of the Niagara bar in East Village. The former vocalist, with The Clash, the guitarist and songwriter was originally immortalized in this spot by graffiti artists Dr. Revolt and Zephyr in 2003. Remarkably, the artwork has remained largely untroubled by any damage, although additional artistic touches have been added over time, such as the New York skyline landscape behind Strummer.

Location 443: the East Village Niagara bar is on the corner of 7th Street at 112 Avenue A, NY 10009

Remembering Joe: the mural on the busy street intersection in East Village

New York

New York City/Manhattan
Leonard Cohen's 'Chelsea Hotel'

The Chelsea Hotel (or Hotel Chelsea as the sign says) is where Leonard Cohen lived when in New York. It's also where he had an affair with fellow resident guest Janis Joplin, the subject of his song 'Chelsea Hotel #2.' Co-written with guitarist Ron Cornelius, the track was included on Cohen's 1974 album New Skin for the Old Ceremony. Sadly, as all hotels do, it has had its fair share of deaths: this is where Welsh writer Dylan Thomas died of pneumonia and where Sex Pistols' band member Sid Vicious's girlfriend Nancy Spungen was infamously stabbed to death. On a more positive note, Arthur C. Clarke wrote 2001: A Space Odyssey here and few hotels have been eulogized in song quite so much with Bob Dylan ('Sara'), Graham Nash ('The Chelsea Hotel'), Ryan Adams ('Hotel Chelsea Nights') all name checking the place that was a magnate for creative types.

❝It was a wonderful place you know. You could come up to the reception desk there with three naked women a bear and a midget and they wouldn't even raise an eyebrow, just hand you your key and say, "Good night Sir"❞

Leonard Cohen recalls his stays at Hotel Chelsea

Location 444: north of Lower Manhattan and Greenwich Village at 222 West 23rd Street, between Seventh and Eighth Avenues, Chelsea, NY 10011. At the time of writing the Hotel Chelsea was closed but this magnificent building is still definitely worth gawping at from the outside

Photographer Robert Scanlon's pictures looking in and outside the hotel that not only attracted rock and roll residents and guests but featured in the songs they wrote about the place

New York City/Manhattan
Dylan on 'Positively 4th Street'

The exact address of Bob Dylan's home at 'Positively 4th Street' was 161 West 4th Street, in Greenwich Village. But whether that's what the title of his 1965 single referred to is anyone's guess. Perhaps the song does draw a line under the criticism Dylan suffered from his folk fan base, who felt betrayed by him at the time, and 4th Street became a symbol of a period in his life he wanted to turn his back on. What's certainly true is that No.161 was the tiny apartment above Bruno's Spaghetti Shop he first rented in 1961 when starting to slowly make an impact on the Greenwich Village folk scene. It was at the club called Gerde's Folk City, formerly at 11 West 4th Street, that he made his professional debut.

Location 445: Dylan's apartment was on the top floor at 161 West 4th Street, Greenwich Village, NY 10014

New York City/Manhattan
Foghat's East Village fishing trip

Although appearing to feel quite at home, when British rock band Foghat moved to New York City in 1975, the band's drummer Roger Earl obviously missed the more rural pursuits such as fishing. For the cover of their 1975 platinum album Fool for the City, Earl is pictured fishing in an open manhole on a seemingly deserted street in the East Village.

Location 446: position yourself outside #292 East 11th Street (the manhole is still there) and you get the same view as on the Foghat cover, East Village, NY 10003

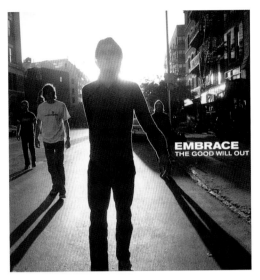

New York City/Manhattan
Embrace snapped in the street

British band Embrace walk down a sunlit West Village street on the cover of their 1998 debut album The Good Will Out.

Location 447: outside the Church of St. Veronica, 149-153 Christopher Street, West Village, New York City, NY 10014

New York City/Manhattan
Paul Simon: 'Feelin' Groovy'

Ever wondered what Simon & Garfunkel were singing about on their 1967 song 'The 59th Street Bridge Song (Feelin' Groovy)'? Well, as many New Yorkers will know, the "bridge" is actually the Queensboro Bridge. And the 'Feelin' Groovy' vibe? The story goes that Paul Simon wrote this upbeat song after returning home to Manhattan across the bridge early one June morning on a really good day. He felt so good about life that he immediately set to work writing what eventually became 'The 59th Street Bridge Song (Feelin' Groovy),' which turned out to be a big hit for Californian outfit Harpers Bizarre enhanced by an arrangement from Leon Russell.

Location 448: pick a stunningly beautiful early morning and travel across the Queensboro Bridge, NY 10044

Tony Loew's photo of fisherman and drummer Roger Earl

New York

New York City/ Manhattan
The Village Vanguard

A mecca for jazz fans since 1935, the Village Vanguard club may not cater much for rock fans but up to 1957 it promoted a wide range of music which would see appearances by country-blues artists such as Lead Belly and folk performers like Pete Seeger. Jazz musicians maintain that one of the secrets of the Village Vanguard's success is the unusual shape of the room and the triangle-type corner where bands set up to let the outstanding acoustics enhance performances. Give your ears a refreshing change and give it a go.

Location 449: the club is at 178 7th Avenue South, Greenwich Village, NY 10014

New York City/ Manhattan
An 'Englishman in New York'

The character Sting was referring to when he wrote and recorded his hit single 'Englishman in New York' was a mixture of himself and the writer and actor Quentin Crisp. The song, which first appeared on the former Police man's 1987 album … Nothing Like the Sun, describes the "illegal alien" and gay eccentric Crisp as he walks Fifth Avenue close to where he set up home in a studio apartment in the Bowery, following his arrival from England aged 72.

Location 450: Quentin Crisp's former home was his apartment at 46 East Third Street, NY 10003

THE FREEWHEELIN' BOB DYLAN

Blowin' in the Wind
Girl From the North Country
Masters of War
Down the Highway
Bob Dylan's Blues
A Hard Rain's-A-Gonna Fall

Don't Think Twice, It's All Right
Bob Dylan's Dream
Oxford Town
Talkin' World War III Blues
Corrina, Corrina
Honey, Just Allow Me One More Chance
I Shall Be Free

New York City/Manhattan
Freewheelin' on Jones Street

Every classic album should have an equally classic cover image and Bob Dylan's Freewheelin' definitely ticks both boxes. Columbia Records photographer Don Hunstein captures the vibe of the album, released in May 1963, perfectly. Un-posed and seemingly carefree and casual, Dylan and girlfriend Suze Rotolo are pictured out wandering the Greenwich Village streets round the corner from their West 4th Street apartment. Carefree they might have been but Rotolo remembered how she'd dressed up to beat the cold. It was a snowy February photo shoot and because Dylan was conscious of his image, he simply wore a thin jacket. By contrast, Rotolo, having wrapped up in several layers including one of Dylan's big, bulky sweaters, thought she looked fat. Perhaps it was all part of Dylan's diffident plan to make his girl cling closer to him in a loving hug.

Location 451: best to visit this iconic spot in winter when the leaves on the trees don't obscure the Freewheelin' view which had Bob and Suze walking northeast up Jones Street to West 4th Street, Greenwich Village, NY 10014

A cold February day as dusk falls in Greenwich Village. Photographer Don Hunstein had exhausted all the options of an indoor shot at the couple's apartment, so they decided to walk round the block and one of popular music's best-loved album cover images was captured

A KNOCK OUT! A HIGH
ENERGY EVENING!
...THE BEST POSSIBLE
SHOW! —— N Y Post

Photo by Robert Scanlon/afghaniscan.com

Welcoming sign: the 250-capacity Cafe Wha?, a key home of the 1960s folk movement and a favorite haunt of Bob Dylan and his extended entourage

New York City/Manhattan
Greenwich Village's Cafe Wha?

It was something of a family affair when David Lee Roth played a special pre-tour warm-up gig with Van Halen at Greenwich Village's Cafe Wha? in 2012. The vocalist's uncle was present at the gig in the legendary rock venue, which was fitting as it was Manny Lee Roth who owned the place back in the 1960s. Cafe Wha? has impeccable rock and roll credentials having hosted Bob Dylan, Jimi Hendrix, and Bruce Springsteen, and a bunch of other big performers at the small street corner basement. Although the name and clientele changed during the 70s and 80s the club got its "Cafe Wha?" name and rock audiences back again in 1987 and today it promises to wow 21st century music fans with three of the greatest house bands in New York City.

Location 452: Cafe Wha? is on the corner of MacDougal Street and Minetta Lane at 115 MacDougal Street in Greenwich Village, NY 10012

❝This is a temple. This is a very special place and I am more nervous about this gig than I would ever be at the [Madison Square] Garden. There is no hiding up here. There are no fake vocals. There is no fake anything ❞

David Lee Roth describes Cafe Wha? to The New York Times

New York

New York City/ Manhattan
The Physical Graffiti building

The building pictured on the cover of Led Zeppelin album Physical Graffiti is in East Village. Designer Peter Corriston reportedly spent weeks trying to find the perfect place for his concept of a cover with multiple windows, each revealing letters forming the title of the 1975 album. The tenement block was the same location Mick Jagger and Keith Richards (with a guest appearance by Peter Tosh) used for The Rolling Stones video accompanying their 1981 hit 'Waiting on a Friend.' Currently, part of this building (the basement of No. 96 St. Marks Place) is a tea room with enough rock and roll memorabilia on the walls to confirm you are in the right vicinity. As if there was any doubt: this establishment is called Physical GraffiTea!

Location 454: 96 and 98 St. Mark's Place, East Village, NY 10009

New York City/Manhattan
The Beastie Boys create Paul's Boutique

The current Three Monkeys bar in the Lower East Side was formerly Paul's Boutique, the title and street corner location of the Beastie Boys' Paul's Boutique album cover photo. The Beastie Boys had the sign made and sourced all the clothing that appeared on the cover - almost everything, even the banjo, came from their own homes. There never was a 'real' Paul's Boutique on this corner at the time of the cover shoot, but restaurant owners cashed in by changing the name once the album made an impact until renaming it The Three Monkeys. The Paul's Boutique name did, however, come from a real Brooklyn clothing business the band heard advertized on a local radio station by deep-voiced DJ Bill Bailey. The 1989 album was a slow burner but was awarded double platinum sales status a decade later.

Location 453: Paul's Boutique became The Three Monkeys in 2007 at 99 Rivington, on the corner of Ludlow Street, Lower East Side, NY 10002

Beastie Boys Michael "Mike D" Diamond, Adam "MCA" Yauch, and Adam "Ad-Rock" Horovitz appear on the inside album cover's 360-degree panoramic street shot. They used the contents of their own homes for the front cover

Right: take tea while 'Waiting on a Friend' at the address made famous on the Led Zeppelin Physical Graffiti album cover

Photo by Robert Scanlon/afghaniscan.com

New York

New York City/ Manhattan

Bob eclipses Bruce at Max's Kansas City

Established in 1965, Max's Kansas City at 213 Park Avenue South was a favorite venue for New York City artists, writers, and glam-rock musicians to eat, drink and play. Andy Warhol, David Bowie, Iggy Pop, and Lou Reed were regulars in the early 1970s but the wider circle of celebrated rock stars also frequented the place. What a night July 18th 1973 must have been Upstairs at Max's Kansas City when Bruce Springsteen gigged here, supported by Bob Marley and The Wailers. The two acts stayed for a 14-night residency and Marley and co. (newly smuggled in from Jamaica and making their New York debut) are reported to have sensationally eclipsed the performances of local boy Bruce. Around this time, punters could well have been served by waitress Debbie Harry, who would also turn performer with Blondie at Max's after she and Chris Stein had first met when Harry's band The Stilettos played their debut gig at the tiny Boburn Tavern on 24th Street. Max's was also where Aerosmith made their New York performance debut, encouraging a watching Clive Davis to sign the band to the Columbia label, and where The Velvet Underground were recorded on a tiny mono cassette recorder with handheld

microphone for what ended up as their 1972 'Live at Max's Kansas City' album. By 1975, with new ownership and the emphasis switched to punk, a new Max's opened on the same site promoting the Sex Pistols, the Ramones, Talking Heads, Television and Blondie. When the newly-formed Beastie Boys (supporting Bad Brains) played this venue's closing night in 1981, Max's wasn't quite finished. When the third Max's opened in 1998, taking over the old Village Gate, the revival was quickly ended. The place still

hosts the same kind of activities, but it is not Max's.

❝WAILERS SERVE UP GENUINE REGGAY❞

New York Times headline accompanying the review of the Springsteen/Bob Marley shows at Max's Kansas City

Locations 455 and 456: the first Max's was at 213 Park Avenue South on 17th Street, Gramercy Park, NY 10003. The second Max's was at 240 West 52nd Street, Midtown, NY 10019

THE VELVET UNDERGROUND LIVE AT MAX'S KANSAS CITY
Featuring: Lou Reed, Doug Yule, Billy Yule, Sterling Morrison

The Max's Kansas City 'house band's' live album featured the club on the cover

New York City/ Manhattan
The world famous CBGB

When club manager Hilly Kristal opened Hilly's on the Bowery in 1970 it made little impact and less money, but the new club that he created at the intersection of Bowery and Bleecker Street became just about the hottest nightclub in New York City. CBGB would become the place to perform and be seen by punk and new wave's movers and shakers, but when it opened for business for the first time in 1973 it was envisioned, as the acronym suggests, as a Country, BlueGrass, and Blues establishment. The second part of the club's title was OMFUG, which stood for "Other Music For Uplifting Gormandizers" but the length of its name meant that the club was more often than not affectionately called "CB's." New talent showcased at the bar were encouraged to play original material and covers were pretty much banned – partly to nurture developing musicians and partly to avoid the club paying royalty checks to ASCAP. The plan worked, and an underground scene of new music involving bands such as Television, The Stilettos (with Debbie Harry), the Ramones, and Talking Heads meant that CBGB had not only a prominent New York profile but an international one as the new wave scene revolved around the club. In addition to the live music, the venue opened a record shop and café next door at CBGB Record Canteen. Sadly, closure of CBGB came via a property rental dispute in 2006. What followed was a wave of nostalgia for a much-loved New York icon, generated by a final-

Bob Gruen

week performance from Blondie and a last-night gig from Patti Smith and various guests on October 15th 2006. The building still stands but the famous red and white out front entrance awning is now preserved in Cleveland's Rock and Roll Hall of Fame and Museum. Look out for the street sign marking Joey Ramone Place outside the former club entrance. Ramone was honored with the sign two years after his death in 2001. Aside from his connections to CBGB, the Ramones vocalist lived nearby for a time in the same apartment block with the band's bass player Dee Dee Ramone.

It's a birthplace. It's like a big womb here. It's very primitive, very primal

Joey Ramone explains what CBGB means to him in a 1994 Rolling Stone interview

Locations 457 and 458: the CBGB address is 315 Bowery, at the intersection with the eastern end of Bleecker Street, Bowery, NY 10003. Just head for the building across the street with the familiar (but not original) curved awning. Fans searching for the Joey Ramone Place street sign will have to crane their necks. A much stolen piece of rock memorabilia, it has now been moved 20 feet off the ground to avoid constant replacement at its position at Bowery and East 2nd Street, close to CBGB and the apartment he shared at 6 East 2nd Street, NY 10003

Deborah Harry was present at the beginning and the end of CBGB

New York

New York City/ Manhattan
Fred Neil on Bleecker & MacDougal

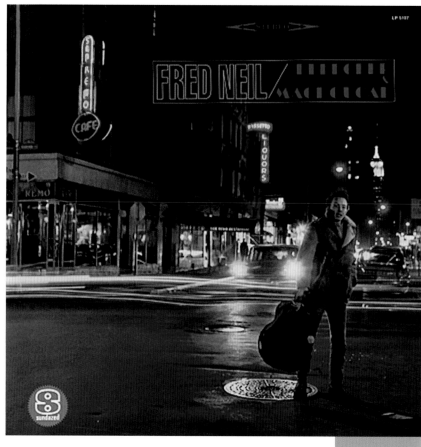

Fred Neil's influential Bleecker & MacDougal album carried a photo on the cover of the Ohio-born singer-songwriter shot at the intersection of two streets (Bleecker Street and MacDougal Street). Although not a commercial success when first released in 1965, Neil's album was an early inspiration to many budding songwriters and musicians at the time and earned a re-issue under new title Little Bit of Rain in 1970. In addition, 'Bleecker Street' was one of a batch of three songs that Paul Simon wrote and first showed Art Garfunkel that ended up on the duo's debut album Wednesday Morning, 3 AM. The cover of the 1964 LP was shot at the Fifth Avenue and 53rd Street subway station.

Locations 459 and 460: Fred Neil's album cover location is at the junction of Bleecker Street and MacDougal Street, Greenwich Village, NY 10012 (the manhole covers on the photograph are a clue to the exact spot). The Simon and Garfunkel album cover shot was snapped at Fifth Avenue and 53rd Street Subway Station, north of Bleecker Street and a few blocks south of Central Park, NY 10022

Looking the part: midnight cowboy Fred Neil at the crossroads

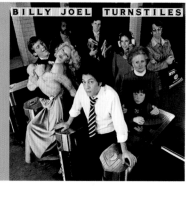

Billy Joel, accompanied by an assortment of characters assembled at Astor Place to represent each one of the songs on Turnstiles

New York City/Manhattan
Billy Joel's Turnstiles

The 'turnstiles' featured on the front and back of Billy Joel's 1976 album of that name are at subway station Astor Place, a structure now on the List of Registered Historic Places in New York City. Joel is pictured standing on the uptown side of the station at a spot just feet from where Paul Simon was photographed seven years later for inside cover shots for his 1983 Hearts and Bones album.

Location 461: the Astor Place subway station is at Astor Place (8th Street and Fourth Avenue), Lower Manhattan, NY 10003

New York City/Manhattan
The Highway 61 Revisited cover

Featuring one of Bob Dylan's familiar penetrating stares, the picture that would later wind up on the Highway 61 Revisited album cover leaves an indelible impression. Daniel Kramer's photograph of Dylan was captured on the steps in front of Dylan's manager Albert Grossman's apartment in Gramercy Park. The apartment was a couple of miles south of the Columbia Records studio on 7th Avenue where Highway 61 Revisited – Dylan's famous departure from acoustic into his mostly electric homage to the blues – was recorded in the summer of 1965.

Locations 462 and 463: Albert Grossman's apartment was at 4 Gramercy Park West, NY 10003. Studio A at the Columbia Records studios was on the seventh floor at 799 7th Avenue (on the southeast corner of 52nd Street), NY 10019, but is no more

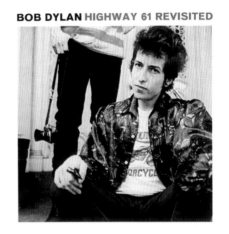

BOB DYLAN HIGHWAY 61 REVISITED

Dylan and friend (Bob Neuwirth) with camera, snapped out front of Albert Grossman's apartment

New York City/Manhattan
Jeff Buckley's home from home

The Irish-owned Sin-é coffee house was where Jeff Buckley (son of singer-songwriter Tim Buckley, who had also played the venue) first made an impact in 1992. His early gigs were performed there amid the clatter of coffee cups, with no stage and often just his guitar a microphone, and amp for company. Sin-é became a real home from home for Buckley. Nurtured by the regular customers and encouraged by the informal surroundings, when he wasn't performing he still hung out at Sin-é, drinking coffee and practicing his next set. With its Celtic connections, owners Shane Doyle and Karl Geary managed to persuade some familiar Irish faces to perform from time to time. Sinéad O'Connor and The Pogues' vocalist, Shane MacGowan, are reported to have given impromptu performances and U2 checked out the place when working in New York City. Opened in 1989, the club moved to larger premises in Williamsburg, Brooklyn, in 2000 and then over to a place on the Lower East Side before shutting for the last time in 2007.

Location 464: although the original Sin-é is no more, the building still stands at 122 St. Mark's Place, East Village, NY 10009

New York City/Manhattan
'The Killing of Georgie' at '53rd & 3rd'

The Ramones song from their eponymously titled debut album '53rd & 3rd' describes a male prostitution hotspot! Although the area around this intersection has changed architecturally since Dee Dee Ramone wrote the song in 1976, the activities he wrote about still remain. It's not the only song with a knife attack at this spot as its theme. Coincidentally, Rod Stewart's powerful song 'The Killing of Georgie (Part I and II)' written describing a gay friend of his who is murdered in a gang attack, was also penned in 1976. Stewart's lyrics for the song he wrote for his A Night on the Town LP describe the murder and emergency of the situation, where "an ambulance screamed to a halt on 53rd and 3rd."

Location 465: as the Ramones, debut album track and the Rod Stewart song says: 53rd Street and 3rd Avenue, Midtown, NY 10022

New York City/Manhattan
Sid Vicious lived and died here

On bail following girlfriend Nancy Spungen's death, Sex Pistols bass guitarist Sid Vicious died at his home here in the West Village. His death, aged just 21, was attributed to a heroin overdose on February 1st 1979.

Location 466: the infamous Sid Vicious apartment was at 63 Bank Street, West Village, NY 10014

New York

New York City/Manhattan
The Bitter End

One of quite a number of intimate, famous Greenwich Village clubs, The Bitter End has one big claim to fame as New York City's oldest rock club – established 1961. Managed and owned by Paul Colby, The Bitter End has nurtured the talents of hundreds of musicians and comedians down the years. The familiar red brick interior has been a backdrop to performances by established talents – Bob Dylan's Rolling Thunder Revue came together here in 1975 - and those building experience like the 14-year-old Lady Gaga, who began with open mic nights here before the place became something of a home base for her between 2005 and 2007. To give some idea of the breadth of music genres catered for down the years, Bill Haley, Randy Newman, Curtis Mayfield, Peter, Paul & Mary, Donny Hathaway, and Pete Seeger are just some of the artists to have recorded live albums at The Bitter End. Big names return from time to time to play in front of a couple of hundred fans, which is exactly what Neil Diamond did at a "secret gig" in 2008 which was broadcast to a wider audience courtesy of speakers out on Bleecker Street.

Location 467: The Bitter End is sandwiched in between the Peculiar Pub and Terra Blues at 147 Bleecker Street, Greenwich Village, NY 10012

Ari Michelson

Above and below left: Neil Diamond outside and inside The Bitter End on the occasion of his 'secret gig'

Below: The Bitter End was an early career home base for Lady Gaga

Ari Michelson

New York City/ Manhattan
Electric Lady Studios

When Jimi Hendrix and his manager Michael Jeffery purchased the Generation Club (formerly the basement nightclub Village Barn) in Greenwich Village it was with the intention of reopening it as a nightspot. The pair quickly changed their plans and decided to create a purpose-built recording studio to exactly meet the legendary guitarist's requirements. By the summer of 1970 the place, kitted out with the latest recording equipment, was ready for business and artist Lance Jost was commissioned to apply the finishing touch – a vast space-themed mural. But Jimi Hendrix would barely get any return on his investment. He managed just four weeks recording there prior to his tragic death in September that same year. The studio did become a popular haunt for a number of big-name bands in the wake of Hendrix's death. Patti Smith's

A collage of Lance Jost's mural inside Electric Lady Studios

Horses (1975), David Bowie tracks 'Fame' and 'Across the Universe,' with John Lennon (for his 1975 Young Americans album), parts of Stevie Wonder's Talking Book (1972), The Rolling Stones' Some Girls (1978), Led Zeppelin's Houses of the Holy (1973) and Physical Graffiti (1975), and AC/DC's Back in Black (1980) were all recorded and/ or mixed here. As popular as ever, Radiohead, Coldplay, Kings of Leon, and Foo Fighters have all worked at Electric Lady Studios in recent times, possibly drawn to the place

❛Thanks to surf pioneer Mike Hynson of The Endless Summer fame, I was commissioned in 1970 by Michael Jeffery, Jimi Hendrix's manager, to create an album cover for the European rock group Moon. Delivering the artwork on July 25th to Jimi's roadie, Gerry Stickells, at a Hendrix concert in San Diego, my imagery of space obviously struck a chord with Jimi, enough for him to request that I paint a mural in his Electric Lady recording studio in New York City. Finally packing my paint brushes on September 19th 1970 to head east and begin work on the mural, imagine my shock when I heard through a friend that Jimi had died the day before in London ❜

Lance Jost

in a respectful attempt to conjure up the spirit of Jimi Hendrix.

Location 468: Electric Lady Studios still operate today at 52 West 8th Street, Greenwich Village, NY 10011

New York City/Manhattan
Tom Waits' Empire Diner cover

The beautiful 50s-style Empire Diner dominates the cover of the 1986 Tom Waits compilation album Asylum Years.

Location 469: currently closed as an eatery (Madonna and Barbra Streisand once dined here), but the iconic building remains at 210 10th Avenue (between 22nd Street and 23rd Street), NY 10011

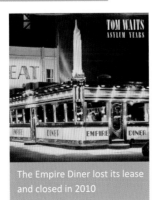

The Empire Diner lost its lease and closed in 2010

New York City/Manhattan
Dave Matthews Band album cover

The album cover for the Dave Matthews Band 1998 chart-topper Before These Crowded Streets was photographed on the rather empty streets of New York City, in the shadow of the Empire State Building.

Location 470: 39th Street and 5th Avenue, NY 10018, would appear to be the spot, but the skyline is ever

changing and has altered much since 1998

New York

The front and back covers of Strange Days, photographed by Joel Brodsky using locals modeling as circus and show performers in Sniffen Court

New York City/Manhattan
The Doors' 'Strange Days' alley

Seemingly inspired by the 1954 Frederico Fellini movie La Strada, The Doors rounded up an assortment of locals and photographed them in the narrow alley at Sniffen Court, Murray Hill, for the cover of their 1967 album Strange Days. The alley is little-changed since the 1960s – even some of the wall art remains. Aside from its rock and roll connections the alley (formerly stables for wealthy local residents) is a rather beautiful little spot, protected but not obscured by some equally impressive wrought iron gates.

Location 471: a private alley, Sniffen Court is in the Murray Hill neighborhood, 150–158 East 36th Street, NY 10016

New York City/Manhattan
The Record Plant and Birdland

The Record Plant recording studios in New York City was the first (in 1968) of the three famous studios of that name to open for business. The L.A. and Sausalito branches opened in 1969 and 1972 respectively and feature in the California pages of Rock Atlas. All three facilities were part of the new more laid back method of recording which also pushed the boundaries technologically in the early rock album boom years around this time. In its first year the New York Record Plant created the perfect environment for the recording of The Jimi Hendrix Experience's Electric Ladyland album. Other significant recording projects that followed included the Record Plant mixing tracks from the Woodstock Festival for soundtrack release, the live onsite capturing of George Harrison's Madison Square Garden Concert For Bangladesh, the recording of Bruce Springsteen's seminal LP Born To Run and the best-selling KISS album, Destroyer. Two rather final Beatles-related Record Plant footnotes: John Lennon was working on new recordings here the day he left for home and was murdered outside his apartment at the Dakota Building and his producer, when in The Beatles, George Martin headed up the Chrysalis Studio Group which owned the place briefly in 1987 before the facility closed soon after. Next to the old Record Plant Studios on West 44th Street is the third and current home of Birdland, the legendary jazz club that got its name from saxophonist Charlie "Bird" Parker. Established in 1949 and still thriving today, it justifiably calls itself The "Jazz Corner of the World".

Locations 472 and 473: about a half mile south of Central Park the Record Plant building still stands at 321 West 44th Street, NY 10036. Next door, still going strong, is Birdland at 315 West 44th Street, NY 10036

New York City/ Manhattan
The Brill Building

The beautiful Brill Building is the place where teams of prolific songwriters met the needs of an escalating demand for new material once the teenage hunger for pop songs became insatiable in the 1950s and early 1960s. Here, publishing firm Aldon Music, formed by Al Nevins and Don Kirshner, employed young writing partnerships Gerry Goffin and Carole King, Howard Greenfield and Neil Sedaka, and many more. Aside from the almost factory-like song-writing production line, the Brill Building's 11 floors housed what was a center for all aspects of the music business during this period. At the height of its success this one location (which was augmented by additional offices a block away at 1650 Broadway) had more than 160 separate music businesses operating at the same time. The musical production line was still just about holding its own in 1969 when Walter Becker and Donald Fagen arrived to add their names to the illustrious list of song writing partnerships that had gone before. They learned more than they made financially and witnessed and participated in the massive music business shift to the West Coast in the early seventies, a switch that saw the duo gain much success as Steely Dan. For the Brill Building, its period of dominance as the home of teenage expression had ended with the emergence of new song-writing talent that recorded his or her own material.

❝Every day we squeezed into our respective cubby holes with just enough room for a piano, a bench, and maybe a chair for the lyricist❞

Carole King

Location 474: a couple of blocks north of Times Square, the still opulent-looking entrance to the Brill Building is at 1619 Broadway on 49th Street, NY 10019

The Brill Building was so called due to the fact that Brill Brothers' clothing store originally occupied the street-level frontage of this magnificent Art Deco structure

Peter Downham

New York

New York City/ Manhattan
Lady Gaga's childhood temple

Fittingly, Lady Gaga's Upper West Side childhood home was no ordinary house. The Pythian Temple, with its mix of Art Deco and Egyptian-style architecture, was where the singer-songwriter (real name Stefani Germanotta) lived with her parents in a triplex apartment complete with terrace from the age of nine. And the flamboyant building had rock and roll history long before Gaga's residency. When the Pythian Temple had a recording facility based here, Buddy Holly, Sammy Davis Jr., and Billie Holiday used the huge auditorium converted by Decca Records, and in 1954 this is where Bill Haley and His Comets cut tracks for one of rock's milestone albums, Rock Around the Clock.

Location 475: the Pythian Temple is at 135 West 70th Street, Upper West Side, NY 10023

Martin Downham

Buddy Holly, Bill Haley, Sammy Davis Jr., and Billie Holiday all passed through the grand entrance to what would later be the front door to Lady Gaga's childhood home

Recorded in the Pythian Temple's Decca studio: the record that shook, rattled, and rolled popular music in the mid-fifties

New York City/Manhattan
U2 Way – on Broadway

Irish rock band U2 already had a strong affinity with New York City before the release of 2009 album No Line on the Horizon. The trio's two-way love affair with the city reached new heights when they guested during a week's consecutive TV appearances on David Letterman's Late Show in March 2009. To mark the event on Broadway, Mayor Michael Bloomberg honored Bono, The Edge, Adam Clayton, and Larry Mullen by temporarily re-naming a stretch of West 53rd Street U2 Way.

The Beatles had Penny Lane, Elvis had Lonely Street, and now we have the street between 10th Avenue and funky, funky Broadway

Bono

Location 476: don't go hunting for it now … the unveiling of the U2 Way sign, attended by the band, was at the junction of West 53rd Street and Broadway, NY 10019. The sign and honor lasted just one week.

New York City/Manhattan
The 2000 Oasis album cover

One of the finest views of the New York City skyline graces the cover of the 2000 album by Oasis. The Standing on the Shoulder of Giants final cover shot is a composite of a number of photos taken over an 18-hour period from the top of the Rockefeller Center looking towards the Empire State.

Location 478: Top of the Rock at the Rockefeller Center, 30 Rockefeller Plaza, Entrance on 50th Street between 5th & 6th Avenues, NY 10112

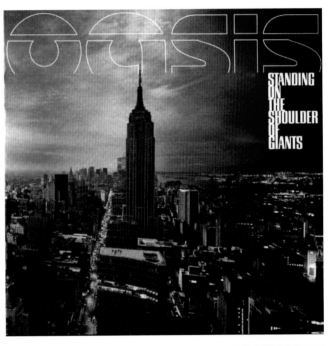

New York City/Manhattan
Suzanne Vega at 'Tom's Diner'

Singer-songwriter Suzanne Vega wrote her 1981 composition 'Tom's Diner' while sat at a table at Tom's Restaurant in Morningside Heights. She formed her song story over a cup of coffee while reading a copy of the New York Post. The nearby Cathedral of St. John the Divine prompted the line about "the bells of the cathedral" and the midnight picnic she wrote about was something Vega had once experienced on the steps of the same building. The song only became a huge hit when British music producer duo DNA remixed the track, featuring Vega's vocals added to a lively Soul II Soul dance beat injection. The outside of the diner will look familiar to fans of TV's Seinfeld. Tom's Restaurant represents the fictional establishment, Monk's Café, in the long-running show.

tom's diner

Suzanne Vega's favorite place for breakfast was the inspiration behind her song

Location 477: Suzanne Vega's favorite diner is in the Morningside Heights neighborhood. Look for Tom's Restaurant at 2880 Broadway, on the corner of 112th Street, NY 10025

New York

New York City/ Manhattan
John Lennon's Dakota apartment

The Dakato has been home to Leonard Bernstein, Rosemary Clooney, and Roberta Flack but its most famous residents have been John Lennon and Yoko Ono. Subletting two apartments on the seventh floor when they moved from The Vilage in 1973, they eventually purchased other apartments, running their business affairs from the Studio One apartment on the ground floor. Tragically, the Dakota is where Lennon was murdered on December 8th 1980. Returning home from a late night recording session at the nearby Record Plant studio, he was approached by Mark Chapman who shot the former Beatle five times. Lennon was able to stagger to the Dakota's security office, scattering the cassette tapes he'd been carrying. Despite efforts to save him by doctors at the local Roosevelt Hospital, his injuries were too serious and he died shortly after 11. pm.

Location 479: the Dakota Building overlooks Central Park at 1 West 72nd Street, NY 10023

John and Yoko lived at Apartment 72, at the very top corner of the Dakota Building, which was constructed between 1880 and 1884. Lennon's murder at the Dakota on December 8th 1980 occurred just three weeks after the release of Double Fantasy, which became a US and UK chart-topper and Album of the Year at the 1982 Grammy Awards

Martin Downham

16-page pullout on John Lennon's life

John Lennon   Double Fantasy   Yoko Ono

DAILY●NEWS
Tonight
Killer stalked him 3 days

EXCLUSIVE: Lennon & suspect

Remembering John: a favorite spot in Central Park for local residents John and Yoko is marked by this Strawberry Fields memorial. Dedicated in 1985, the area features this mosaic designed by artists from the Italian city of Naples

Martin Downham

New York City/Manhattan
Strawberry Fields Garden of Peace

After John Lennon's murder outside the Dakota Building where he lived, a memorial to the former Beatle was created across the street in Central Park. Funded by wife Yoko Ono and referencing two of Lennon's best-loved songs, the memorial includes a landscaped area of the park named Strawberry Fields which features a large circular mosaic with the single word 'Imagine' in the center. This spot has become a much-visited place of pilgrimage where Lennon and Beatles anniversaries are celebrated, and those of other fondly remembered musicians.

Location 480: the 2.5-acre Strawberry Fields area is near Central Park West, between 71st and 74th Streets, NY 10023

New York City/Manhattan
Harlem's Apollo Theater

Harlem's renaissance is in full swing they say. The neighborhood is looking pretty good these days, and at the heart of it is the world famous Apollo Theater. It's an institution that knows its own value in the wider scheme of things and plans are already underway to collect together memorabilia and documents associated with its glorious history as part of the Apollo Theater Archive Project. Familiar to all Americans as the home of the long-running TV variety series Showtime at the Apollo, this old building has helped provide just about every black music legend with their introduction to the stage – even Jimi Hendrix won

an amateur night contest here in 1964. In a precursor to the 21st century reality TV talent shows, a feature of the Apollo during Amateur Nights was the top-hatted man, "The Executioner," who would remove performers from the stage if the noisy Apollo audience disapproved of them. It is unlikely James Brown ever suffered this indignity. Few performers have had a more obvious association with the Apollo. His seminal album, Live at the Apollo, recorded at the theater in 1962 and released a year later, was a huge success. He followed it up with Volume II, released after a second live performance here in 1967. When he died in 2006 his

body was transferred to the Apollo stage, where he lay in state in an open gold casket. Vast crowds queued to file past and pay their last respects to "The Godfather of Soul" who had made his debut in exactly the same spot 50 years earlier.

❝Our whole [Kick out the Jams] thing was based on James Brown. We listened to Live at the Apollo endlessly on acid❞

MC5 guitarist Wayne Kramer

Location 481: the Apollo is less than a mile north of Central Park at 253 West 125th Street, Harlem, NY 10027

The signs above Harlem's world famous temple of entertainment, which began its life as a burlesque theater in the early 20th century before becoming the Apollo Theater in 1934

New York City/ Manhattan
'Spanish Harlem' and 'Angel of Harlem'

'Spanish Harlem' and 'Angel of Harlem' are two big hit songs associated with the East Harlem area of northeastern Manhattan. 'Spanish Harlem,' written by Jerry Leiber and Phil Spector and produced by Leiber and Mike Stoller, was first made famous by Ben E. King, who grew up in Harlem from the age of nine. Of the many subsequent covers, Aretha Franklin's, a decade later, has been the most commercially popular. Her version became a million-seller following its release in 1971. Harlem was also where the legendary jazz singer and songwriter Billie Holiday spent her teenage years and first began performing in and around Harlem at the Alhambra Bar and Grill, the Bright Spot, Brooklyn Elks Club and, significantly, Covan's on West 132nd Street, where producer John Hammond first heard her. Impressed, he arranged Holiday's first recording session, teaming her up with Benny Goodman which gave the Philadelphia-born singer her first modest hit. Billie Holiday had obviously made quite an impression on U2. The Irish band's 1988 'Angel of Harlem' hit single documented Holiday's hard life in addition to name-checking NYC landmarks and Holiday's fellow jazz greats Miles Davis and John Coltrane.

Location 482: Spanish Harlem, Harlem, or East Harlem is north of Central Park in northeastern Manhattan, NY 10035

Photo by Robert Scanlon/afghaniscan.com

New York

The kids are asleep: The Who were snapped against this stone memorial, a photo that would later appear on the album and movie packaging for The Kids Are Alright

New York City/Manhattan
The Who asleep at Morningside Heights

The Who soundtrack double album, The Kids Are Alright, has a cover shot at the Carl Schurz Monument in Morningside Heights. The band were pictured in 1979, apparently asleep in front of a stone bass relief tableau high up on the memorial site by photographer Art Kane.

Location 483: the memorial is at Morningside Park at West 116th Street and Morningside Drive, Morningside Heights, NY 10027

New York City/Manhattan
Duke Ellington's statue

The Washington D.C.-born band leader Duke Ellington, who died aged 75 in 1974, is remembered by a statue in Central Park situated close to the imposing red brick townhouse he lived in for many years on the corner of Riverside Drive and West 106th Street. The work of sculptor Robert Graham, the striking piece has Ellington elevated on three tall columns supporting the figure of the band leader standing next to his piano.

Locations 484, 485, and 486: a mini Duke Ellington tour could take in the corner of Manhattan's Riverside Drive and West 106th Street where he lived, NY 10025, the street renamed for him as Duke Ellington Boulevard (formerly West 106th Street), NY 10025, and the Central Park memorial to Ellington which is near Fifth Avenue and 110th Street, NY 10029, an intersection named Duke Ellington Circle, NY 10029

New York City/Queens
The Run-DMC Street

Hollis is hip-hop central, which is why local outfit Run-DMC have been honored with a street named for them. The street corner in question (now Run-DMC JMJ Way) was chosen due to its close proximity to the Hollis Hip-Hop Museum at Hollis Famous Burgers restaurant. Sadly that closed, and all plans by the entrepreneur who ran the place to open a hip-hop walk of fame along Hollis Avenue have seemingly been put on hold. This neighborhood was also immortalized in Run-DMC's 1987 single 'Christmas in Hollis.'

Location 487: check out the street sign at what was 205th Street and Hollis Avenue, Hollis, NY 11412

New York City/ Queens
The B52's at the Unisphere

The B-52's stood in line in front of the Unisphere on the cover of their 1998 album Time Capsule. The 140-foot-high representation of Earth was created to mark the beginning of the space age at the 1964-65 New York World's Fair.

Location 488: at Flushing Meadows-Corona Park, the Unisphere is in the northern section of the park close to both Arthur Ashe Stadium and Louis Armstrong Stadium, Queens, NY 11368

The B-52's grab a photo opportunity in front of the world's largest global structure

New York City/Queens
The Beatles at Shea Stadium

Despite its dismantling in 2009, Shea Stadium remains a milestone venue for pop music in general and The Beatles specifically. The baseball and football stadium hosted the famous Beatles concert (attracting a then record-breaking 55,600 attendance for a music gig) just 16 months after it opened for business in April 1964. Thanks to the excitement generated by The Beatles, it wasan age where rock and roll groups were more important than movie stars and indeed politicians and the only way to deliver the band securely to the venue was by helicopter and onto the field inside a Wells Fargo van before they kicked off their 12-number set at 9.16 p.m. Acknowledged by almost everyone as The greatest band in the world, they returned to Shea Stadium in August 1966 and attracted a 45,000 crowd to witness their final appearance on the East Coast, but it is the concert on August 15th 1965

that is remembered as the screaming, record-breaking climax to the "Fab Four"s tours of North America. As it turned out, The Beatles' Shea Stadium attendance record would be eclipsed in 1983 by another British band at the height of their powers. On August 18th 1983, The Police headlined a gig supported by Joan Jett and The Blackhearts and R.E.M. which drew 70,000 fans to the enlarged stadium. There's no plaque or musical reminder of the structure's importance in music history. If you want to stand in the exact spot where John, Paul, George, and Ringo played back in the summer of 1965 you have to dodge the vehicles in the parking lot of the New York Mets, Citi Field stadium, built on the old Shea Stadium center field.

Location 489: 126th Street and Roosevelt Avenue, Flushing, Queens, NY 11368, but don't expect to find a Beatles marker

Port Jefferson
The Long Island Music Hall of Fame

The Long Island Music Hall of Fame is a not-for-profit organization set up to educate the people of Long Island, which in this case includes the four counties of Suffolk, Nassau, Kings, and Queens. A museum (still currently in the planning stage) is expected to house two floors of exhibits, including the piano donated to the LIMHoF by Billy Joel, one of the Hall of Fame's first inductees in 2006.

Location 490: Port Jefferson is on the northern coastline of Long Island, 65 miles east of New York City. When completed, the museum will be situated in the building on the corner of Main Street and East Main Street, Port Jefferson, NY 11777

New York City/ Queens
The Ramones' 'Rockaway Beach'

The largest urban beach in the USA was the subject of the Ramones' highest-charting single on the Billboard Hot 100. The 1977 hit 'Rockaway Beach' was written by Dee Dee Ramone, whose fellow band member Johnny Ramone claimed he was the act's "only real beachgoer." Dee Dee's lyrics describe the ten-mile bus ride the band members would have taken to the beach from their homes in Forest Hills.

Location 491: Rockaway Beach runs along the South Shore of Long Island, Queens, NY 11693

New York

Vista
The church of the Blue Oyster Cult

The thoroughly Gothic Episcopal Chapel of St. Paul in the small town of Vista appears on the cover of Blue Öyster Cult's highest, charting US album. Peaking at No. 22, the 1975 live set ÖOn Your Feet or on Your Knees features a Cult Cadillac on the front which deposited the band members who appear inside the building and gatefold sleeve.

Location 494: approximately five miles south of South Salem, the Episcopal Chapel of St. Paul still stands near the fork of Route 123 and Elmwood Road, Vista (near Lewisboro), NY 10590

Still standing: the church of the Cult, photographed by John Berg back in 1975

Trumansburg
The GrassRoots Festival of Music & Dance

The type of bands selected to play the GrassRoots Festival of Music & Dance every July are "a difficult to nail down group of musicians and artists who lean toward roots related and world music" according to the committee. A great initiative by the local community in 1991, when the festival first began by raising money for the AIDS support organization AIDSwork, GrassRoots has slowly grown to an event with national awareness.

Location 493: Trumansburg is a village 12 miles northwest of Ithaca. The Finger Lakes GrassRoots Festival of Music & Dance is held annually at the Trumansburg Fairgrounds, Trumansburg, NY 14886

New York City/ Queens
Fountains of Wayne in Utopia

The New York City-formed Fountains of Wayne named their 1999 album Utopia Parkway for the stretch of road that runs north to south in the borough of Queens, through the suburban middle-class neighborhood of Utopia.

Location 492: Utopia Parkway runs right through the Queens neighborhood named Utopia at NY 11365

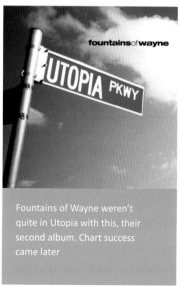

Fountains of Wayne weren't quite in Utopia with this, their second album. Chart success came later

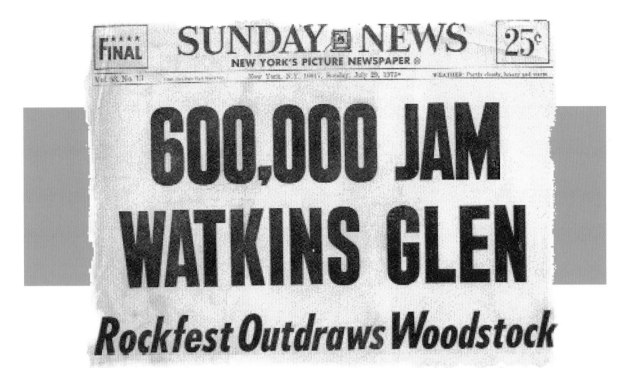

Watkins Glen
The record-breaking Summer Jam

Bigger than Woodstock, the Summer Jam in 1973 at this New York raceÖtrack was recognized by the Guinness Book of World Records as the largest audience for a rock festival at that time. An estimated 600,000 music fans poured into the Watkins Glen International racetrack to see performances by The Allman Brothers, The Band, and the Grateful Dead, although only 150,000 of that number were ticket holders. The 450,000 who did not pay for a $10 ticket had little problem entering the site once early arrivals intent on making it a free concert broke down the 6-foot-tall barbwire-topped perimeter fences. What followed was what must have been the biggest crowd for a sound-check when around 350,000, already packed in the day before the scheduled start on July 28th, witnessed The Band (who hadn't played live for 18

months) and the Dead running through their rehearsals. The next day the huge, still growing gathering experienced a mixture of music and torrential rain, and an epic jam performed by members of all three bands.

❝We've played them all, Woodstock, Isle of Wight, The Train Festival, and there's nothing to touch it. I've never felt this way about any of them. In fact I thought all the others were a drag ❞

The Band's Robbie Robertson nominates Summer Jam as his festival favorite

Unsurprisingly, the concert generated plenty of negative feedback among the local population. Tens of thousands of cars were abandoned along routes 14 and 414 and for three or four days

the inhabitants of Watkins Glen and Finger Lakes were without mail, fire, or police services. The general disruption resulted in lawsuits against the concert organizers but thankfully no one had died on the site. There was, however, one tragic death in the sky above the festival during The Band's set. Skydiver Willard J. Smith crashlanded in flames when the colored flares he was carrying strapped to his leg exploded in mid-air. In 2011, after a 38-year absence of rock music, Phish played their Super Ball IX festival here in front of 48,000.

Location 495: upstate New York, 90 miles southwest of Syracuse at what was in 1973 the home of the United States Grand Prix. The Watkins Glen International automobile racetrack is at 2790 County Route 16, Watkins Glen, NY 14891

New York

Douglas Gilbert

Woodstock/Bearsville/West Saugerties
Bob Dylan and the Woodstock community

Looking for the location of the 1969 Woodstock Festival round these parts? You need to redirect your search to Bethel, 67 miles southwest of this town of 5,000 Woodstock inhabitants, who are more than likely a tad weary of repeating this information!

This remote Catskill Mountains community is where Bob Dylan escaped to the country to reclusively write and eventually reboot his life after his legendary

motorcycle accident in 1966. Peter Yarrow (the "Peter" in folk-singing trio Peter, Paul & Mary) and his family still own the plot of land where Bob Dylan first came to stay in the Woodstock area back in 1963. At Yarrow's invitation, he and girlfriend Suze Rotolo were guests at his mother's summer cabin below Ohayo Mountain. Eager to make his escape from the summer heat of Greenwich Village and hang out and write in Woodstock's

countrified artistic community, Dylan's arrival coincided with a mini folk music boom in the town. The local Café Espresso began folk nights that proved successful enough to encourage the likes of Tom Paxton and Ramblin' Jack Elliott to venture north and perform here. Dylan would drop by the café, play chess, and write songs on a typewriter at the café's upstairs 'White Room.' Those songs would wind up on albums Another Side of Bob Dylan

At the intersection near Tinker Street and Tannery Brook Road, Woodstock, Bob Dylan gives John Sebastian a lift on the 500cc Triumph Tiger 100SS motorcycle he crashed two years later in 1966

(1964) and Bringing It All Back Home (1965). Dylan lived at the café and felt so comfortable in the Woodstock community that he purchased his own mountainside property on Camelot Road in 1965, called Hi Lo Ha. His dark cedar brown Arts and Crafts-style mansion with distinctive blue window frames was a convenient distance from the Bearsville home of his manager Albert Grossman, who'd moved to the area a year earlier with his wife Sally. The Grossmans' property provided the location for some iconic photo shoots. Sally Grossman is the girl who sat next to Dylan in the living room, pictured on the cover of his Bringing It All Back Home album. Not someone who seemingly took any kind of guidance from his record company, it's a surprise to find that Sally Grossman's appearance on the cover was because Columbia wanted a woman in the picture. The Bearsville house's garden is where the 1966 John Wesley Harding cover portrait of Dylan was shot. It was in July that year when Dylan's famously symbolic motorcycle accident occurred on a riverside track en route from his Camelot Road home to Bearsville. No one but Bob Dylan and his doctor knows how serious his injuries were but it led to a period of hardly any contact with the

Being [in Woodstock] in the summer, it's pretty amazing; it's definitely a vibe. By the time we were done in Bearsville, we were like 'Lord of the Flies.' We were communing with the deer

Rob Thomas (Matchbox Twenty) on the recording of the 2002 album More than You Think You Are

outside world and creative space that enabled him to work on a new project with a bunch of musicians now calling themselves The Band. A nearby house with basement recording facilities shared by Richard Manuel and Rick Danko was where Dylan and The Band recorded hundreds of songs, resulting in the much-bootlegged Basement Tapes, and eventually Music from Big Pink. The "Big Pink" referred to in the title is the house itself, in West Saugerties, which was pictured inside the cover of the 1968 album. Dylan's final home in the area, before his deteriorating relationship with manager Albert Grossman led him to vacate Woodstock, was on Ohayo Road in 1970. When Albert Grossman died in 1986 he left the neighbourhood a substantial and practical legacy. His Bearsville Studios (where The Band, Janis Joplin, Paul Butterfield, Patti Smith, R.E.M., Phish, and Matchbox Twenty all recorded) and the former hay barn he re-opened as the Bearsville Theater stand alongside restaurants and a bar, and a video studio developed originally by Todd Rundgren. There are other great music personalities connected to the area – ahead of the Woodstock Festival in 1969 Jimi Hendrix rented a large white house on the corner of Wiley Lane and another near the village of Shokan, and ▶

New York

The 'Big Pink' house in West Saugerties whose owners Don and Susan LaSala embrace and continue its musical history

rehearsed in the Tinker Street Cinema – but it is the sometimes mythical and hugely creative characteristics of Bob Dylan that are most associated with this unspoilt New York state community.

Location 496: the now dilapidated Yarrow family cabin where Dylan first stayed in Woodstock is at the intersection of Broadview Road and Hill 99 off the Ohayo Mountain Road, Woodstock, NY 12498

Location 497: The Café Espresso is little changed apart from its name which is now the Tinker Street Café at 59 Tinker Street. The upstairs 'White Room' is currently occupied by The Center for Photography, Woodstock, NY 12498

Location 498: the Grossmans' house was and still is off the Glasco Turnpike on Ricks Road, in the tiny hamlet of Bearsville, a mile west of the center of Woodstock, NY 12498

Location 499: Dylan's Camelot Road

property at Byrdcliffe is the last property on the right-hand side of a narrow road that becomes a trail, Woodstock, NY 12498

Location 500: the motorcycle accident location, some say, was almost immediately outside the Grossmans' property – others are sure it was up near Saw Kill River on the downhill stretch of Striebel Road, Bearsville, NY 12409 … take your pick.

> ❝A pink house seated in the sun of Overlook Mountain in West Saugerties, New York. Big Pink bore this music and these songs along its way. It's the first witness of this album that's been thought and composed right there inside its walls ❞
>
> *Words from the cover of The Band's Music from Big Pink*

Location 501: the beautifully preserved 'Big Pink' house is on a bumpy private road at 56 Parnassus Lane, West Saugerties, NY 12477. Saugerties is about five miles northeast of Woodstock

Location 502: Bob Dylan's Ohayo Mountain Road home is back from the road south of Woodstock, NY 12498

Location 503: Bearsville Studios (A and B) on Speare Road are slated for sale as a private residence but the Turtle Creek barn (Studio C) where The Band recorded is still functioning at a spot farther down the hill at the top of Ricks Road, Woodstock, NY 12498

Location 504: the 250-seater Bearsville Theater, is at 291 Tinker Street, Woodstock, NY 12498

Location 505: Jimi Hendrix's house was 12 miles west of Woodstock near Shokan, at the end of Traver Hollow Road, NY 12412

North Carolina

Asheville
Moogfest and Moog factory tours

This city in western North Carolina was home to the inventor of the Moog synthesizer, Robert Moog, who was buried in the city's Lou Pollack Cemetery following his death in 2005. Every October a festival in his honor is staged throughout various venues in Asheville, where Moog spent the final 30 years of his life. Moogfest has staged performances by keyboard wizards Brian Eno, Keith Emerson, Edgar Winter, and Thomas Dolby. The Moogfest venues over recent years have been spread around Asheville, at the Animoog Playground, Moog workshops at Moogaplex, and the Moog Music factory, where you can play a Moog or Theremin and take a tour. For those who want to learn even more about this unique brand of electronic music, watch out for news of the amazing Moogseum, which is in the planning stage.

Bob Moog with Moogfest performer Keith Emerson

Location 506: Moogfest is staged around the city of Asheville, which is 130 miles west of Charlotte. The Moog factory is situated at 160 Broadway Street, Asheville, NC 28801

Asheville
The Bele Chere festival

At the end of July, 250,000 music and art lovers descend on the streets of downtown Asheville for the largest free festival in the southeast. Its name, Bele Chere, derives from ancient Scottish dialect words meaning "Beautiful Living," something this festival has practiced well since the first event in 1979. The festival has helped revitalize a rundown business district into a thriving center for eating, shopping, and entertainment. The music on show may not be made by the biggest names in rock but the variety and sheer weight of numbers taking to the stages makes it hard not to find something you'd want to see. With band names from the recent schedules like Baby Rattlesnakes, Grown Up Avenger Stuff, and Doc Aquatic, what's not to like?!

Location 507: downtown Asheville, NC 28801

North Carolina

Doc Watson, permanently playing his favorite Gallagher guitar

Alex Hallmark

Greensboro
OMD's '88 Seconds in Greensboro'

British band Orchestral Manoeuvres in the Dark created a song about the infamous massacre that took place in Greensboro on November 3rd, 1979. The tragic events occurred when five participants in a civil rights protest march were shot dead by Ku Klux Klan and Nazi Party members. The catalyst for the 88-second incident becoming the subject of an OMD song was '88 Seconds in Greensboro,' a British World in Action TV documentary watched by the band's Andy McCluskey, who then wrote the song that appeared on their 1985 hit album Crush.

❛I'd seen a TV program about the incident. I was stunned — an average suburban setting with all this carnage suddenly transpiring❜

OMD's Andy McCluskey

Location 513: in the center of town, the massacre took place on Everitt Street, Greensboro, NC 27401

Boone
The Doc Watson statue

The eight-times folk and ethnic Grammy-winning guitarist and songwriter Doc Watson is remembered by a statue in his home town of Boone, in the Blue Ridge Mountains. Watson was born ten miles east of here in Deep Gap on March 3rd 1923 and died on May 29th 2012. Blind almost from birth, Watson became a super-skilled guitarist, famous for his flatpicking style of playing.

This extraordinary musician – "Just one of the People" as the plaque next to his statue modestly describes him - was presented with the National Medal of Arts by President Bill Clinton in 1997.

Location 509: Boone is 100 miles northwest of Charlotte. The statue is on the corner of King Street and Depot Street, 642 West King Street, Boone, NC 28607

❛He was not really happy about having his portrait sculpture done. But as we talked and I took photos, Doc began to warm to the idea of a sculpture. He decided he needed to be portrayed in his concert clothes, so he changed into them and I took more photos. Then he decided he needed to be playing his favorite Gallagher guitar, so we went to his house, got the guitar, and made more photos. When any guitar was in his hands, he was constantly playing and singing. He made two more requests: first that a plaque be placed on the sculpture reading "Just one of the People," and second that I not make his hair too long❜

Sculptor Alex Hallmark

Chapel Hill
James Taylor's homesick anthems

When singer-songwriter James Taylor was three years of age his family moved to this rural spot in North Carolina. When recalling his childhood in Chapel Hill and the surrounding area he described his emotional attachment by explaining, "I feel as though my experience of coming of age there was more a matter of landscape and climate than people." His vivid memories of "the red soil, the seasons, and the way things smelled" all conjured up a sense of homesickness when he found himself in Europe writing songs when signed to The Beatles' Apple label. The song 'Carolina in My Mind,' from Taylor's 1968 eponymous debut album, reflects his longing for the place he had left behind and became something of an anthem for the state of North Carolina and the university based at Chapel Hill, where his father was Assistant Professor of Medicine. The James Taylor connections to Chapel Hill are permanently established through the Chapel Hill Museum's exhibition of memorabilia and the nearby James Taylor Bridge named in his honor in 2003. 'Copperline,' the opening track on his platinum-selling 1991 album New Moon Shine, is another autobiographical song, in which Taylor remembers key moments from his childhood and the family home at Morgan Creek.

Locations 510, 511, and 512: the museum is in downtown Chapel Hill at the intersection of East Franklin and North Boundary Streets, 523 East Franklin Street, Chapel Hill, NC 27514. James Taylor's 11-room architectural gem of a childhood home is a mile south of the center of Chapel Hill at 618 Morgan Creek Road, NC 27517. It's a private residence, so please respect the current owners' privacy. The James Taylor Bridge is half a mile west of the house on Route 15-501, NC 27517

Belhaven
Little Eva's gravestone

Eva Narcissus Boyd, best known for her 1962 signature hit 'The Loco-Motion' and her name change to Little Eva was born (in 1943) and buried (in 2003) in Belhaven. Local monument-maker Quincy Edgerton created the stone memorial to her at the Black Bottom Cemetery when he heard that the cemetery and markers had fallen into disrepair. The stonework he finished and had erected in 2008 carries the message "Singing with the Angels" and is topped off by an image of a locomotive in full steam and a "Locomotion" inscription.

Location 508: Belhaven is east of the state, near the Atlantic coast. The Black Bottom Cemetery is at the junction of Old Country Road and Pine Street, Belhaven, NC 27810

A kiosk close to this statue of John Coltrane enables visitors to hear the sounds the great man created with his saxophone

High Point
The John Coltrane Statue

The statue of the legendary jazz saxophonist stands in the town of High Point, where John Coltrane grew up and first picked up the instrument that would make him world famous. That defining moment came at William Penn High School, close to his childhood home at 118 Underhill Street. Born in nearby Hamlet in 1926, his family moved 90 miles north to High Point within three months of John's arrival. The 8-foot likeness of Coltrane was erected in 2006 on the date of what would have been his 80th birthday.

Location 514: High Point is a little over 10 miles southwest of Greensboro. The statue stands on Commerce Avenue and Hamilton Street, High Point, NC 27262

North Carolina

Meg Rogers

Tryon
Nina Simone's hometown statue

Nina Simone was born in Tryon and died in France. Her ashes were scattered in Africa, and seven years after her death her home town erected a statue as a memorial to this remarkable performer. But not all her ashes were scattered in Africa. Inside the extraordinary, hollow-bodied sculpture, created by Zenos Frudakis, is a bronze heart into which Frudakis poured the singer's remaining ashes before welding closed the statue.

Location 516: at the Nina Simone Plaza, 54 South Trade Street, Tryon, NC 28782

Born and remembered in Tryon: Nina Simone surveys the traffic on Trade Street

Kannapolis
The North Carolina Music Hall of Fame Museum

Among the exhibits on display are outfits worn by Nina Simone and Clyde McPhatter, and much memorabilia on George Clinton, Roberta Flack, and James Taylor. The dream of a museum was made a reality through an inquiry by musician and entrepreneur Mike Curb and support from his Curb Family Foundation in 2006.

Opening in 2009, the museum, which has free admission, is housed in the town's former police station, court rooms, and jail.

Location 515: less than 30 miles northeast of Charlotte. The museum is at 109 West A Street, Kannapolis, NC 28081

McNair Evans

Wilkesboro
MerleFest

Founded in 1988, MerleFest is a roots music event that draws attendances of more than 80,000 to the small town of Wilkesboro on the campus of Wilkes Community College, for which the festival is a major fundraiser. This annual April shindig is named for musician Merle Watson, son of Doc Watson (see Boone, North Carolina, Rock Atlas entry), who died aged 36 in a farm tractor accident in 1985. There are few, if any, larger and better festivals to attend in the USA

❛When Merle and I started out we called our music 'traditional plus,' meaning the traditional music of the Appalachian region plus whatever other styles we were in the mood to play. Since the beginning, the people of the college and I have agreed that the music of MerleFest is 'traditional plus'❜

Doc Watson

if you are into folk and bluegrass music in a big way. Linda Ronstadt, Elvis Costello, Willie Nelson, Robert Plant, The Doobie Brothers, and Bruce Hornsby have all played the festival which has promoted a new genre all of its own, which Doc described as "traditional plus" music.

Location 517: 85 miles north of Charlotte. MerleFest is held at Wilkes Community College, South Collegiate Drive, NC 28697

Wilkesboro blues: Leon Russell plays the dusk slot at MerleFest 2013

North Dakota

Fargo
AC/DC at the Fargodome

Technically not a dome at all, the Fargodome opened on December 2nd 1992 and has attracted touring rock legends of the order of Aerosmith, Guns 'N' Roses, The Rolling Stones, Bon Jovi, Van Halen, and Bruce Springsteen ever since. When rock veterans AC/DC played the 21,692-capacity venue on January 17th 2009 they set a Fargodome record for the highest-grossing concert, filling every seat and raking in $1,870,334 in ticket sales, boosted by the enormous success of their recently released album Black Ice.

Location 518: the Fargodome is located approximately five minutes north of the downtown business district at 1800 North University Drive, Fargo, ND 58102

Above: AC/DC rip up the Fargodome

Below: the Fargodome where AC/DC set a venue attendance record in 2009

Wyndmere
Where Motley Crue created a one-man revolution

Here the rock landmark is a book. You surely won't want to visit the place but Wyndmere (named for the English Lake Windermere) is the town where farm boy turned author Chuck Klosterman was raised and cultivated his love of heavy metal through early exposure to Mötley Crüe's 1983 breakthrough album, Shout at the Devil. This led to Klosterman penning his amusing memoir, Fargo Rock City: A Heavy Metal Odyssey in Rural North Dakota. Is there a better way to understand the musical geography of this rock bypassed state? Stephen King agrees!

Location 519: Wyndmere is about 60 miles south of Fargo,. ND 58081

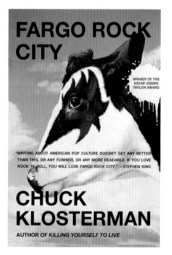

FARGO ROCK CITY

WINNER OF THE ASCAP-DEEMS TAYLOR AWARD

"WRITING ABOUT AMERICAN POP CULTURE DOESN'T GET ANY BETTER THAN THIS, OR ANY FUNNIER, OR ANY MORE READABLE. IF YOU LOVE ROCK 'N' ROLL, YOU WILL LOVE FARGO ROCK CITY." - STEPHEN KING

CHUCK KLOSTERMAN

AUTHOR OF KILLING YOURSELF TO LIVE

Bobak Ha'Eri

Ohio

Cincinnati
The Shake It Records store

Shake It Records started life as a record label back in 1978 before branching out to add a record store business in 1999. That Northside record store was switched to premises with three times the space in 2001 when they moved to their current address nearby on Hamilton Avenue. With about 30,000 CDs and 8,000 vinyl records there's plenty of choice for anyone seeking out obscure independent releases. The store's enthusiasm for Chicago post-punk art-rock, Ethiopian boog-a-loo, rockabilly, vintage soul, R&B, blues, punk/hardcore, classic country, 60s garage and psych, reggae/dub/rocksteady, vintage ska, krautrock, creative hip-hop, electronica, straight ahead rock 'n' roll, vintage bop, cool and avant garde jazz, cult soundtracks, and Afrobeat/funk gives you some idea of what you can expect amid the 3,200 square feet of floor space.

Location 520: in the Northside neighborhood, a short distance from downtown Cincinnati at 4156 Hamilton Avenue, Cincinnati, OH 45223

Cincinnati
The MidPoint Music Festival

With attendances at the MidPoint Music Festival rising from 13,500 in 2008 to double that figure in 2012, this is a festival most definitely on the up. Its reputation has grown on the back of its uncanny ability to find bands that post-MPMF get tagged "next big thing" by the music press. In addition to new talent, the festival has attracted stellar names of the caliber of Dinosaur Jr., Booker T. Jones, and Grizzly Bear. The annual event is spread over three days at the end of September, and spread around various locations with a main stage in Washington Park. So, if you end up listening to a band that isn't quite your cup of tea at one place, the chances are you'll find something right up your street round the very next corner.

Location 521: downtown Cincinnati, with the main stage at Washington Park, 1230 Elm Street, Cincinnati, OH 45210

Cleveland
The Walk of Fame

In 2012, the first sidewalk plaques were unveiled honoring inductees in the Rock and Roll Hall of Fame. The 24-inch diameter replica gold records are to be embedded in sidewalks all over the downtown area over the coming years, one for each Hall of Famer. Recent inductees that have gold discs already along Lakeside Avenue include Beastie Boys, Guns N' Roses, and the Red Hot Chili Peppers. The programe will continue with plaques scheduled to appear from the east bank of the Flats to East 17th Street, and from the Rock Hall to Progressive Field.

Location 522: the first of more than 280 sidewalk plaques planned for the downtown area were embedded and unveiled outside the Cleveland Public Auditorium, Lakeside Avenue, OH 44114, a short walk from the Rock and Roll Hall of Fame

Columbus
Rock on the Range festival

The Rock on the Range festival's slogan, "Where Rock Lives" is not an idle boast. Some festivals mix and match genres and promote variety. Not this one. Ever since ZZ Top, Velvet Revolver, Puddle of Mudd, and Evanescence power-chorded their way to opening the first Rock on the Range in 2007, this festival's intentions have been clearly defined. The bands that have followed down the years - Stone Temple Pilots, Korn, Limp Bizkit, Adelitas Way, and Slash – certainly haven't deviated from the festival's mission statement. Around 70,000 music fans attend the three-day event in May. A second Rock on the Range festival takes place in Winnipeg, Canada, every year a month later.

Location 523: the festival is held at Crew Stadium (about four miles north of downtown Columbus), 1 Black and Gold Boulevard, Columbus, Ohio 43211

Ohio

Cleveland
The Rock and Roll Hall of Fame Museum

The world famous Rock and Roll Hall of Fame was established on April 20th 1983 and its museum was opened on September 1st 1995. As a popular music visitor attraction it's hard to beat. With its spectacular glass pyramid-style architecture and adjoining towers and cubes, this striking structure is appropriately sited in the city where rock and roll's first concerts took place. Cleveland hosted The Moondog Coronation Ball on March 21st 1952, organized by disc jockey Alan Freed, the man responsible for coining the phrase "rock and roll." There's a historical marker which describes this momentous moment outside the museum. The 55,000 square feet of exhibition space inside the museum includes a special wing for the elite artists inducted into the Hall of Fame. Surprisingly, the annual induction of new artists is not always held at the Cleveland building - New York and Los Angeles have hosted the event – and current plans are set to schedule induction ceremonies only once every three years at the actual Hall of Fame base in Cleveland. The museum spans seven levels, where all the expected stage clothing, instruments of rock, and memorabilia are exhibited. From a Rock Atlas point of view, the exhibit displaying the cities that have most influenced rock and roll is particularly fascinating, featuring the key facts as to why Memphis, Detroit, London, Liverpool, San Francisco, Los Angeles, New York, and Seattle have contributed so much. One of the RRHF's most important functions is the archiving of written and film material documenting the history of rock and roll. This library and archives are housed separately in the Metro Campus of Cuyahoga Community College in downtown Cleveland.

Locations 524 and 525: the Rock and Roll Hall of Fame Museum is on the waterfront of Lake Erie in downtown Cleveland at 1100 Rock and Roll Boulevard, Cleveland, Ohio 44114. The RRHF Library and Archives are two miles southeast of the museum at the Metro Campus of Cuyahoga Community College, 2809 Woodland Avenue, Cleveland, OH 44115

The not-for-profit, educational Rock and Roll Hall of Fame requires a six-hour visit if you are to experience just about all it has to offer, including Pink Floyd's The Wall exhibit, which dominates this area of the museum

Ohio

Youngstown
Bruce Springsteen's 'tricky territory'

The history of Youngstown's industrial past was articulated by the track of the same name on Bruce Springsteen's album The Ghost of Tom Joad. The city's steel industry history (from prosperity to decline) was a carefully researched story-telling project of Springsteen's which provided the 1995 album with its stand-out track. Less than a year after the song's release, Springsteen made an emotional stop on the Ghost of Tom Joad Tour to play the song as part of a concert at Youngstown's 2,600-capacity Stambaugh Auditorium, which sold out in record time. His respectful telling of the lives of the Youngstown people was well received by the city, and during an extended stay to visit the local places of historic interest he was presented with the key to the city by Mayor Patrick Ungaro, himself a champion in the regeneration of Youngstown. The inscribed six-inch-long plastic gold key later became an exhibit in the Rock and Roll Hall of Fame Museum in nearby Cleveland.

❝You get into tricky territory when you write a song about someone's home town. You don't want to get it wrong❞

Bruce Springsteen on his 'Youngstown' story telling

Location 528: listed in the Register of Historic Places, the grand Greco-Roman-style Stambaugh Auditorium is north of downtown Youngstown at 1000 5th Avenue, Youngstown, OH 44504

Dave Grohl's special visit to Warren in 2012

Warren
David Grohl Alley

Nirvana drummer and Foo Fighters frontman Dave Grohl didn't call Warren, Ohio, home for very long but it was his birthplace and where he grew up as a young child before his family headed east to Virginia. He clearly loves the place, even more so lately since the powers that be decided to honor him by giving him the key to the city and naming one of its thoroughfares 'David Grohl Alley'. The more artistic among his fanbase have treated the alley as a blank canvas for some striking graffiti and chalk imagery to express their appreciation of Warren's famous son. Reports that the alley was to be structurally graced with a pair of Dave's drumsticks - the world's largest – have so far been unfounded.

❝To the wonderful city of Warren, from the bottom of my heart I'd like to thank you all so much. For the childhood memories, for my family, for my very own alley, for the world's largest drumsticks, and for all of your support: but, most of all for being such a great community. One that makes me proud to say I am from Warren, Ohio!"❞

Dave Grohl

Location 527: Warren is 60 miles southeast of Cleveland. For David Grohl Alley, head for the junction of Park Avenue and Market Street. The alley connects South Park Avenue with Main Avenue South West, Warren, OH 44483

North Lawrence
The Rock N Resort Music Festival

The Rock N Resort Music Festival is a great place to still see some great names from the golden age of rock. Grand Funk Railroad, Edgar Winter, The Guess Who, Blue Öyster Cult, Cheap Trick, and Kansas are the kind of heritage bands that have made this July two-day event tick in the past. In recent times the emphasis has been on younger metal acts such as Papa Roach and Buckcherry.

Location 526: North Lawrence is 50 miles south of Cleveland. The festival is at 13190 Patterson Road, North Lawrence, OH 44666

Oklahoma

Okemah
Woody Guthrie's birthplace

Sixth Street, Okemah, is said to be the birthplace of folk singer and songwriter Woody Guthrie (1912-1967), who alongside his prodigy Bob Dylan ranks as a hugely influential American icon. The city celebrates the man with a free annual festival and there's a statue in downtown Okemah. A further reminder of Guthrie can be found on a grassy bank which was once his two-story, six-room childhood home. Here, a carved tree memorial spells out "WG," "Okemah," and the title of his most famous song, "This Land is Your Land." If you want to seek out Woody's headstone (complete with engraved cartoon likeness) in the city's cemetery, it's in the Guthrie family plot.

Locations 529, 530, and 531:
Okemah is 65 miles south of Tulsa. The statue is on West Broadway Street near the junction with South 4th Street, Okemah, OK 74859. The wooden carving is on the site of Guthrie's childhood home on the south side of West Birch Street, Okemah, OK 74859. The headstone with Woody's name and dates of birth and death has been placed at the Guthrie family plot in Okemah's Highland Cemetery, which you can find by taking Woody Guthrie Boulevard north out of Okemah, North 3770 Road, OK 74859

Locations across town include the Brick Street Cafe, the Rocky Road Tavern, and the Crystal theater, with an outdoor main stage at the Pastures of Plenty, under the white water tower

Oklahoma

Oklahoma City
Flaming Lips Alley

The Flaming Lips were formed in Norman, 20 miles south of Oklahoma City, a fact honored by the city who named a street after the band in 2007. A city perhaps best known for cowboys, college football, and oil wells also has newly dedicated streets in the Bricktown district which recognize two other local musicians, country singer Vince Gill and jazz guitarist Charlie Christian.

❝I never considered I should deserve as much as a lamp post. It's one of these great little secrets – you stumble upon us. I think it could be the greatest alley in the universe ❞

Wayne Coyne responds to suggestions as to why something bigger than an alley wasn't named after the band

Location 533: Flaming Lips Alley is marked by street signs, located off Mickey Mantle Drive, just north of the Bricktown Ballpark, Oklahoma City, OK 73104

Photo: Jason Bondy

Flaming Lips frontman Wayne Coyne in the "greatest little alley in the universe"

Tulsa
The Woody Guthrie Museum and Archives

The Woody Guthrie Center, home of the Woody Guthrie Archives, is in the Brady Arts District of Tulsa. The George Kaiser Family Foundation, a Tulsa-based philanthropic organization, purchased the archives in December 2011 from Woody Guthrie Publications in New York and imported them to Woody's native Oklahoma. Collected here are lyrics, books, artwork, letters and postcards, manuscripts, Guthrie's personal journals, photographs, handwritten songbooks, and his annotated record collection. The center will also feature state-of-the-art interactive material on Woody's life, art, and legacy and will include Oklahoma's only permanent exhibit on the Dust Bowl. Perhaps the single-most important item in the collection is Woody Guthrie's original handwritten copy of 'This Land is Your Land.'

Location 535: 65 miles north of Woody Guthrie's Okemah birthplace. The Woody Guthrie Center Museum and Archives are at 102 East Brady Street, Tulsa, OK 74103

Muskogee
Merle Haggard's 'Okie from Muskogee' and the Oklahoma Music Hall of Fame & Museum

The modestly sized city of Muskogee was where folk guitarist Leo Kottke grew up, 2005 American Idol winner Carrie Underwood was born, and where the Oklahoma Music Hall of Fame was established in 1997, followed by its museum in 2003. That said, nothing appears to eclipse Muskogee's fame on the world stage as much as Merle Haggard's often-dubbed redneck anthem 'Okie from Muskogee'. Haggard had few connections to the place until the song was a smash hit in 1969 but Muskogee was the lyrical epitome of a pro-troops-in-Vietnam sentiment prevalent at the time in small town, middle America. Merle Haggard was inducted into the Oklahoma Music Hall of Fame in the organization's debut year and features in the museum, alongside a long list of other Oklahoma-born music legends, including David Gates (born Tulsa), Vince Gill (born Norman), Jesse Ed Davis (born Norman), and Leon Russell (born Lawton).

Location 532: Muskogee is 50 miles southeast of Tulsa. The Oklahoma Music Hall of Fame & Museum is housed in the old Frisco Freight Depot at 401 South 3rd Street, Muskogee, OK 74401

Talihina
The Kings of Leon family tree

To say that religion played a significant part in the upbringing of the Kings of Leon band members and other Talihina residents is an understatement. Their tiny home town, which brothers Caleb, Nathan, and Jared Followill, and cousin Matthew Followill, look on as their family base, has a population of just 1,211 and the area is served by one Catholic and 13 Protestant churches. The brothers' father Ivan was a preacher and took his three sons on the road, traveling to tent revivals and churches across Oklahoma and further south. The shacks, forest, and creeks around Talihina formed the boys' playground. It's a location they still revisit today for their annual family reunion to visit Grandpa Leon, whose name (along with dad Ivan's middle name) the boys took when naming their band. Their

fascinating and extraordinary family background is best understood by watching the absorbing documentary movie Talihina Sky, released on DVD in 2011. 'Talihina Sky' is also the title of a track on the band's 2003 debut album Youth & Young Manhood and their EP, What I Saw, released that same year.

Location 534: the family reunion grounds are private but the boys' uncle, Ralph Followill, owns a popular bar, the R-Bar, at 52550 US Highway 271, OK 74571

Top: the Talihina town billboard
Left: the Talihina Followill family: (top left to right) Nathan, Matthew, Cambo (Matthew's father), Ivan (Nathan, Caleb and Jared's father), Caleb and Jared. Seated at the front are Grandpa Leon and Grandma Mildred Followill

Photo: Jamie Daughters

Washita County
The 'Wichita Lineman' song story

The storyline inspiration for Jimmy Webb's 'Wichita Lineman' didn't come from the actual towns called Wichita, in Kansas and Texas, and not from the Wichita Mountains of Oklahoma. "Wichita" was used by the songwriter in the lyrics only because it sounded a whole lot better than "Washita." That was the name of the county where he was driving one day across the Oklahoma prairie and saw a lineman in the distance working on one of the endless line of telephone poles beside the road. Conjuring up a "picture of loneliness," partly from his own experience of a lost love, he imagined what call that Washita County lineman might have been making on the phone at the top of the pole that day and created one of popular music's most affecting love songs. The first and most successful rendition of 'Wichita Lineman' was by Glen Campbell, whose single and album of that name made their chart debuts in 1968. Webb had been asked specifically by Campbell to write another geographical song like his earlier Webb-penned hit 'By the Time I get to Phoenix' and wrote 'Wichita Lineman' in an afternoon while drawing on the "prairie gothic images," as he called them, of Washita County.

The Wichita Lineman album which topped both the Billboard pop and country charts in 1968

Location 536: New Cordell is the administrative center of Washita County, OK 73632

Oregon

Jason Quigley

At your service: Jackpot! owner Larry Crane

Portland
Larry Crane's Jackpot! Recording Studio

With the simple principle that if you treat recording as a service industry the artists will surely come, The Decemberists, The Shins, Eddie Vedder, R.E.M. (demoing their final album Collapse into Now) and Sonic Youth have all used Jackpot! Recording Studio, opened in Portland in 1997. The owner and engineer, Larry Crane, knows a thing or two about how to create the perfect recording environment and founded Tape Op magazine.

❝I started Jackpot! in 1997 for all my musician friends who wanted me to open a place for them to record at. We're in the heart of a vibrant city, and surrounded by amazing Portland food, coffee, and microbrews. It's a great part of that! ❞

Larry Crane

Location 537: Jackpot! is at 2420 South East 50th Street, Portland, OR 97206

Turner
Tim Hardin's gravestone

Performer and writer of classic songs including 'Reason to Believe' and 'If I were a Carpenter,' Tim Hardin is buried in Turner, Marion County, Oregon. Born in Eugene in 1941, his career was blighted by heroin abuse, which caused his death in 1980 when he was living at 625 Orange Drive in Hollywood, California. Marked by a simple gravestone with the inscription "He Sang from His Heart," he is buried in the Twin Oaks Cemetery (60 miles north of his birthplace) in Turner.

Location 541: the Twin Oaks Cemetery is at Witzel Road, east of downtown Turner, OR 97392

Portland
Bon Iver's 'Holocene'

'Holocene' is a single on Bon Iver's 2011 album Bon Iver, Bon Iver. Each track on the album, which peaked at No.2 on the Billboard 200 chart, was said by frontman Justin Vernon to represent a place and Holocene was a bar in Portland "where I had a dark night of the soul."

Location 538: Holocene is a music and arts venue, nightclub, and events space on the east side of Willamette River, 1001 South East Morrison Street, Portland, OR 97214

Portland
Beatles meet Beach Boys

Shortly before their only concert appearance in Oregon, The Beatles experienced a serious incident. As the Lockheed Electra airplane carrying the 'Fab Four' neared Portland, one of the four engines caught fire. Fortunately they touched down safely, but not before a panicked John Lennon had written a few last messages and stashed them in a film canister for safe keeping. Portland's Memorial Coliseum hosted The Beatles' historic appearance on August 22nd 1965 when 19,936 lucky ticket holders watched two shows scheduled for 3.30 p.m. and 8.30 p.m. In the downtime between the two shows the British quartet met their American rivals The Beach Boys for the first time. Four of the band, Mike Love, Carl Wilson, Al Jardine, and Bruce Johnston enlisted the help of Portland radio DJ Steve Brown to get to meet The Beatles after traveling hot foot from California the day before the shows. When the two groups got together on Sunday evening they traded their experiences and trivial stuff about cars, girls, and homes, backstage at the Coliseum. No doubt the topics of conversation also included each group's respective current hits – The Beatles were racing up the Billboard Hot 100 with 'Help' and The Beach Boys were enjoying the recent chart success of their own summer surfing anthem 'California Girls.' Alan Ginsburg was also in attendance to watch the gig and was inspired to write his poem 'Portland Coliseum.'

> ❛The next 45 minutes to an hour will never leave my memory. Here I am in the company of eight of the most recognized people on the face of the Earth. There were no leaders of countries, no presidents that I'd ever been aware of that had the attention that The Beatles and The Beach Boys had paid to them ❜

KISN Radio DJ Steve Brown

Location 539: the Memorial Coliseum (now the Veterans Memorial Coliseum) is at the junction of North Winning Street and North East Wheeler Avenue, Portland, OR 97227

Joe Cotter's extraordinary sculpture of Jerry Garcia, in the grounds of the McMenamins resort in Troutdale

Troutdale
The Jerry Garcia statue

There's a bronze statue of the one-time Grateful Dead guitarist Jerry Garcia at the McMenamins Edgefield resort here in Troutdale. This amazing piece of sculpture – Garcia appears to have been created as half guitarist, half tree man – is by artist Joe Cotter, who was commissioned to make the seven-foot statue in 1998.

Location 540: Troutdale is 15 miles east of Portland. The McMenamins resort is a mile or so west of the center of Troutdale at 2126 South West Halsey Street, Troutdale, OR 97060

Pennsylvania

Allentown and Bethlehem
Billy Joel's 'Allentown'

Billy Joel's gritty hit song 'Allentown' should really have been titled 'Bethlehem.' The 1982 single from his Nylon Curtain album became something of a blue-collar anthem with its references to the declining steel industry in this part of Pennsylvania. However, Allentown itself had no steel industry to speak of, with nearby Bethlehem the base for the Bethlehem Steel Corporation, the second-largest U.S. steel producer until decline and closure in 1995. The sentiment of Joel's song rang true enough but, using artistic licence he called it 'Allentown' because the word was easier to rhyme and no doubt sounded more like a steel town than

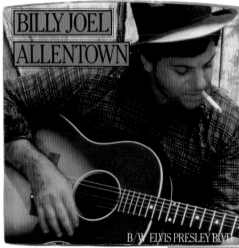

The single that put Allentown on the map

Bethlehem to the wider world. The Allentown community embraced the song's success and the Mayor even presented

Joel with the key to the city. Whatever the title it was the documenting of the struggle suffered by the local community that mattered, and on a visit to perform at a sold-out concert at Bethlehem's Stabler Arena Joel received a validatory five-minute standing ovation after he'd encored with 'Allentown.' This venue has another claim to fame. The 'live' segments of Bon Jovi videos 'Bed of Roses' and 'In These Arms' were shot here.

Location 542: Allentown and Bethlehem are 60 miles north of Philadelphia. The Stabler Arena is a couple of miles southeast of downtown Bethlehem, at 124 Goodman Drive, Bethlehem, PA 18015

Canonsburg
The Perry Como statue

Canonsburg's proud claim is that it is "America's Small Town Musical Capital." It certainly is if you're a fan of Perry Como, Bobby Vinton, and The Four Coins, who all hail from this coal and steel town 20 miles southwest of Pittsburgh. There's a Perry Como statue (erected in 1999) with dedicated paving blocks and a street named after the young Perry where he once owned a barber shop. Look out for the town's music history imaginatively written on tree grates, which tell the story of the songs made popular by the area's famous hit-makers. The Canonsburg town clock even plays the hit tunes on the hour.

Location 544: the statue is in front of the Canonsburg Municipal Building at 68 East Pike Street, PA 15317. What was once Third Street was renamed Perry Como Avenue in 1977

Frazer
Jim Croce's grave

After his tragic death as a result of a plane crash in Natchitoches, Louisiana, singer-songwriter Jim Croce was buried at the Haym Solomon Memorial Park, close to the suburbs of Philadelphia where he grew up. For fans who wish to visit the place, his memorial is a stylish, square floor plaque simply inscribed with his name and dates: "Jim Croce – 1943-1973."

Location 547: Frazer is about 20 miles west of downtown Philadelphia. Haym Salomon Memorial Park and Community Mausoleum is at 200 Moores Road, Frazer, PA 19355

Ted Colegrove

Jaime R. Cser

Bethlehem
The nation's largest free festival

Musikfest is held in downtown Bethlehem every August and is touted as the nation's largest free music festival, attracting up to one million people to the former industrial hotbed. Although 300 artists perform on 14 different stages throughout the city over ten days, not all are free to watch. For headline acts such as the current year's crop of Avenged Sevenfold, Skillet, Styx, Foreigner, and Peter Frampton you will need to pay for tickets to their gigs at the Sands Steel Stage.

Location 543: fourteen stages are scattered across the city. The Sands Steel Stage is at 101 Founders Way, Bethlehem, PA 18015

Chester
"The cradle of Rock 'n' Roll"

Bill Haley (who lived a few miles outside Chester from the age of seven in Boothwyn) and His Comets can lay claim to being the first rock 'n' roll band. Haley was musical director of Chester radio station WPWA during the forties, where he first imagined merging genres like rhythm and blues and country music that would lay the foundations of a new American genre that would sweep the nation. The music that led to massive fifties hits 'Crazy Man, Crazy,' 'Shake Rattle and Roll,' and rebel teen anthem 'Rock Around the Clock' was formed, tested, and developed in the Delaware Valley. According to the still musically active Comets guitarist Johnny Kay, "This area is where it started and that's kind of been forgotten." Kay is adamant, "this area actually is the cradle of rock 'n' roll. It was right there in Chester, Pennsylvania. This is where it started and it doesn't get enough credit."

Locations 545 and 546: Chester is 25 miles southwest of downtown Phildelphia. The WPWA radio station was on Route 352 Edgemont Avenue, Chester, PA 19013. Close by was the home Haley moved to when he could afford Melody Manor, at 3190 Foulk Road, PA 19061

Philadelphia
The Bessie Smith headstone

Born in Chattanooga, Tennessee, Bessie Smith (1895-1937) was the so-called 'Empress of the Blues' whose association with Philadelphia began in the 1920s when her recording career took off and she lived in the city. Her early death, caused by an automobile accident on Route 61 between Memphis and Clarksdale, was followed by a funeral with thousands of mourners filing past her coffin to pay their respects. Astonishingly, this blues icon's grave lay unmarked without a headstone until 1970, when the 1960s incarnation of Bessie Smith, Janis Joplin (who felt she owed so much to Bessie Smith musically), and Bessie's former employee, Juanita Green, paid for a headstone with the inscription '"The greatest blues singer in the world will never stop singing." Dory Previn paid tribute to Janis Joplin's act of kindness and devotion in 'Stone for Bessie Smith,' a track from her 1971 album Mythical Kings and Iguanas.

Location 548: Bessie Smith's gravestone is at Mount Lawn Cemetery near Sharon Hill, a borough west of downtown Philadelphia, at 84th Street and Hook Road, Sharon Hill, Philadelphia, PA 19079

Pennsylvania

Philadelphia
Live Aid at the John F. Kennedy Stadium

Demolished after more than 70 years of hosting top sporting action and some of the most memorable music concerts of all time, the John F. Kennedy Stadium was a grand, neo-Roman-style structure with a capacity of 102,000 seats. A reported 99,000 were present in the stadium for the historic Live Aid concert on July 13th 1985. Other massive concert events in the stadium's history include The Beatles' appearance in 1966 when 21,000 attended, Yes and Peter Frampton topping the 1976 Bicentennial Concert bill which attracted 130,000, The Rolling Stones (supported by Peter Tosh and Foreigner) in 1978 drawing 100,000, and Pink Floyd in 1987, whose crowd topped the 120,000 mark. A much smaller indoor venue, the Wells Fargo Center now occupies the site, where Bruce Springsteen has sold out the place a record-breaking 50-plus times.

Location 549: the John F. Kennedy Stadium site is now occupied by the indoor sport and concert venue called the Wells Fargo Center at South Broad Street, Philadelphia, PA 19148

For whom the bell tolls: It tolled for the John F. Kennedy Stadium when, shortly after the Grateful Dead's headlining concert there on July 7th 1989, the huge outdoor venue was condemned as unsafe and later demolished. Crimson White & Indigo is the Dead's concert recording from that day

Philadelphia
aka Music store

There's plenty of space to move around in (not always the case in cramped record stores these days) at this light and airy record shop in Old City, Philadelphia. It's all about the music here, with the motto "Rock is our life," which means no toys or memorabilia. The knowledgable aka staff write helpful suggestions on some of the records' plastic wrappers to direct you to side projects or sound-a-like bands.

Location 550: aka is on the west side of the Delaware River at 27 North 2nd Street, Philadelphia, PA 19106

Philadelphia
David Bowie and the 'Sigma Kids'

In 1967, Cameo-Parkway Studio chief engineer Joseph Tarsia sold all his possessions to set up his own studio. A year later he founded Sigma Sound Studios and helped launch and sustain the Philly soul sound made famous by artists of the caliber of The O'Jays and The Delfonics. This in turn attracted superstars keen to tap into the Philly vibe such as David Bowie and Madonna. When Bowie recorded his Young Americans album there, in the late summer of 1974, his daily trips to Sigma from the nearby Barclay hotel were noted by his fanatical Philadelphia fans. Over the weeks of recording, Bowie built up a rapport with the "Sigma Kids," as he called them, who faithfully hung around the hotel and outside Sigma for a glimpse and often a chat with their hero. So successful was this Philadelphia hub of creativity, Joseph Tarsia opened a second Sigma Sound Studios in New York City, which operated for over a decade until the mid-1980s. The Philadelphia studio still stands today although Tarsia sold that business in 2003.

Locations 551 and 552: the Sigma Sound building is at 212 North 12th Street, in downtown Philadelphia, PA 19107. If you want to stay in the Barclay hotel where David Bowie wrote songs and rested while recording at Sigma Sound you are out of luck. The building, on the southeast corner of Rittenhouse Square, PA 19103, has now been converted to condominiums

Pittsburgh
Jerry's "fine used" records

The facts are impressive. Jerry Weber has been serving the vinyl junkies of Pittsburgh for more than 30 years and claims to have two million vinyl records in his store to tempt you. And yes, it is all "fine used" vinyl, as the shop sign proudly says outside. No CDs, no new vinyl, but the customers seem to like it that way. Ben Folds is a regular and Robert Plant bought an old-fashioned suitcase record player off Jerry on a visit to the place.

❝A guy came in and asked if we had any scuba-diving records. He wanted album covers with scuba divers on them. There are probably four albums in the whole world with scuba divers on the covers! ❞

Jerry Weber talking to Goldmine magazine

Location 558: Jerry's Records is about four miles east of downtown Pittsburgh, in the historic Squirrel Hill neighborhood, at 2136 Murray Avenue, Pittsburgh, PA 15217

Sharon
The Vocal Group Hall of Fame Museum and Theater

The Vocal Group Hall of Fame honors all members of singing groups, and since it was founded in 1997has inducted the likes of rock bands Crosby, Stills & Nash, the Eagles, The Beatles, and The Beach Boys. The future looks uncertain for the museum (currently closed) but the organizers are hopeful a location (possibly the impressive Columbia Theater) will be found soon.

Location 559: Sharon is about 15 miles northeast of Youngstown, Ohio. The Columbia Theater is at 82 West State Street, Sharon, PA 16146

Philadelphia
Sister Rosetta Tharpe's home marker

From the 1940s to the 1960s, gospel and blues artist Sister Rosetta Tharpe (1915-1973) was unique. A large imposing figure of a woman playing an electric guitar, she lived the final period of her life in Philadelphia, where an historic marker paid for by her fans and friends stands outside her former home. The 'Godmother of Rock and Roll' is buried in the city's Northwood Cemetery.

Location 556: the marker is outside her former home at 1102 Master Street, in North Philadelphia, PA 19122. Northwood Cemetery is at 1501 Haines Street, Philadelphia, PA 19126

Philadelphia
The Walk of Fame

There are 106 rectangular bronze plaques on the Avenue of the Arts in Philadelphia, each one dedicated to an artist that has contributed to the city's great musical timeline. Solomon Burke, Chubby Checker, Jim Croce, Bill Haley, Daryl Hall, Joan Jett, John Oates, Todd Rundgren, and Phil Spector are just some of the movers and shakers who have been honored in this way by the not-for-profit Philadelphia Music Alliance.

Location 557: the Walk of Fame is in the heart of Philadelphia, all along the Avenue of the Arts on South Broad Street, between Walnut Street and Spruce Street, Philadelphia, PA 19102

Joan Jett at her Walk of Fame plaque unveiling on South Broad Street

RockAtlasUSA

Rhode Island

Newport
Dylan at the Newport Folk Festival

In addition to its important history, the Newport Folk Festival's location makes it an outstanding place to experience live music, situated at the mouth of Newport Harbor with panoramic views of the Newport Bridge and the East Passage. Folk music has been closely associated with Newport since 1959, when the now world famous Newport Folk Festival was founded by George Wein. Already a successful festival organizer through his work on the Newport Jazz Festival, Wein tried his hand at folk with an impressive board of directors which included Pete Seeger and Albert Grossman. The Newport Folk Festival was boosted by the publicity surrounding new, upcoming sixties folk stars Joan Baez and Bob Dylan. Making his Newport debut in 1963 as a guest of Baez prompted many to single out this Dylan performance as a key moment in popular music history. He returned for a much anticipated second performance a year later but caused a storm with his electric folk-rock here in 1965 when backed by the Paul Butterfield Blues Band and Mike Bloomfield. Folk fans were horrified as he abandoned pure folk and muddied it with guitars and amps. Interesting

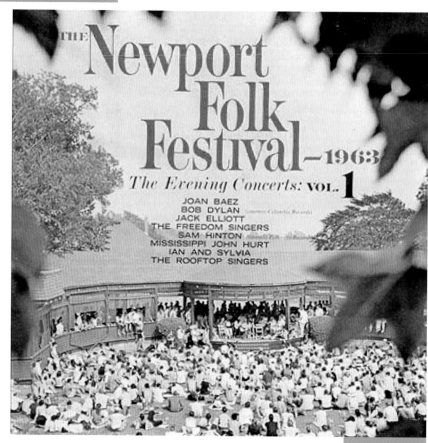

to note, then, that at the 50th anniversary Newport Festival in 2009 Newport was awash with the electric folk sounds generated by a new wave of acts such as The Avett Brothers, The Decemberists, and Fleet Foxes.

Locations 557 and 558: 75

miles south of Boston, MA. Fort Adams is located at Harrison Avenue, Newport, RI 02840. The first two appearances by Bob Dylan at the Newport Folk Festival were made when the festival took place two miles northeast at Freebody Park, off Memorial Boulevard, RI 02840

The original festival site at Freebody Park

Brittany Wilkes, Rhode Island Music Hall of Fame

Pawtucket
The Rhode Island Music Hall of Fame Museum

Newly opened, this free museum consists of beautifully designed information panels on the 17 acts so far inducted into the Rhode Island Music Hall of Fame. In addition, there's a "Music of the Ocean State" exhibit with record labels, record covers, and sheet music depicting songs about Rhode Island and/or composed by Rhode Islanders, and another area where visitors can use a listening station to hear the music of the inductees. In it's early stages of development, the exhibition is currently two-dimensional only but will grow to include actual items of memorabilia over time. Among the most recent inductees into the Hall of Fame, at only this volunteer organization's second ceremony in 2012, were Newport's famous chart band The Cowsills.

Location 559: Pawtucket is 4 miles northeast of Providence. The Rhode Island Music Hall of Fame is at 999 Main Street, Pawtucket, RI 02860

The Cowsills on stage during their performance at the second annual Rhode Island Music Hall of Fame induction ceremony and concert. Right: The Cowsills at the unveiling of their exhibit at the Rhode Island Music Hall of Fame

Brittany Wilkes, Rhode Island Music Hall of Fame

RockAtlasUSA

South Carolina

Columbia
Hometown recognition for Hootie & The Blowfish

A regular feature of all Hootie & The Blowfish gigs around the world is their simple allegiance to the town where they were formed – "We are Hootie & the Blowfish from Columbia, South Carolina." Only fair, then, that Columbia should recognize its rock 'n' roll global promotion by creating a monument to the band. The 25th-anniversary archway art piece has a granite floor plaque shaped as a giant guitar pick, with stainless-steel spires reaching 16 feet into the sky interconnected with musical stanzas.

Location 560: the sculpture (unveiled in 2010 with the band and hundreds of fans present) is at the corner of Harden Street and Santee Avenue, Five Points, SC 29205. A stretch of Santee Avenue has been renamed Hootie & The Blowfish Boulevard

HOOTIE & THE BLOWFISH

Above: South Carolina's finest rock and roll export, Hootie & the Blowfish
Right: the floor space below the Hootie & the Blowfish sculpture is this large annotated guitar pick

South Dakota

Sioux Falls
South Dakota's Rock and Roll Museum

The South Dakota Rock and Roll Music Association run a small but perfectly formed free museum. It features memorabilia relating to the state's much-loved artists such as Bobby Vee, Myron Lee and The Caddies and Dee Jay & The Runaways. These are just three of the acts that have been inducted into the recently formed SDRRMA Hall of Fame. With its sparse population, the Association's chairman and founder, Don Fritz, admits that South Dakota hasn't produced a mass of famous musicians but he proudly promotes one claim to fame. "We probably had more ballrooms per capita than any place in the USA." Several of these are still in use and have a lot of music history. Two in particular are the Spearfish Pavilion in Spearfish and the Arkota Ballroom (now called the Shrine El Riad) in Sioux Falls.

Location 561: the South Dakota Rock and Roll Museum is situated inside the Washington Pavilion in downtown Sioux Falls, on the corner of 11th Street and Main Avenue, SD 57104

The free museum honoring South Dakota's finest, in downtown Sioux Falls

RockAtlasUSA

Tennessee

Chattanooga
The Riverbend Festival

The Riverbend Festival dates back to 1982 and has grown from a lengthy five-night affair to the current, even lengthier, nine nights, which draw a reported 600,000 in June to the banks of the Tennessee River in Chattanooga. Foreigner, The Beach Boys, and Sheryl Crow are just some of the classic rock acts who have graced the festival with their presence in recent years.

Location 563: the festival site is at 200 Riverfront Parkway, downtown Chattanooga, TN 37402

The Riverbend Festival attracts up to 80,000 people a night to the banks of the Tennessee River

Camden
The Patsy Cline memorial

An engraved memorial stone marks the spot where 29-year-old singer Patsy Cline was killed in a tragic accident along with three other nationally known country performers. "On this site, March 5 1963, Patsy Cline, Cowboy Copas, Hawkshaw Hawkins, Randy Hughes, lost their lives in a plane crash. In loving memory July 6 1996," read the words on the memorial.

Location 562: Camden is 100 miles west of Nashville. The memorial stone is on Mount Carmel Road, TN 38320. The site is served by a small parking area

Photo: DaxTxcb

Memphis
The Isaac Hayes gravestone

A large pictorial bronze plaque decorates the gravestone
of Isaac Hayes, who was born in Covington, Tennessee,
and died in Memphis in 2008.

Jackson
Carl Perkins memorial plaque

Rock and roll pioneer Carl Perkins, who inspired
so many ground-breaking musicians including The
Beatles, was born in Tiptonville, Tennessee, in 1932.
All that marks his passing in 1998 is a small bronze
plaque on the tomb wall in a Jackson cemetery,
about 70 miles northeast of his birthplace.

Location 564: Ridgecrest Cemetery is a few miles
north of downtown Jackson, TN 38305

Location 565: the gravestone is at the Memorial Park
Funeral Home Cemetery, 13 miles east of downtown
Memphis at 5668 Poplar Avenue, Memphis, TN 38119

Memphis
Elvis' 'Heartbreak Hotel' home

When Elvis Presley's career skyrocketed around 1956 he spent some
of the money he earned from the success of 'Heartbreak Hotel' on a
new home for himself and his parents, at Audubon Drive, Memphis.
Purchased for $40,000, the single-story ranch-style property gave
him only limited privacy from his increasing fanbase, and after just 13
months he up-sized to the grander security of Graceland.

Location 566: about ten miles from Graceland and the center of
Memphis, at 1034 Audubon Drive, Memphis, TN 38117

ROCK ATLAS USA EDITION **237**

Tennessee

FIRE DESTROYS CASH'S FORMER HOME

CHERYL TATUM / GANNETT TENNESSEE

The former home of Johnny and June Carter Cash, being renovated by Barry Gibb, burns to the ground in Hendersonville.

House was family haven and a magnet for artists

Hendersonville
The homes of Johnny Cash

This Sumner County city has seen many musicians make it their home. Roy Orbison, Conway Twitty, Dan Seals, Taylor Swift, and Chris Henderson (3 Doors Down) have all lived hereabouts, enjoying the convenient closeness to Nashville. But Hendersonville's most famous resident was Johnny Cash, who lived in his home on the banks of Old Hickory Lake. Cash and wife June Carter lived in the house on the lakeside for most of their 35-year marriage. Both died in 2003 and the property was then purchased by Barry Gibb of the Bee Gees. Sadly, before Gibb could move in, the distinctive house burned to the ground while renovations were in progress. Little trace of the home remains where Cash hosted his legendary guitar jams with other music legends in his round lakeside room. Across the street his mother's former home still

stands. Here Johnny Cash spent his last days when the lake house became too difficult to negotiate in his wheelchair. This ranch house was nicknamed "Mama Cash's House" by the family and housed some of the family's most important items of memorabilia, including Cash's gold record for 'I Walk the Line.'

Locations 567, 568, and 569: Hendersonville is 20 miles northeast of Nashville. The site of Johnny Cash's lakeside home is at his old address at 200 Caudill Drive, Hendersonville, TN 37075. The ranch house where Cash spent his last days is across the street at 185 Caudill Drive, Hendersonville, TN 37075. Johnny and June Carter Cash are both buried at Hendersonville Memory Gardens, 353 East Main Street, Hendersonville, TN 37075

C. Taylor Crothers

Above: The Bonnaroo Music & Arts Festival fills up with 80,000 happy campers
Below: Red Hot Chili Peppers in a "Bonnaroovian" groove

Manchester
The caring, sharing Bonnaroo festival

This is a festival that exudes goodwill. Read "The Bonnaroovian Code" on the website, which gives you a warm feeling inside even before you have set foot at the actual event which takes place every June in 700 acres of Tennessee countryside. The vibe is not dissimilar to that which saw Glastonbury become a roaring success. Like the UK's premier eco-friendly festival, Bonnaroo is located on a farm where, over four days and on more than ten stages, you get music, art, a mini film festival and, as the organizers predict, "a feeling of overwhelming happiness".

Location 570: Manchester is about 40 miles northwest of Chattanooga and the festival site is just east of Manchester at 1560 New Bushy Branch Road, TN 37355

C. Taylor Crothers

Tennessee

Keith Miles

Memphis
Sun Studio

The world famous Sun Studio is a surprisingly small red brick building on the corner of Union Avenue and Marshall Avenue in Memphis. This is where Alabama-born record producer, promoter, and businessman Sam Phillips set up a recording facility in 1950 and then set about creating his Sun Records label and Sun Studio. Now a visitor attraction which draws holidaying families and wide-eyed rock stars eager to stand in the very room popular music history was made, the Sun Studio tour takes about 50 visitors at a time. The tour takes you downstairs into the room where Elvis Presley, Jerry Lee Lewis, and Johnny Cash cut some of America's most remarkable records. In more recent times, many rock musicians have tried to capture the spirit of historic recordings like Elvis' 'That's All Right' (1954) and arguably the first rock and roll record, 'Rocket 88' (1951), by booking session time here. U2 made the trip to Sun Studio in 1987 to record a contribution to a Woody Guthrie memorial album. Then, with Memphis-born producer Jack Clement at the helm they later set about borrowing microphones and guitars from the era when Clement had worked with Elvis, Carl Perkins, and Jerry Lee Lewis to record tracks for their 1988 album Rattle and Hum. The Sun recording sessions for tracks such as 'Angel of Harlem' and 'When Loves Come to Town' were also filmed, showing up on the Rattle And Hum movie, released that same year.

Location 571: Sun Studio is a mile east of the center of Memphis at 706 Union Avenue, TN 38103

Tennessee

The Classical Revival-style house was built in 1939 on the estate named after Grace Toof, the aunt of the then owner's wife

Elvis Presley Bu $100,000 Home

MEMPHIS, Tenn., March 23 —Rock and rolling Elvis Presl came a country squire today chasing a $100,000 country res for himself and his parents,.

The 22-year-old guitar stru said he was swapping in his pr smaller Memphis home as part ment on the modern two-story bedroom establishment.

The new home, boasting a fou garage, is located on a 13½ tract of land in Whitehaven sout Memphis near the Mississippi s line.

The property is adjacent to church. When notified of the s: pastor Howard Stevens said he v "pleased" to have the controvers pelvis pulsating singer as a nei; bor.

Memphis
Elvis' Graceland

Aside from the White House, Elvis Presley's Graceland is America's most famous home. Since opening to the public as a hugely popular tourist attraction five years after the 'King of Rock n' Roll''s death in 1977, the house and grounds have attracted an estimated 15 million visitors. Aside from the obvious attractions of the house itself, the grounds are the final resting place of Elvis, his parents, and his grandmother. Each grave is represented by an impressive memorial and plaque and Elvis' still-born twin brother, Jesse Garon Presley, is also remembered by a smaller plaque. Graceland may have been the place where Elvis literally lived, loved, and died but he wasn't the property's first owner. In fact, the name of the estate

(dating back to 1861, when it was a Hereford cattle farm) came from Grace Toof, the daughter of S. E. Toof, the then owner. The house called Graceland was built much later in 1939 when Grace's niece, Ruth Moore and her husband Dr. Thomas D. Moore, constructed a home specifically with the playing and listening of music in mind. "Our entire home is centered around music," Mrs Moore told a local reporter in 1940. Built on a hill surrounded by a grove of oak trees, the house's musical history is exactly what must have attracted Elvis when checking out the place as a potential home in 1956. Easily affordable at $100,000 (he sold his previous Memphis home on Audubon Drive for more than half that), Elvis and his parents moved across to Graceland

in April 1957. Gladys, Elvis' mother, immediately set to work introducing some chickens and hanging out the Presley family washing in the backyard while Elvis turned his attentions to more expensive needs. A swimming pool, perimeter walls, and iron gates were all constructed in the first year while he was often away from home filming his third movie, Jailhouse Rock. The main two-story building was created in the Classical Revival style, with single story wings either side. The house's most striking feature is the central projecting portico and impressive columns. Highlights of Graceland's museum of treasures include the den-like Jungle Room complete with waterfall, the Trophy Room, showcasing everything from

Tony Bradshaw

contracts to bubble gum cards, the Automobile Museum, and the Elvis aircraft (JetStar and the Lisa Marie Convair 880). The stables where Elvis would saddle up and ride down to the iconic, music-note-designed gates to sign autographs are still standing, but the most poignant reminder of the man himself is the eternal flame housed in a glass case at the top of his grave. The vast majority of visitors to Graceland do so through the main gates with a ticket, but one of the most famous trespassers to have scaled the wall and dropped into Graceland was a young Bruce Springsteen. In 1976, the New Jersey rock star caught a cab from downtown Memphis, where he had played a concert on his Born to Run Tour, and jumped the wall before finding Graceland's front door. Springsteen didn't even get the chance to knock and was politely but firmly led back to the street by Elvis' security guards. As it happens, Elvis was in Lake Tahoe and wasn't even home that night. So, the heir apparent in many people's minds to Elvis' crown as the 'King of Rock n' Roll' never got to meet his hero.

Keith Miles

Keith Miles

Despite the misconceptions that Graceland might be a tacky commercial venture with little class or style, no admission fees or souvenirs are in evidence on the property itself and all tickets, food, and drink concessions, and the shuttle bus to the house, are situated across the street. This creates a surprisingly reverential and calm atmosphere throughout the house and estate, like most other museums you might visit. The difference here is that you

Top: Elvis' remains were originally buried in Forest Hill Cemetery but he's now been reburied at Graceland. Above: Elvis' original pink Cadillac

are walking in Memphis in a very special home and garden belonging to the world's most-loved music star. In June 1971, to honor their famous resident, the Memphis City Council officially renamed Highway 51 South "Elvis Presley Boulevard." Twenty years later Graceland became the first rock and roll location to be listed by the National Register of Historic Places when it gained that status in 1991. In 2006 it was

Later on, I used to wonder what I would have said if I had knocked on the door and if Elvis had come to the door. Because it really wasn't Elvis I was goin' to see, but it was like he came along and whispered some dream in everybody's ear and somehow we all dreamed it

Bruce Springsteen recalls the night he jumped the wall into Graceland

designated a National Historic Landmark.

Location 572: nearer the Mississippi state line than downtown Memphis, which is ten miles to the north, Graceland is situated (naturally) on 3764 Elvis Presley Boulevard, Highway 51 South, TN 38116

Tennessee

Memphis
The Rock 'n' Soul Museum

The Memphis Rock 'n' Soul Museum is the place to head for to get a comprehensive overview of the Memphis music experience. You can explore the early forms of popular music as the rural field hollers and sharecroppers of the 1930s begin a timeline that leads to the explosion of sound that came out of Sun, Stax, and Hi Records during Memphis' musical heyday. If you want to find out more about influential Memphis artists Elvis Presley, B.B. King, Carl Perkins, Jerry Lee Lewis, Isaac Hayes, Otis Redding, Johnny Cash, Sam & Dave, Al Green, and The Bar-Kays, you've come to the right place. Visitors can take the digital audio tour guide (packed with more than 300 minutes of information) through seven galleries. Executive director John Doyle sums up the museum's value when he says: "The exhibition, created by the Smithsonian Institution, involves much more than guitars and drumsticks. It tells the story of musical pioneers who, for the love of music, overcame racial and socio-economic barriers to create the music that shook and shaped the entire world."

Location 573: at 191 Beale Street (Suite 100), on the corner of the legendary Highway 61 at the FedExForum sports and entertainment complex in downtown Memphis, TN 38103

Memphis
'Walking in Memphis' and the W.C. Handy statue

Singer-songwriter Marc Cohn wrote 'Walking in Memphis' about a trip he made to the city in 1986 when he visited Graceland, heard the Reverend Al Green preach the gospel, and sought out the statue of 'Father of the Blues' W.C. Handy. Equally important in terms of the song's inspiration was his life-changing encounter with a singer and pianist, Muriel Witkins, who he met at a restaurant outside Memphis. Cohn's 1991 hit was covered, most prominently, by Cher in 1995 and Lonestar in 2003.

Location 574: the W.C. Handy statue is in Handy Park on Beale Street, Memphis, TN 38103

Memphis
Elvis' favorite barber shop and movie theater

Jim's barber shop on Main Street was the place where the teenage Elvis Presley had his hair cut right up until his early twenties, when overpowering fan worship made it safer for him to get it cut at Graceland. Next door but one was the grand Malco theater, (formerly the Orpheum theater and now with that name once more), which Elvis hired after hours to watch movies.

Locations 575 and 576: although Jim's barber shop no longer exists as a business on the premises the building at 207 South Main Street still stands, next door but one to the Malco/Orpheum theater 203 South Main Street, Memphis, TN 38103

Memphis
The Elvis Presley statues

Yes, there are two statues of Elvis Presley in Memphis. The Beale Street action pose statue of 'The King' by artist Andrea Lugar replaced an earlier, more sedate likeness by Eric Parks which moved to the Welcome Center, where you can also see an excellent statue of bluesman B.B. King.

Locations 577 and 578: the statues are on Beale Street, between Main Street and 2nd Street, Memphis, TN 38103, and at the Welcome Center, 119 North Riverside Drive, Memphis, TN 38103

Below: Booker T. Jones paid tribute to The Beatles' Abbey Road album by covering it track for track. Left: as Abbey Road was EMI's studio so McLemore Avenue was the location of Stax's. The original Stax building is now the Stax Museum

Memphis
The Stax Museum in Soulsville

Although the original Stax recording studio was demolished in 1989, in 2003 the Stax Museum of American Soul Music was fittingly opened on the same site. A highlight of a visit to the museum is the replica of the famous Stax Studio A. The unusual sloping floor of this unique recording studio has been accurately reconstructed. The slope was once the seated area inside the Capitol Theatre before Stax took over the building. The golden age of Stax and its seemingly endless output of soul classics began in the early 1960s with Booker T. and the MGs, Otis Redding, Rufus Thomas, and Sam & Dave all laying down memorable soul and R&B hits here on McLemore Avenue, Memphis. These artists are just some of those featured in the 2,000 interactive exhibits in the museum.

Location 579: the museum is two miles southeast of downtown Memphis at 926 E McLemore Avenue, Memphis, TN 38106

Tennessee

Nashville
Jack White's Third Man Records

A six-mile journey north of his home is where Jack White's extraordinary Third Man Records building stands. The distinctive black frontage, topped off by a 50s-style radio mast sculpture radiating air waves, houses a visitor-friendly vinyl record store, Third Man record label office, photo studio, dark room, live music venue, and recording booth. Inside what White claims was once a candy factory is now a candy store for vinyl lovers, furnished with various odd exhibits that portray Jack's fascination for taxidermy. Decorating the familiar, brightly painted Jack

Third Man HQ: a haven for vinyl lovers

White décor are stuffed buffalo and giraffe, shrunken heads, and tribal masks.

Location 584: in south-central Nashville at 623 7th Avenue South, Nashville, TN 37203

Memphis
Jeff Buckley's Memphis Zoo memorial

One of the most unusual memorials to a long-gone musician can be found at the Memphis Zoo. In a corner of the Sumatran tiger enclosure are two small black plaques in memory of Jeff Buckley. The Californian singer-songwriter, who died aged just 30 in 1997, had been a frequent visitor to the zoo and even had an interview scheduled to become a volunteer zookeeper around the time of his death. Buckley drowned in a swimming accident in the Wolf River nearby.

Location 580: the plaques are on the stone wall in the Sumatran tiger enclosure, Memphis Zoo, Midtown, 2000 Galloway Avenue, Memphis, TN 38112

Memphis
The Goner and Shangri-La record stores

Memphis is blessed with two popular record stores that featured in a recent Top 30 list by Rolling Stone magazine. You can get pretty much anything you're looking for at both, but Goner Records is a particularly good place to head for if you want the broadest selection of garage rock. There's even a Goner Records label where they champion the best new raw talent from that department and the annual Goner Fest which champions the local bands they represent. Shangri-La Records buys and sells virtually any genre on vinyl and CD formats and the equipment to play it on. The store is actually a three-room detached house and it has traded from the same address for more than 25 years.

Locations 581 and 582: Goner Records is at 2152 Young Avenue, Memphis, TN 38104, and Shangri-La Records is less than 2 miles north at 1916 Madison Avenue, Memphis, TN 38104

Memphis
Furry Lewis' gravestone

The gravestone of bluesman Walter "Furry" Lewis is engraved with an illustration of an acoustic guitar alongside the inscription "When I Lay My Burden Down." This headstone, which towers over a smaller stone inscribed with the simple description "Bluesman," was purchased by fans. Lewis, who was born in 1893 and only died in 1981, was immortalized in song by Joni Mitchell's 1976 Hejira LP track, 'Furry Sings the Blues.' The song was inspired by Mitchell's meeting with Lewis in Memphis in 1975.

Location 583: the Hollywood Cemetery is a short distance east of Interstate 69, accessed from Hernando Road, TN 38106

Nashville
The Johnny Cash Museum

Opened in 2013, this well presented new museum has all the usual artefacts and memorabilia you would expect to see associated with the 'Man in Black.' However, organizers have come up with some ingenious ways of preserving precious fragments of the life of Johnny Cash. When fire destroyed almost all of the Cash family's lakeside home at Hendersonville, a brick wall and the house's iron gates were restored for exhibition at the museum.

Location 585: The Johnny Cash Museum is in the center of Nashville at 119 Third Avenue South, Nashville, TN 37201

Nashville
Metallica Live at Grimey's

Recorded in 2008 and released in 2010, Live at Grimey's is a nine-track special record Metallica released capturing a performance the band made in the basement of this popular Nashville record store. Around 150 fanclub members and friends of the band crammed into the space below Grimey's New & Preloved Music record shop on the eve of Metallica's headlining spot at the Bonnaroo festival.

Location 586: Grimey's is at 1604 8th Avenue, South Nashville, TN 37203

Nashville
Jack White in the Hank Williams neighborhood

So regularly was White Stripes, Raconteurs, and Dead Weather man Jack White traveling from his home town, Detroit to Nashville that he eventually settled in the music capital, a short distance from the former home of country legend Hank Williams. The seven-acre property is a 10-minute drive south from White's Third Man record label and record store business near central Nashville. In keeping with the taxidermy theme and décor at Third Man, the property sports the trademark red and white livery associated with the man and his fondness for exotic creatures, like the stuffed hyenas that decorate the ground floor. Rural but close enough to the city, the house, recording studio, guesthouse, and workshop reportedly cost more than $3 million when White purchased the place in 2005.

Location 587: private residence - 5055 Franklin Pike, south of Nashville in the Oak Hill area, TN 37220

In a still from the movie It Might Get Loud (2009), Tennessee guitar-maker Jack White demonstrates how to go about constructing one using blocks of wood, string, a hammer and nails, and a Coke bottle

Nashville
The Grand Ole Opry

Country music's most famous stage is at the Grand Ole Opry house in Nashville. Before 1974, the weekly star-studded country concert was held at the former Union Gospel Tabernacle, the red-brick Ryman Auditorium. In a bid for some spiritual continuity, organizers cut a large circle of the timber stage when the concert moved to larger premises (at the Grand Ole Opry across the city) and inlaid the section in the new stage.

Location 588, 589 and 590: the Ryman Auditorium building still stands near the center of Nashville at 116 5th Avenue, Nashville TN 37203. A very short walk south takes you to the Country Music Hall of Fame Museum at 222 5th Avenue South, Nashville, TN 37203. The currently operating Grand Ole Opry is on the city's eastern outskirts at 2800 Opryland Drive, Nashville, TN 37214

Tennessee

Nashville
Chet Atkins' statue

A statue of country music guitar legend Chet Atkins stands on the corner of Fifth Avenue and Union Street in Nashville. Created by sculptor Russell Faxon, the life-size bronze statue was unveiled back in 2000 in the presence of country stars Vince Gill, Charlie Pride, and Atkins himself. Faxon's statue comprises the seated figure of Atkins hunched over his guitar, with an empty stool next to him for anyone who wishes to sit next to the country superstar. Nashville has also honored the man with a street named for him and the city-wide music festival that also bears his name. Responsible for playing a major part in developing the famous 'Nashville Sound' through producing and performing, Atkins was actually born 200 miles east of Nashville in Luttrell, Tennessee.

Location 591: the statue is outside the Bank of America building on the corner of Union Street and Fifth Avenue in downtown Nashville, TN 37219

Nickajack Cave
Johnny Cash's redemption

Singing legend Johnny Cash was in a pretty low place in 1967. "A walking vision of death," due to amphetamine and barbiturate addiction, is how he described himself in his autobiography. In October that year he decided to commit suicide, planning to lose himself in the deep recesses of a cave system on the Tennessee River. Nickajack Cave is a place he knew well, having previously explored the huge underground caverns and tunnels when searching for native American and Civil War artefacts with childhood friends. Aside from being a safe haven for a colony of 100,000 rare gray bats, the place was an extremely unsafe environment for any human intent on crawling for hours with the ultimate aim of ending it all. Leaving his Hendersonville home he set off on his suicide mission, driving southeast for two hours before parking his jeep outside the entrance to Nickajack Cave. Walking and crawling he headed aimlessly into the underground isolation. Cash's mission looked to have reached its tragic conclusion when his flashlight batteries finally expired, leaving him utterly alone and in total darkness. However, according to Cash, the black out had an unexpectedly profound effect on him. Laying there in the gloom, he was overtaken by a sense that although he'd given up on God, God hadn't given up on him. Astonishingly, realizing he was to die on God's terms and not his own, he began a long crawl to eventual safety, to be met by his mother and wife, June Carter, outside the cave. Both had apparently come to look for him, sensing that all was not well. On the road back home, Cash made a pledge to kick his addiction and commit himself to God. Within a month he was performing in front of fans without the aid of pills for the first time in more than a decade. Country star Gary Allan recorded a ballad of Cash's experience, 'Nickajack Cave (Johnny Cash's Redemption),' for his Tough All Over album in 2005.

Location 592: about five miles east of South Pittsburgh, Nickajack Cave is a wildlife refuge, operated by the Tennessee Wildlife Resources Agency, just north of Chattanooga. The cave is closed to protect the bats but you can view it from the Maple View Recreation Area, TN 37380

Above: the Tennessee Historical Commission marker. Right: the album the husband and wife duo recorded shortly before Cash's 1967 redemption in Nickajack Cave

The sign in the photograph reads:

2B 7

NICKAJACK CAVE

5¼ miles southeast was the town of Nickajack or Anikusatiyi, destroyed by Ore's force, Sept. 14, 1794. The town occupied a space between the river and the cave in which was a storehouse for plunder. It was also used by the Confederacy during the War Between the States as a source of saltpeter.

TENNESSEE HISTORICAL COMMISSION

Sevierville Convention & Visitors Bureau

Sevierville
The Dolly Parton statue

According to local tourist marketing types, Sevierville is "Where Smoky Mountain Fun Begins." The place certainly appeals to Dolly Parton, whose family roots are here. In 1987, watched by her proud parents, Dolly unveiled the striking statue of herself in front of the Sevierville courthouse. The Dollywood theme park is in nearby Pigeon Forge. Some of her earliest shows were at WIVK radio station in nearby Knoxville, and the still-open-for-business Walker's Grocery Store in Sevierville.

Location 594: located between Asheville (North Carolina) and Knoxville (Tennessee) on Interstate 40, Sevierville's Dolly Parton statue is on the lawns at the corner of Court Avenue and Commerce Street, TN 37862

"I just wanted to depict the joy of her as a young girl from the mountains of Tennessee who loved her music so," said sculptor Jim Gray

Nutbush
Tina Turner's birthplace

The tiny rural community of Nutbush is where Tina Turner was born, raised, and immortalized in the 1973 hit single 'Nutbush City Limits.' The song was credited as a record release by "Ike [her husband] and Tina Turner" but the lyrics were all Tina's – written autobiographically about her time growing up in Nutbush. She was raised by her grandmother here and also in nearby Brownsville. The State Route 19 between the two places was designated and signed "Tina Turner Highway" in 2002. There's no surviving childhood home to visit but the nearby Spring Hill Baptist Church, where she first sang in public, still stands.

Location 593: Nutbush is 60 miles northeast of Memphis. The Spring Hill Baptist Church is three miles west at 237 Springhill Road, toward Ripley, TN 38063

Texas

Austin
Stevie Ray Vaughan's memorial statue

Though born in Dallas, blues rock guitarist Stevie Ray Vaughan, who was tragically killed in a helicopter crash in 1990, is immortalized by a statue in Austin, the city where his career in music took off when he moved there, aged 17. The eight-foot bronze memorial is the work of sculptor Ralph Helmick and shows SRV in an almost heroic pioneering pose, featuring poncho, wide-brimmed hat, and guitar by his side.

Location 596: the memorial statue is in the Auditorium Shores park, on the banks of the Colorado River (known as Lady Bird Lake as it goes through town). The exact location of the statue is west of South 1st Street and north of West Riverside Drive, TX 78704

Unveiled in 1993, Ralph Helmick's statue of Stevie Ray Vaughan has its own bronze shadow for when the sun fails to shine in Austin

Will Howcroft Photography

Austin
Waterloo Records

British visitors will immediately feel at home on approaching the Waterloo record store in Austin. The building does a great job disguising itself as Waterloo underground tube station in South London. Waterloo first opened its doors in 1982, a time before Austin became the world mecca for music folk it is today. Voted 'Best Record Store' by The Austin Chronicle every year since it began trading, the place doesn't just offer an amazing selection of music to buy; it also has an envious history of in-store performers, who have included Sonic Youth, Nirvana, and Queens of the Stone Age.

Location 597: Waterloo Records is in downtown Austin at 600 North Lamar Boulevard, Austin, TX 78703

Amarillo
The Texas city big in Britain

When Neil Sedaka and Howard Greenfield wrote 'Is This the Way to Amarillo,' neither of them could have quite expected the enduring success the song would enjoy. When the UK's Tony Christie recorded it, his single release became a decent enough hit across Britain and most of Europe in 1971. But the joyfully bouncing song with this large Texas city at the heart of it just wouldn't ever seem to lose its appeal. In 2005 it became a million-selling British chart-topping charity single and the "sha-la-la" chorus still rates as one of the most popular chants sung by European sports fans. It might not have been such a success if Sedaka had stuck with his earlier plan to title the song 'Is This the Way to Pensacola.' Lyrically, nothing much rhymed with that Florida city, so the story of Amarillo and girlfriend "Sweet Maria" who waits for her lover to return there is now embedded in British pop history.

Location 595: 350 miles northwest of Dallas in North Texas, TX 79107

Austin
South by Southwest and the Austin City Limits Music Festivals

Spring and fall deep in the heart of Texas is when the music world comes to Austin. The South by Southwest (SXSW) arts and technology shindig every spring has a music element that showcases more than 2,000 performers at 100-plus venues throughout Austin. This huge event attracts huge stars – Bruce Springsteen and Dave Grohl were keynote speakers at the 2012 and 2013 music festivals. An estimated 16,000 register from around the world to talk about, listen to and watch music, making Austin the center of the music universe in March. The Austin City Limits Music Festival is a spin-off from the hugely successful Austin City Limits live television music series and transforms Austin into the live music capital every October. Depeche Mode, Muse, and Kings of Leon were just some of the heavyweights scheduled to appear in 2013.

Locations 598, 599 and 600: SXSW is spread throughout much of downtown Austin, TX 78701. The Austin City Limits Music Festival is centered around Zilker Park at 2100 Barton Springs Road, Austin, TX 78746

Neil Young and Crazy Horse rock Austin City Limits by night in 2012

Cambria Harkey

Texas

Clete, Willie, and Willie

Austin
Willie Nelson's statue

Although born in Abbott, a tiny town 130 miles north of Austin, the statue of Willie Nelson stands on the newly named Willie Nelson Boulevard in Austin, the city he has called home since 1971.

> ❝ Willie Nelson is a modern hero to so many of us; his quiet strength and fine work has touched everyone who knows him and his music, and the Willie Nelson monument will continue to act as a tactile beacon for all who adore him. It remains an honor and a privilege to have been chosen as the sculptor of Willie ❞
>
> *Clete Shields*

Location 601: the statue is in downtown Austin, outside the Moody Theater, home of the Austin City Limits studio, 310 West Willie Nelson Boulevard (formerly 2nd Street), Austin, TX 78701

Crockett
The Lightnin' Hopkins statue

The electric and country-blues musician Lightnin' Hopkins (1912-1982) is honored by a concrete statue here in Crockett, where he played when scuffling for a living before his career led him to grander venues including Carnegie Hall. He was born Sam John Hopkins in Centerville, 30 miles west of Crockett, and went on to become a prodigious recording artist who the young Jimi Hendrix reportedly listened avidly to when first discovering the blues. The epitaph on his gravestone at Forest Park Lawndale cemetery in Houston reads "Here lies Lightnin', who stood famous and tall, he didn't hesitate to give his all."

Location 603: 110 miles north of Houston. The statue is opposite Camp Street Cafe & Store where Hopkins played for tips in the 1940s, at 215 South 3rd Street, Crockett, TX 75835

China Grove
The Doobie Brothers' "sleepy little town"

'China Grove' is, according to the lyrics of the Doobie Brothers song, a "sleepy little town, down around San Antone." A track on the band's 1973 album The Captain and Me, 'China Grove' was written by the band's vocalist and guitarist Tom Johnston, who has claimed in interviews that he thought he'd made the place up until someone told him that it really existed "down around" San Antonio and reflected that it must have lodged in his subconscious. With its memorable chugging guitar riff, 'China Grove' gave the band their third Top 20 single and helped establish them as one of America's biggest FM radio rock bands.

Location 602: China Grove is a tiny town 10 miles east of downtown San Antonio. China Grove, TX 78263

Dallas
Texas Music Alley

Ten legendary Texans who have made a significant contribution to popular music are the subject of sculptures to be admired in the city's West End Historic District. Fans of "Blind" Lemon Jefferson, Roy Orbison, and Buddy Holly will be pleased to see their favorites among those musicians chosen for this honor. The sculptures are the work of Texas artist William Easley, whose first three pieces were unveiled in the Texas Music Alley in 1992.

Location 604: West End Historic District, Munger Avenue and North Market Street, Dallas, TX 75202

Dallas
Stevie Ray Vaughan's childhood home and grave

Born in Dallas in 1954, bluesman Stevie Ray Vaughan was buried in the city's Laurel Land Memorial Park after his early death in a helicopter accident in 1990. His childhood home was in the Oak Cliff district of the city. The small bungalow where he lived from 1955 to 1972, and first picked up a guitar aged seven, still stands.

Locations 605 and 606: Stevie Ray Vaughan's childhood home is about five miles southwest of the center of Dallas at 2557 Glenfield Avenue, Oak Cliff, Dallas, TX 75233. The Vaughan Estate marks the family graves at Laurel Land Memorial Park, eight miles south of Dallas, 6000 South R. L. Thornton Freeway, Dallas, TX 75232

Don Henley returns to Linden and rides one of the floats at the Cass County Wildflower Festival Parade in 2001

Paul Ridenour

Galveston
The Vietnam war song now luring tourists

The writer of the 1969 hit 'Galveston,' Jimmy Webb, and its singer, Glen Campbell, may have had different interpretations on the lyrical meaning but there's no doubting the song is all about a soldier in Vietnam yearning for his girl back in the Texas city of Galveston. Webb dressed the song with anti-war tones but Campbell always sang it as a soaring patriotic number. The lyrics describe the coastal city's beach with sea waves crashing, and more than four decades after 'Galveston' hit No. 4 on the Billboard Hot 100 the Texas Gulf Coast island purchased the rights to make it the official song of its 2013 tourism campaign.

Location 607: Galveston is 50 miles southeast of Houston. The beach front is at Galveston Island, TX 77554

Gilmer and Linden
Don Henley's hometown discovery

With a population of little more than 4,000, the small Texas town of Gilmer has helped supply the music world with four people who have contributed greatly to four very different genres of music. Eagles founding member Don Henley, blues guitarist Freddie King and singer Johnny Mathis were all born locally, and singer-songwriter Michelle Shocked was raised here. Although born in Gilmer, Henley grew up 40 miles northeast in an even smaller farming town called Linden. He has lived for many years in California, but Henley returns to his childhood home community regularly and is clearly enthralled by the history of Linden, and has even been quoted as saying that he'd like to research more information about two legendary musicians he discovered had been born in the town.

❛I discovered something remarkable about my hometown and its environs. I have found documentation which shows that legendary blues guitarist T-Bone Walker and renowned ragtime composer Scott Joplin were both born on the outskirts of Linden, Texas, the little community where I was raised. I don't think that any of the townsfolk were even remotely aware of this until recently. Growing up, we always thought that nothing ever happened around there, but evidently that isn't true ❜

Don Henley

Locations 608 and 609: both towns are in northeastern Texas. Gilmer is TX 75644 and Linden TX 75563

Texas

Artist David Adickes hopes to eventually place his huge homage to The Beatles at Cleveland's Rock and Roll Hall of Fame

Paul Ridenour

Houston
The giant Beatles statues

A curious giant statue of John, Paul, George, and Ringo stands tall in Texas' largest city. Each of the four Beatles (apart from Ringo Starr, who is sat at his drum kit) is represented by a 36-foot-high white figure created by artist David Adickes who famously created the even taller 67-foot statue of politician Sam Houston which towers over the good people of Huntsville, 70 miles away. There is pictorial evidence to suggest that 'Paul McCartney' was blown clean over during

damage caused by Hurricane Ike in 2008. The "real" Beatles' only noteworthy connection to the city is the two concerts they played at the Sam Houston Coliseum on August 19th 1965.

Location 611: The Beatles stand outside David Adickes' studio amid his equally huge busts of American presidents, two miles north of downtown Houston at 2500 Summer Street, Houston, TX 77007

Houston
The Free Press Summer Fest

As music festivals go, Houston's Free Press Summer Fest might be in its infancy, but attracting large crowds and stellar headline acts hasn't apparently been a problem. The whole idea began in 2009 and has mushroomed into a two-day annual, early June event where The Flaming Lips, Weezer, and The Avett Brothers have all headlined. The 2012 festival drew more than 90,000 revellers to Eleanor Tinsley Park, where The Flaming Lips performed the Pink Floyd classic album The Dark Side of the Moon, a regular feature of their set on the festival circuit that summer.

Location 612: the festival entrance at Eleanor Tinsley Park is in downtown Houston at 500 Allen Parkway, Houston, TX 77019

Fort Worth
McCartney's return with Wings over Texas

On May 3rd 1976, Paul McCartney stepped out on an American stage to perform for the first time since The Beatles' final San Francisco concert in 1966. Date one of the Wings Over America Tour was an historic affair, a fact not lost on the sell-out audience inside the Tarrant County Convention Center in Fort Worth. Before Wings could play a single note the arena erupted with a 15-minute ovation directed at the returning Beatle. Other rock-worthy events that have taken place here include the concert filming for Metallica's 1998 DVD Cunning Stunts and the post-Exile on Main St Rolling Stones Convention Center gig with Stevie Wonder as support in 1972. Led Zeppelin loved the place so much they played it five times in seven years from 1970 to 1977. Fittingly, the final date on ZZ Top's 89-show Worldwide Texas Tour, which featured a Texas-shaped stage, livestock, and rattlesnakes, was here at Fort Worth's premier arena for rock in 1977.

Location 610: the Tarrant County Convention Center (now renamed the Fort Worth Convention Center) is in downtown Fort Worth at 1201 Houston Street, Fort Worth, TX 76102

Lubbock
Buddy Holly's hometown

Lubbock is where Buddy Holly was born in 1936 and buried in 1959. Significantly it was also the place where rock and roll chemistry was made in 1955 when the aspiring Holly opened the bill at concerts by Elvis Presley and Bill Haley and His Comets and absorbed their music to create his own unique sound. There's a number of ways fans can pay tribute to the singer with the famous hiccupping vocal delivery in Lubbock. First, to learn everything you didn't know already about Holly, head for the Buddy Holly Center, a museum in a renovated former railroad depot devoted to West Texas music. The Buddy Holly gallery features memorabilia presented in an area shaped like a guitar, defined by curving, piano-finished cherry wood exhibit cases. You'll learn about his birthplace, a building long gone but remembered by an historical marker, and his home on 37th Street, which is thankfully still standing. The most photographed Buddy visitor attraction is the 8-foot bronze statue of the man and his guitar which stands above a Walk of Fame honoring a number of West Texas musicians, actors, and artists, including Waylon Jennings, Bobby Keys, and Roy Orbison. Buddy Holly's gravestone – engraved "Holley" in keeping with his real birth name – is in the City of Lubbock Cemetery.

Locations 614, 615, 616, 617 and 618: The West Texas city of

Lubbock is more than 300 miles west of Dallas. The Buddy Holly Center is at 1801 Crickets Avenue, Lubbock, TX 79401. The statue is also on Crickets Avenue, across the street from the Buddy Holly Center, on the corner of 19th Street, TX 79401. Holly's birthplace is at 1911 6th Street, Lubbock, just north of downtown Lubbock, TX 79403 and his home is slightly south of downtown Lubbock at 1305 37th Street, Lubbock, TX 79412. The City of Lubbock Cemetery is a mile or so east of downtown at 2011 East 31st Street, Lubbock, TX 79404

Grant Speed's Buddy Holly statue on Crickets Avenue

Robert D. Waller

La Grange
ZZ Top's whorehouse hit

Known variously as the Chicken Ranch, Miss Edna's Boarding House, and probably some unkinder names, the bordello on the edge of La Grange was the subject of ZZ Top's 1973 hit single 'La Grange.' The band's bass player, Dusty Hill, says that inspiration for the song came from the establishment which was later featured in the movie The Best Little Whorehouse in Texas, starring Dolly Parton and Burt Reynolds.

> *La Grange is a little bitty town, and little towns in Texas are real conservative. But they fought against it. They didn't want it closed, because it was like a landmark. It was on a little ranch outside of town, the Chicken Ranch. Anyway, we wrote this song and put it out, and it was out maybe three months before they closed it. It pissed me off. It was a whorehouse, but anything that lasts a hundred years, there's got to be a reason*
>
> *Dusty Hill in an interview with Spin magazine*

Location 613: La Grange is 65 miles southeast of Austin. Two or three miles east of downtown La Grange, TX 78945. The 'shack outside La Grange,' that home out on the range', as the song says, closed in 1974

Texas

Pampa
The Woody Guthrie Folk Music Center

The Harris Drugs Store on South Cuyler Street in Pampa, where Woody Guthrie once worked and performed his music, is now the Woody Guthrie Folk Music Center. Pampa was where the young Guthrie attended high school, bought his first guitar and got married. Every year on the anniversary of Guthrie's death (October 3rd) Pampa celebrates his life and extraordinary cultural legacy with musical tributes. The center is a haven for students of the man's work, encouraging visitors to read and research the life of Woody Guthrie and play their own music.

Location 619: Pampa is 55 miles northeast of Amarillo. The Woody Guthrie Folk Music Center is at 320 South Cuyler Street, Pampa, TX 79065

Janis Joplin's family home is just one of several points of interest on the Janis Joplin Road Trip map, available from the local Convention & Visitors Bureau

Justin Carrasquillo Photography

Port Arthur
Janis Joplin's home town

Although the first childhood home of Port Arthur-born singer Janis Joplin was demolished in 1980, the family home she lived in from the age of four, on 32nd Street, has thankfully survived and is marked by an historic marker in the front yard. The legendary blues-rock singer, who was born in 1943 and died in 1970 – the same year her family moved out of their Port Arthur home – is remembered by the music exhibits associated with her at the city's Museum of the Gulf Coast.

Among those exhibits is a replica of Joplin's psychedelically decorated 1956 Porsche Cabriolet and a multi-headed bronze representation of Janis by Texas sculptor Douglas Clark. Plans to turn the site of her first home into a 'Piece of My Heart' memorial where fans can visit to celebrate the life of one of America's greatest female singers appear to have stalled. However, you can pick up an excellent Janis Joplin road trip map, featuring the Port Arthur schools, churches, and cafes she frequented, at the the Port Arthur Convention & Visitors Bureau.

Locations 620, 621, and 622: Port Arthur is 90 miles east of Houston. Janis Joplin's first home, where the 'Piece of My Heart' memorial may one day be constructed is at 4048 Procter Street, Port Arthur, TX 77642. Her way-marked childhood home is at 4330 32nd Street, Port Arthur, TX 77642. The Museum of the Gulf Coast is at 700 Procter Street, Port Arthur, TX 77640

San Antonio
Robert Johnson at the Gunter Hotel

Determined to establish the exact location for Robert Johnson's historic recordings in 1936, the San Antonio Blues Society and Robert Johnson Blues Society erected a commemorative marker here at the Gunter Hotel. Room 414 was used for Johnson's actual recordings, while the engineers directed operations through a connecting door in room 413. The hotel is now listed on the National Register of Historic Places and attracts many inquisitive visitors. John Mellencamp booked into room 414 and recorded tracks for his 2010 album, No Better Than This. Absorbing the atmosphere created by the room's historic past, Mellencamp recorded in mono and the LP's third track, 'Right Behind Me,' was written, he revealed, "just for this room."

Location 623: the Sheraton Gunter hotel is in downtown San Antonio at 205 East Houston Street, San Antonio, TX 78205

Rooms 414 and 413 of the Gunter Hotel illustrates the cover of Robert Johnson's King of the Delta Blues Singers, Vol. II

Wink
The Roy Orbison Museum

When you drive through the small town of Wink in Texas, the Roy Orbison Drive sign and a small, low-level building with images of one of the world's most popular singers on the walls indicate that this is the place where Orbison belonged and where its 900 residents obviously still love him. Born 350 miles northeast of here in Vernon in 1936, Wink is where the young Roy Orbison grew up amid the "football, oil fields, oil, grease, and sand," as he put it. The building with images of the 'Big O' on

the outside houses the lovingly ramshackle collection of memorabilia that is the Roy Orbison Museum. If it's not open when you visit, it quickly can be if you request a look around at the nearby Wink City Hall. The Orbison family home where Roy lived from aged 10 is marked in an empty plot of land where the house once stood by an historical marker. Roy's first band, The Wink Westerners, was formed while he was a student at high school and they once opened for Slim Whitman at the now

rather neglected (but still standing) Rig Theater.

Locations 624, 625 and 626: Wink is 50 miles west of Odessa. The Roy Orbison Museum is at 213 East Hendricks Boulevard, Wink, TX 79789, and the Rig Theater is next door. The historical marker which shows the spot where Roy Orbison once lived is at 105 North Roy Orbison Drive (formerly 102 Langley Way), Wink, TX 79789

Utah

Wendover
Ry Cooder's drag race cover

Photographer Robert Wilson Kellogg shot the picture that appears on the cover of Ry Cooder's 2008 album I, Flathead. The famous Bonneville Salt Flats, near Wendover, on the western edge of Utah, is where the picture was taken, a good deal farther east than where the Californian salt-flat drag-racer, the subject of the tracks on the concept album, did his thing.

Location 628: off Highway 80 near the town of Wendover, UT 84083

I, FLATHEAD
Ry Cooder
The Songs of Kash Buk and the Klowns

The world of the 1940s Californian racer captured in Utah. The "Flathead" referred to in the album title is the Ford Flathead engine

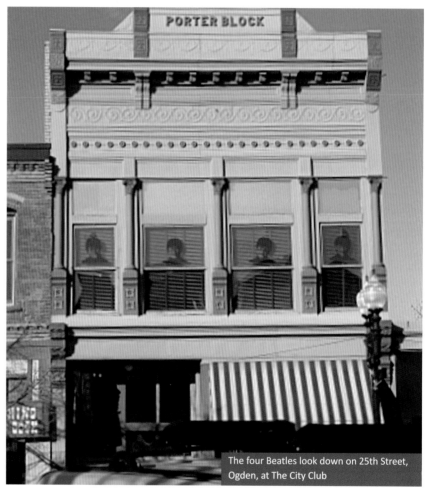

The four Beatles look down on 25th Street, Ogden, at The City Club

Ogden
Cocktails and memorabilia at The City Club

More than a themed restaurant, The City Club in Ogden is an eatery and Beatles museum combined. You can choose from a selection of Beatles-themed cocktails – a rum-based Maxwell Silver Hammer anyone? - while surrounded by an amazing collection of 'Fab Four' memorabilia and artwork.

Location 627: The City Club is in the Porter Block building, in downtown Ogden, at 264 25th Street, Ogden, UT 84401

Vermont

Burlington
Phish Food and Nectar's

Rock band Phish were formed in Burlington in the early 1980s, and there's a link to another Burlington claim to fame. When Ben Cohen and Jerry Greenfield started their ice-cream business in the city, Phish and Ben & Jerry's joined forces to create the ice-cream company's special flavor, Phish Food. When the band started to break big with their first album release on major label Elektra, they didn't forget their roots. They named their 1992 album A Picture of Nectar, after the bar Nectar's in Burlington where proprietor Nectar Rorris booked them for their earliest residency.

Location 629: Burlington is Vermont's largest city and is in the north of the state. Nectar's lounge and retaurant is still a great music venue, boasting the world's best gravy fries as an added inducement to visit. The venue is at 188 Main Street, Burlington, VT 05401

Rock and roll ice-cream from Burlington

The Nectar Rorris tribute album: Phish's 1992 album cover visually pays homage to the man and venue that helped establish the band, formed at The University of Vermont in Burlington

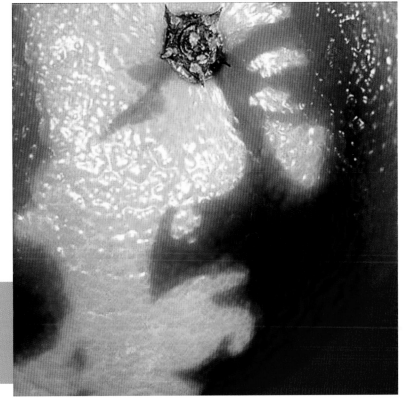

Virginia

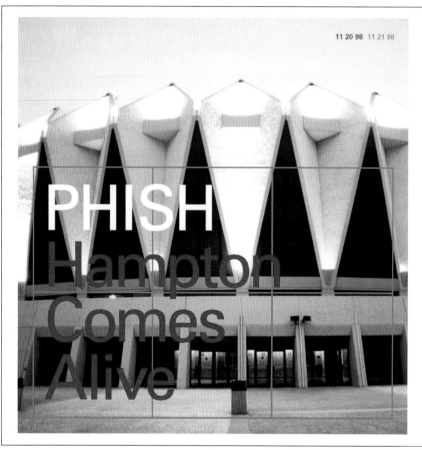

11 20 98   11 21 98

PHISH
Hampton
Comes
Alive

The album, which went to No. 4 on the Billboard chart, and the Rock Atlas author in an unconvincing attempt to emulate the cover shoot of one of his favorite LPs at Manassas station

Hampton
Phish and The Stones at the Coliseum

When Vermont band Phish called it a day in 2004 it looked unlikely they would ever perform again following an emotional final concert in front of 65,000 on a farm in Coventry, VE. But, back they came in 2008 with three reunion concerts at Hampton Coliseum and a six-disc live album, Hampton Comes Alive, which pictured the venue on the cover. In 1981 The Rolling Stones played two nights at the Coliseum, remembered for two distinctly different reasons. The gigs were filmed for the first pay-per-view TV music event and included the famous incident when Keith Richards attacked a misguided fan who attempted to get to Mick Jagger, whacking the stage invader with his Telecaster!

Location 630: the Hampton Coliseum is at 1000 Coliseum Drive, VA 23666

Manassas
The Stills station photo shoot

When Stephen Stills assembled a supergroup of some of America's finest musicians in 1971 there was the usual problem of what to call themselves. Eventually, for the release of the outfit's debut album – a critically acclaimed double LP with sides devoted to blues, country, and rock - Stills settled on the title "Manassas," a place in Virginia that had witnessed a significant turning

point in the American Civil War. For the album cover Stills, who knew his history when it came to the battles of Bull Run, had the band line up for a photo at the railroad station under the "Manassas" sign, which conveniently (and typographically) titled their first record.

Location 631: Manassas is 30 miles west of the center of Washington D.C. The Manassas railroad station is downtown at 9431 West Street, Manassas, VA 20110

❝As I recall we drove out to the Manassas railroad station very early one morning. It may have been [photographer] Ira Wexler's idea to shoot at the station. We didn't name the band until way after the photo shoot, maybe later that day or later that week. Great album cover shot and great album ❞

Chris Hillman, Manassas

Janet Roberts

Washington

Picture: Jennifer Huber/SoloTravelGirl.com

Aberdeen
Kurt Cobain – under the bridge

'Come As You Are' exclaims the Aberdeen roadside sign welcoming visitors to the birthplace and hometown of Kurt Cobain (1967-1994), courtesy of Nirvana's 1992 hit single. It's also the hometown of Nirvana's bass player, Krist Novoselic, who moved to this small former logging and fishing city aged 14 and set about creating what would become the world's most famous grunge band with Cobain. The Young Street Bridge over the Wishkah River is perhaps the nearest thing you might get to any location that carries a positive connection to the talented but troubled Cobain. It was here, under the rickety old bridge's south approach, that he wrote his songs and where some of his ashes were scattered following his

dramatic suicide in Seattle in 1994. A sculpted guitar memorial was unveiled in the park close by the bridge in 2011 and there's a sign displaying lyrics and a stone marker remembering the man who many regard as the last truly great rock star.

Locations 632 and 633: Aberdeen is 100 miles west of Seattle. Now a private residence, Kurt Cobain's childhood home (from 1968 to1976) is at 1210 East First Street, Aberdeen, WA 98520. The southern approach to the Young Street Bridge and the Riverfront Park sculpture are near the intersection of Stanton Street and East 2nd Street, Aberdeen, WA 98520

The Kurt Cobain memorial sculpture is a representation of a 2.5-meter Fender Jag-Stang guitar, designed by Cobain. The stone sculpture is the work of local artists Kim and Lora Malakoff

Kirkland
Natural habitat of Fleet Foxes

The last day of school at Kirkland Junior High for Robin Pecknold and Skyler Skjelset was a significant date in the timeline of Fleet Foxes' development. That was the day their friendship began and grew over the summer vacation before guitars were bought and a band (The Pineapples) was formed at Lake Washington High School. They made their debut at the Old Fire House Teen Center, followed by Victor's Coffee Co. in neighboring Redmond and The Lyons' Den in Bothell before expanding their line-up and sound. Their first gig billed as Fleet Foxes came at Neumos in Capitol Hill in Seattle, and by 2008 their unique take on folk-rock had shaped debut album Fleet Foxes.

❝The Northwest is such a beautiful and inspiring place. I can't imagine the music sounding the same if we grew up somewhere like L.A. or New York. Growing up in Kirkland was part of that ❞

Skyler Skjelset, Fleet Foxes

Locations 634, 635, 636, 637, and 638: Kirkland Junior High School is at 430 18th Avenue, Kirkland, WA 98033. Lake Washington High School is at 12033 North East 80th Street, Kirkland, WA 98033. The nearby Old Fire House Teen Center is at 16510 North East 79th Street, Redmond, WA 98052, Victor's Coffee Co. is at 7993 Gilman Street, Redmond, WA 98052, and The Lyons' Den at 10415 Beardslee Boulevard, Bothell, WA 98011

Inside the pagoda-like Jimi Hendrix memorial at Renton

Obert Sorsten

Renton
The Jimi Hendrix memorial

When Jimi Hendrix died in London on September 18th 1970 his body was flown home to Renton and buried in the Greenwood Memorial Park, with a single stone marker. This stone marker and the legendary guitarist's remains were later moved to a new spot in the same cemetery, where the impressive Jimi Hendrix memorial stands at the center of what is now a Hendrix family plot. The memorial, which features images of Hendrix and his autograph, comprises three pillars and a domed roof flanked by a sundial. Despite its architectural merits, there's a feeling something is missing. Plans for the memorial were reported to have included a statue of Hendrix in the center, but that idea has yet to become reality. The lack of a statue certainly doesn't deter the thousands of fans who make a pilgrimage to this spot every year.

Location 639: Renton is 10 miles southeast of Seattle. The Greenwood Memorial Park is at 350 Monroe Avenue North East, Renton, WA 98056

Washington

George
The Gorge at George

Few music venues can rival The Gorge Amphitheatre's spectacular location. Music fans and recent headliners like Foo Fighters, Mumford & Sons, and Jack White who make the trip to the annual Sasquatch! Music Festival are treated to a panorama featuring the Columbia gorge canyon, Columbia River, and the distant Cascade mountain range. Two live albums recorded here have covers depicting this location's scenic view. The Gorge, by the Dave Matthews Band, recorded in 2002, was a three-nighter released on CD and DVD in 2004. The natural amphitheatre's sloping lawns also played host to and witnessed three of Pearl Jam's most memorable concert appearances, which the band recorded and released as Live at the Gorge 05/06 as a seven-disc set.

Location 640: the tiny city of George is 150 miles southeast of Seattle. The Gorge Amphitheatre is at 754 Silica Road North West, George, WA 98848

Packaged with the best view in rock on the cover, three dates in September 2005 and July 2006 captured Pearl Jam at their best at the Gorge.

Right: The George Amphitheatre's stunning view can be enjoyed by more than 20,000 music fans

George

Esty Ketsy

Seattle
The final home of Kurt Cobain

Now a private residence, the beautiful house where Kurt Cobain lived during his final days still stands in an up-market neighborhood in Seattle, although the adjacent garage where he committed suicide and was discovered dead on April 8th 1994 has been demolished. Fans who make the pilgrimage to Seattle mostly make for nearby Viretta Park, especially on Cobain's birthday (February 20th)

and the anniversary of his death, to sit on the two heavily inscribed park benches, lay flowers, and leave tokens to remember the grunge-rock legend.

Locations 641 and 642: Kurt Cobain's final home was at 171 Lake Washington Boulevard East, Seattle, WA 98127. Viretta Park is at 151 Lake Washington Boulevard North, Seattle, WA 98127

Kurt Cobain's final home. Courtney Love had the garage, where husband Kurt was discovered dead, demolished in 1996

The Jimi Hendrix jacket on display at the EMP's Hear My Train a Comin': Hendrix Hits London exhibition

Dave Matthews looking back at Seattle on the Fremont Bridge

Seattle
Dave Matthews' solo debut

Some Devil by Dave Matthews (sans band) was very much a made-in-Seattle project. Recorded at the city's Studio Litho, the 2003 album's cover photo of Matthews was snapped on Seattle's Fremont Bridge.

Locations 644 and 645: the Fremont Bridge is north of downtown Seattle at the northwestern corner of Lake Union. Studio Litho is a little way farther north from the bridge at 348 North West 54th Street, Seattle, WA 98107

Seattle
Emerald City Guitars

Good customer service is evidently high on the agenda in this vintage guitar shop, run by Jay Boone since 1996. "Don't be scared, no one's on commission" is the appealing pledge. It's a sales technique that attracts avid guitar collectors from around the world, including Billy Gibbons (ZZ Top), Thom Yorke, and Colin and Jonny Greenwood (Radiohead), Limp Bizkit, Joe Bonamassa, and Lemmy, to name an excitable few.

Location 646: Emerald City Guitars is in the heart of the historic Pioneer Square district of Seattle, half a block west of 1st Avenue at 83 South Washington Street, WA 98104

Seattle
Hendrix and much more at the Experience Music Project

An extraordinary sheet metal structure, the Experience Music Project (now known simply as EMP) houses the world's largest collection of Jimi Hendrix memorabilia and an ever-changing menu of other rock artefacts and themed exhibitions. This pop culture museum with a difference was opened in 2000 by Paul Allen (co-founder of Microsoft Corp. with Bill Gates), whose personal collection of guitars, stage gear, and lyrics formed the basis of the items on view.

Location 643: the Experience Music Project is situated on the campus of the Seattle Center park, next to the iconic Space Needle tower at 325 Fifth Avenue, Seattle, WA 98109

Washington

Seattle
The Jimi Hendrix statue, school, and park

There's a bronze statue of Seattle-born Jimi Hendrix in the Capitol Hill district, created by Seattle artist Daryl Smith. It captures the wilder side of the legendary musician with him typically down on his knees, ringing the very last drop of expression out of his guitar. Sadly there's no Jimi Hendrix childhood home to visit. That was torn down long before anyone would have appreciated the value of it, but Seattle's James A. Garfield High School does remember its former pupil with a bust of Jimi, despite the fact that he got expelled. Then there's the Jimi Hendrix Park, which is still a work in progress but nearing its goals of enriching a thriving multi-cultural community in its location adjacent to the Northwest African American Museum and grounds of the former Colman School.

Locations 647, 648, and 649:
Jimi's statue is at 1600 Broadway, near the corner of Pine Street, Seattle, WA 98122. James A. Garfield High School (Quincy Jones is also a former pupil) is at 400 23rd Avenue, Seattle, WA 98122. Jimi Hendrix Park is a mile southeast of downtown Seattle at 2400 South Massachusetts Street, Seattle, WA 98144

'Wild Thing': Jimi Hendrix on Seattle's Broadway

Reynaldo Schneck

Seattle
Fishing Beatles and Zeppelin at the Edgewater

The Edgewater hotel is Seattle's home from home for the world's rock stars. Although Led Zeppelin, The Beach Boys, David Bowie, KISS, Rod Stewart, R.E.M., and The Rolling Stones have all stayed at this hotel on a pier on Elliott Bay, it was the arrival of The Beatles that made the earliest and biggest impact. You can still book The Beatles' Suite 272, but the room's 1964 fixtures and fittings present when the band stayed here are now replaced by album covers, photos of the 'Fab Four' and a plaque commemorating their visit to play the nearby Seattle Center Coliseum (now the Key Arena at Seattle Center). After The Beatles checked out, the thick orange and yellow carpets from room 272 were pulled up, cut carefully into small squares and sold to raise money for children's charities at the local MacDougall's department store. The hotel has, in the past, actively encouraged guests to fish from the bedroom windows, an invitation The Beatles accepted according to photographic evidence at the time. Less well documented (certainly not photographically, anyway) is the infamous 1969 Led Zeppelin story where a groupie, a large fish, and a sexual act are now written in rock legend, but in several different ways depending on who is telling this tale of debauchery. The band's second visit to the Edgewater in 1973 got them temporarily banned after they reportedly hid around 30 mudsharks or dogfish about the hotel premises and tossed furniture and bed clothes into the water below. These days the hotel is a quirky, luxurious, and respectable place to stay and the band's Robert Plant has been a regular guest down the years.

Location 650: the Edgewater hotel is on a pier at the north end of the waterfront at 2411 Alaskan Way, Pier 67, Seattle, WA 98121

Right: The Beatles fish from their Edgewater hotel bedroom windows. Below: The Beatles Suite as it is today

Photo courtesy of The Edgewater Hotel

West Virginia

Beckley
The West Virginia Music Hall of Fame Exhibition

There's a permanent exhibition of the rich musical history of West Virginia at the Governor Hulett C. Smith Theater in Tamarack. Run by the West Virginia Music Hall of Fame and funded by a grant from the state's Humanities Council, it features memorabilia and information on local artists such as singer-songwriter Bill Withers. Punk group Th' Inbred and funk pioneer and co-founder of Parliament/Funkadelic, Fuzzy Haskins, also feature.

Location 651: the Governor Hulett C. Smith Theater is in Tamarack, a tourist destination arts and crafts facility located at Exit 45 above the Beckley service area of the West Virginia Turnpike, at 1 Tamarack Park, Beckley, WV 25801

A Columbia Records press picture of West Virginian Bill Withers who was born in the tiny community of Slab Fork, 12 miles southwest of Beckley. He is now remembered in the town's West Virginia Music Hall of Fame exhibition

Oak Hill
The Hank Williams memorial

On January 1st 1953 in Oak Hill, 29-year-old Hank Williams Sr. made his last stop on his last tour. Across the road from Burdette's Pure Oil service station there's a plaque dedicated to Hank by his fans, who, as the memorial says, "wish to keep his memory and music alive forever." It was at this service station where his driver, 18-year-old student Charles Carr, first discovered Hank was dead. He pulled over into the now demolished gas station, which some fans later hoped might be converted into a Hank Williams museum, to discover that the already sick Williams had passed away in the back seat.

Location 653: Oak Hill is 50 miles southeast of Charleston. The memorial is outside the public library at 611 Main Street, Oak Hill, WV 25901

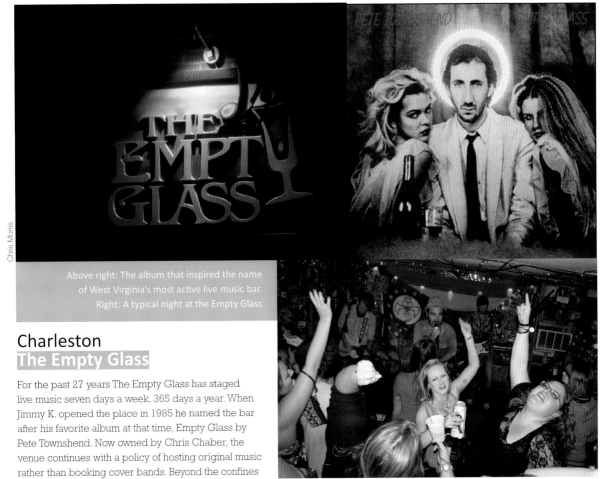

Chris Morris

Above right: The album that inspired the name of West Virginia's most active live music bar.
Right: A typical night at the Empty Glass

Chris Morris

Charleston
The Empty Glass

For the past 27 years The Empty Glass has staged live music seven days a week, 365 days a year. When Jimmy K. opened the place in 1985 he named the bar after his favorite album at that time, Empty Glass by Pete Townshend. Now owned by Chris Chaber, the venue continues with a policy of hosting original music rather than booking cover bands. Beyond the confines of West Virginia, The Empty Glass is well known on the national touring circuit and has attracted some big names. When British soul singer Joss Stone recorded at the NPR Radio Program Mountain Stage a block away, she came over to The Empty Glass for the regular post Mountain Stage Jam and jammed most of the night.

Location 652: in the center of Charleston, The Empty Glass is at 410 Elizabeth Street, WV 25311

❝A lot of our regular touring acts tour the whole country and come back and tell us of bands as far as California asking them about The Empty Glass. The name is much bigger than the venue itself. I think the success and longevity of The Empty Glass lies in the fact that it does focus on original music. There is no other bar in West Virginia that I know of that has live music seven days a week ❞

Jason Robinson, The Empty Glass

Talcott
John Henry's statue

The folk hero John Henry was a steel-driving former slave immortalized in song by everyone from Mississippi John Hurt to Bruce Springsteen. He died working on a tunnel more than one mile long, which began construction at Big Bend in 1870. There's a statue of him wielding his hammer at the town's John Henry Historical Park.

Location 654: Talcott is 100 miles southeast of Charleston. The statue stands west of town in John Henry Historical Park, near the entrance to the Big Bend railroad tunnel, WV 25951

Wisconsin

Eau Claire
Bon Iver's happy home

Aside from being (weird fact alert) the self-proclaimed 'Horseradish Capital of the World,' Eau Claire is the spiritual and practical home of Bon Iver. The band's singer-songwriter, Justin Vernon, has a close association with Eau Claire that has lasted all his life. The man is tattooed with Wisconsin and absorbs a love of the state that unusually precludes traveling almost anywhere else to make his music. The band's first album released in 2007, For Emma, Forever Ago, was the unplanned result of a three-month period of convalescence akin to hibernation which Vernon spent in his father's cabin, 70 miles east of Eau Claire in Medford. The second album, Bon Iver, Bon Iver (2011), was another local project recorded in a studio Vernon built with his brother Nate at Fall Creek, just 10 miles east of Eau Claire. April Base Studios (three miles from the house where he grew up and ten minutes from the bar where his parents first met) was constructed at a property that was formerly a veterinary clinic. After much reconstruction work, the building's indoor pool became the recording studio.

Location 655: Eau Claire is 90 miles east of Minneapolis. Ten miles east of Eau Claire is April Base Studios, which has hosted recordings by many local Wisconsin artists but is not open to the public and is little-promoted. Fall Creek, WI 54742

The Wisconsin-born artist Gregory Euclide created the Bon Iver, Bon Iver album cover using pine cones, seeds, melted snow, and other natural Wisconsin materials

❛Whenever I get home from tour and I'm driving in Eau Claire I kinda just do some fist pumps because I'm happy to be there ❜

Justin Vernon (Bon Iver)

Green Bay
Ballroom memorial

The Riverside Ballroom in Green Bay is where the Winter Dance Party Tour featuring Buddy Holly, Ritchie Valens, and The Big Bopper played the penultimate date of a grueling, freezing tour schedule that ended in tragedy. All three rock and roll stars were killed in the infamous 'Day the Music Died' plane crash on February 3rd 1959 in Iowa. The Riverside Ballroom performance on February 1st is commemorated by a life-size, two-dimensional, stainless steel figure of each of the three musicians who died two days later at the end of this unhappy tour.

Location 656: Green Bay is about 110 miles north of Milwaukee. The Riverside Ballroom is at 1560 Main Street, Green Bay, WI 54302

Madison
Otis' tragedy plaque

Lake Monona is where the plane carrying soul singer-songwriter Otis Redding and The Bar-Kays crashed on December 9th 1967. Following a search for survivors the next day, Redding's body was recovered from the icy waters. His death aged just 26, which is marked by a lakeside plaque here, occurred in the period a few days after he wrote '(Sittin' on) the Dock of the Bay' and before the song shot to the top of the Billboard Hot 100 when released in early 1968.

Location 657: the dedicated seating area and Otis Redding plaque is on the rooftop at the Monona Terrace Community and Convention Center, One John Nolen Drive, Madison, WI 53703

Madison
Joni Mitchell takes to the ice

The cover of Joni Mitchell's album Hejira features the wintry landscape of Lake Mendota, and although the singer-songwriter appears to be standing on the frozen lake, the cover comprises several separate shots. Booked to appear at the Dane County Coliseum (now Veterans Memorial Coliseum) on February 29th 1976, Joni Mitchell's visit to Madison coincided with a devastating storm that brought trees and power lines crashing down and left half a million people without electricity for several days. With the tour at an end, this natural phenomenon did, however, encourage Joni to head out to Lake Mendota and take to the ice in a pair of borrowed skates. The frosty, misty conditions were a photographer's dream and rock lensman Joel Bernstein was on hand to capture the now famous pictures of the black, raggedy figure of Joni skating on the bleak, icy landscape. Disappointingly, this shot was rejected in favor of the composite cover that was eventually agreed on. A second photographer, Norman Seeff, shot the portrait of Mitchell back in the comparative comfort of Madison before the combined concept of all three was completed by an airbrush artist.

Location 658: Madison is 80 miles west of Milwaukee. The Hejira cover shots were taken from the frozen southern half of Lake Mendota at University Bay, Elm Drive, Madison, WI 53706, pointing at the then frosty trees on Picnic Point

JONI MITCHELL   Songs Of A Prairie Girl

Joni Mitchell takes to the ice on Lake Mendota on March 4th 1976 for a picture eventually used on the cover of a 2005 compilation album. The Hejira cover portrait was a composite of several photos

Wisconsin

Milwaukee
The seven-room Rave/Eagles Club

Looking more like city hall than a music venue, the Eagles Club was built in 1926 and in its heyday echoed to the sounds of boxing, swimming, and bowling. This grand building, which was added to the National Register of Historic Places in 1986, now has the ability to host seven different events all at the same time. There's The Rave Hall, Penthouse Lounge, The Eagles Hall, The Rave Bar, The Rave Vibe Room, and Rockstar Lounge for all sizes of musical entertainment. But it is The Eagles Ballroom, with its 25,000 square-foot wooden dance floor, that has hosted a veritable rock who's who down the years. Bob Dylan, Coldplay, Green Day, Marilyn Manson, and Matchbox Twenty are just some of the star names to have played under this vast domed ceiling. The place has also nurtured debut US-touring British bands like Oasis and Blur.

Location 659: 2401 West Wisconsin Avenue, Milwaukee, WI 53233

Milwaukee
The beer (and song) that made Milwaukee famous

Country songwriter and producer Glenn Sutton's most successful song was 'What's Made Milwaukee Famous (Has Made a Loser out of Me).' The hit's lyrics were inspired by the long-running Schlitz beer commercials that read 'Schlitz: the beer that made Milwaukee Famous.' The song was a favorite of Jerry Lee Lewis and Rod Stewart who had chart success with it in the US (1968) and the UK (1972), respectively.

Location 661: there are still plenty of breweries in Milwaukee but the Schlitz factory production line in the city ceased long ago. On the original site, Schlitz Park remains a center for employment at 1555 North Rivercenter Drive, Milwaukee, WI 53212

The slogan that inspired Glenn Sutton's mournful song

Milwaukee
The world's largest music festival

The shore of Lake Michigan has a 75-acre permanent site for what Guinness World Records has identified as the world's largest annual music festival at a single location. Summerfest is certainly big. With 900,000 fans enjoying 800 acts appearing on 11 stages over 11 days in June and July it's hard to disagree with them. The earliest Summerfest in 1968 was a move by Milwaukee Mayor Henry Maier to revitalize the downtown area by emulating Munich's Oktoberfest, swapping beer for music as the main attraction. Then spread over 35 different locations, the festival now concentrates all the fun in one central park area named, fittingly, after the mayor who started the whole thing. Hosting the larger bands are the two biggest Summerfest venues, the 23,000-seater Marcus Amphitheater and the 10,000 capacity BMO Harris Pavilion next door. Since the turn of the century, Nine Inch Nails, Prince, Steely Dan, and Bon Jovi have all headlined Summerfest.

Location 660: Summerfest is held at the Henry Maier Festival Park, 200 North Harbor Drive, Milwaukee, WI 53202

Milwaukee
The Beatles under the weather

Local WOKY 92-AM DJ Bob Barry visits The Beatles at the Coach House Motor Inn

The Beatles' first tour of America in 1964 was a punishing affair. Their tour schedule was unrelenting. Hugely popular and too valuable to be given much time off, they were still too early into their development as rock stars to make too many demands to music business bosses, who controlled their every move. So it was no surprise that on arrival in Milwaukee for their only concert in Wisconsin they were a little under the weather. Their September 4th concert had been a 12,000 sell-out a week after the tickets had gone on sale in April. At their Coach House Motor Inn press conference, The Beatles were already starting to suffer the effects of a cold and John Lennon, who had a sore throat, failed to appear at all. But the show at the Milwaukee Auditorium went ahead, followed by dinner at the hotel and the administering of antibiotics (and possibly amphetamines), ready for a flight the following day to fulfil the next tour date in Chicago. Before leaving Milwaukee, Paul McCartney delayed the band's departure from the Coach House Motor Inn to put in a thoughtful telephone call to a fan in the local St. Francis Hospital. Although she had a ticket for the Beatles concert, 14-year-old Christy Cutler was too sick to attend and McCartney chatted for several minutes in an effort to raise the girl's spirits. It worked. At the time, the Milwaukee Journal reported that the girl "wanted to take the telephone home with her. And then the nurses cried."

Ringo made a lot of wisecracks, but Paul was the most talkative. Overall they were very intelligent, very hip, and seemed older than their early 20s, which was about my age at the time

Milwaukee DJ Bob Barry talking to local music historian Ted Schaar about his two visits to The Beatles' hotel

Locations 662 and 663: the Milwaukee Auditorium has had a multi-million-dollar down-size conversion since The Beatles appeared there and is now called The Milwaukee Theatre at 500 West Kilbourn Avenue, Milwaukee, WI 53203. The futuristic-looking Coach House Motor Inn is now a Marquette University dorm at 19th Street and Wisconsin Avenue, WI 53233

Wisconsin

Waukesha
Les Paul's hometown

Les Paul, the man who invented the solid-bodied electric guitar, was born and is buried here in Waukesha. In 2013 the Gibson Guitar Corporation chose Waukesha as that year's GuitarTown, a public arts project that saw ten 10-foot-tall, beautifully created guitars displayed around town. More permanently, Les Paul's Waukesha history can be best understood by visiting some or all of the 12 locations on a Les Paul tour of the town. Still standing are his birthplace, childhood home, the renamed Les Paul Performance Center in Cutler Park (where he performed in his youth), and the Prairie Home Cemetery where he is buried. The Waukesha County Museum has an excellent, new, permanent exhibition devoted to the man and, farther afield, Discovery World in Milwaukee is well worth a visit if your interest in Les Paul knows no bounds. Here a timeline-based display called Les Paul's House of Sound tells you pretty much everything you need to know about this great Wisconsin man's contribution to popular music. His most visited memorial, though, is the road that serves as a beltway to the city of Waukesha called "Les Paul Parkway."

Locations 664, 665, 666, 667, 668, 669, and 670: Waukesha is 20 miles west of Milwaukee. Les Paul's birthplace is at 109 North Street, Waukesha, WI 53188. His childhood home is at 3320 West St. Paul Avenue, Waukesha, WI 53188. The Les Paul Performance Center is at Cutler Park, Wisconsin Avenue, and Maple Avenue, Waukesha, WI 53186. Waukesha County Museum (with a new Les Paul exhibit) is at 101 West Main Street, Waukesha, WI 53186. The Prairie Home Cemetery is at 605 South Prairie Avenue, Waukesha, WI 53186. Les Paul Parkway starts at East Moreland Boulevard as Highway 164 and becomes Highway 59 on the eastern side of town, Waukesha, WI 53186. Les Paul's House of Sound is 20 miles away at Discovery World, 500 North Harbor Road, Milwaukee, WI 53202

Left: the autographed Les Paul Goldtop guitar on display at the Waukesha County Museum's Les Paul exhibit. This guitar was signed by the 18 musicians who played at the 2005 Carnegie Hall concert to mark Les Paul's 90th birthday. Among the signatures are those of his godson Steve Miller, Peter Frampton, Joe Satriani, and Kenny Wayne Shepherd

Right: Waukesha's famous son, Les Paul, in a Capitol Records publicity shot

‛I set my sights high and with determination. If you believe in yourself, you need only reinforce all your dreams ›

Les Paul's message on his gravestone for all visitors to contemplate

Wyoming

Cheyenne
Neil Young and the National Guard to the rescue

On August 29th 1985, Neil Young and The International Harvesters played a benefit concert for the people of Cheyenne to help the victims of Wyoming's catastrophic floods that claimed the lives of 12 residents and farmers. Young, whose long-time friend and producer David Briggs was born in Douglas, Wyoming, and whose self-titled debut album opened with the instrumental track 'The Emperor of Wyoming,' was flown into the state's capital together with his band's equipment courtesy of the National Guard, who helped set up the stage at the city's Frontier Park grandstand. After expenses – Young played for free - a total of $117,772 was donated to local organizations and charities who had responded to the disaster. More than a year later, Young was honored in a ceremony in Cheyenne when Mayor Don Erickson presented him with a key to the city for his volunteer work in performing at the aptly named Silver Lining Concert.

Location 671: the outdoor rodeo arena is less than two miles from downtown Cheyenne off Interstate 1-25, Central Avenue, Exit 12, WY 82001

Wyoming State Tribune

❝There's something different about it, having the government help us get there so we can help the farmers. The National Guard's gonna help us load and unload, get in and outta the place, help us set up the stage. It's interesting❞

Neil Young describes the build-up to the highly unusual Cheyenne gig to the New Musical Express' Adam Sweeting

Left to right: volunteer performers at Cheyenne's 1985 Silver Lining concert, Michael DeGreve, Bruce Hauser, and Neil Young, were all honored at a ceremony a year after the event

Visit us online for more information

Preview of UK Rock Atlas
Additional US entries
Preview of U2 Rock Atlas (Ireland)
Rock Atlas App
Rock Atlas Facebook/blog
www.facebook.com/rockatlas
www.rockatlas.com

If you want to find out more about Rock Atlas, go online to visit the Rock Atlas Facebook page or Rock Atlas website. Here you will be able to get regular updates on new books such as the U2 Rock Atlas, featuring the band's special locations in Ireland, Rock Atlas Apps and join in the Facebook blog by commenting on our posts and making your own suggestions for new Rock Atlas location entries. Also online you'll find additional locations and the stories behind them that are not included in more than 1,300 entries currently in the UK and Ireland and USA books.

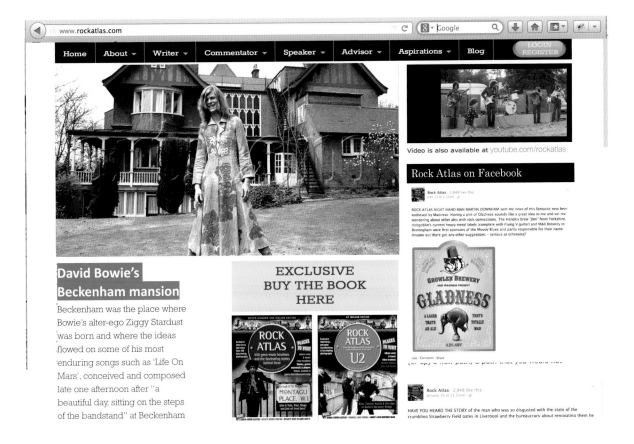

David Bowie's Beckenham mansion

Beckenham was the place where Bowie's alter-ego Ziggy Stardust was born and where the ideas flowed on some of his most enduring songs such as 'Life On Mars', conceived and composed late one afternoon after "a beautiful day, sitting on the steps of the bandstand" at Beckenham

Index

Index

Index

Index

Index

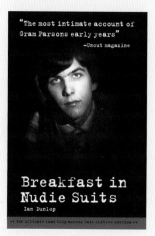